Tort Liability in Warfare

Tort Liability in Warfare

States' Wrongs and Civilians' Rights

Haim Abraham

OXFORD
UNIVERSITY PRESS

OXFORD
UNIVERSITY PRESS

Great Clarendon Street, Oxford, OX2 6DP,
United Kingdom

Oxford University Press is a department of the University of Oxford. It furthers the University's objective of excellence in research, scholarship, and education by publishing worldwide. Oxford is a registered trade mark of Oxford University Press in the UK and in certain other countries

Published in the United States of America by Oxford University Press
198 Madison Avenue, New York, NY 10016, United States of America

British Library Cataloguing in Publication Data

Data available

Library of Congress Control Number: 2024944350

ISBN 9780198893356

DOI: 10.1093/9780191997051.001.0001

Printed and bound by
CPI Group (UK) Ltd, Croydon, CR0 4YY

MIX
Paper | Supporting responsible forestry
FSC® C013604

For Eden

Acknowledgements

This book benefited from the generosity and support of many friends, mentors, and colleagues, who gave their time and shared their insights on various drafts and ideas and without which it would not come to light. I am grateful to Arthur Ripstein, David Dyzenhaus, Ernest Weinrib, Eden Sarid, and Omri Ben-Zvi, who offered sophisticated in-depth comments and insights on the entire manuscript and whose suggestions and observations helped me see the bigger picture as well as the smaller details. I also benefited greatly from feedback and discussions on draft chapters with Allan Beever, Gabriella Bloom, Bruce Chapman, John Goldberg, Maria Lee, Paul Mitchell, Naama Ofrath, and Jennifer Page, whose fresh takes gave new perspectives to my project and advanced it significantly. Conversations with Greg Bowley, Jutta Brunnée, John Enman-Beech, David Enoch, Maytal Gilboa, Ugljesa Grusic, Alon Harel, Larissa Katz, Dimitrios Kyritsis, Karen Knop, Sophia Moreau, Donal Nolan, Jason Neyers, James Penner, Stephen Pitel, Ariel Porat, Matthew Taylor, and Emmanuel Voyiakis assisted me in honing arguments and idea, and I am indebted to them for these conversations.

Materials included in this book were presented at Brunel University London, Goodenough College, Harvard University, London School of Economics and Political Science, McGill University, Oxford Brookes University, Stanford University, Tel-Aviv University, The Hebrew University of Jerusalem, University of Florida, University of Haifa, University of Oxford, University of Sydney, University of Westminster, University of Zurich, and Yale University. I thank the members of those audiences for their comments, suggestions, and questions.

I gratefully acknowledge the Social Science and Humanities Research Council of Canada for a Vanier Canada Graduate Scholarship and the University of Haifa Minerva Center for the Rule of Law Under Extreme Conditions for their support that enabled some of the work on which this book builds.

My greatest thanks is to my husband Eden Sarid, for making sure that I stay focused, on point, accurate, coherent, well-fed, and amply supported. This book would not exist without him.

Contents

1
Introduction

I. Why Torts?

If a person carelessly injures you or damages your property, ordinarily she will have to compensate you for your loss. This norm is enshrined in tort law, the body of law that is applied by courts in civil cases to provide compensation for individuals wronged by others, and it echoes familiar and intuitive notions. Individuals are not in a position to unilaterally take something from, or do something to, another person, and if they act in this way, then they are obliged to revert the effects of their wrongful conduct.[1] In doing so, the normative relationship between the parties is restored, and individuals' rights and social standing as free and equal agents are vindicated.[2]

Yet, if such injuries are inflicted by states on civilians during warfare, civilians are unable to obtain a remedy in tort for their injuries. But why is that? A practical answer would be twofold. First, under international law, states do not owe a duty to private individuals to compensate them for inflictions of losses during war, and individuals do not have a right to compensation against states. Second, in many common law jurisdictions, states enjoy special immunities from tort liability, which bar claims in domestic tort law for wrongs that states inflict on civilians while engaging in warfare.

Nevertheless, the practical answers do not address the more fundamental conceptual question: could and should tort liability be imposed, and compensation be awarded, for losses inflicted during combat? In this book, I show that the answer to this question is 'yes' and that addressing the question of domestic tort law's applicability to address wrongs inflicted on civilians through warfare is crucial.

[1] See, for instance: Allan Beever, *A Theory of Tort Liability* (Hart Publishing 2016) 19–21; Ernest J Weinrib, *The Idea of Private Law* (OUP 2012) 104; Arthur Ripstein, *Private Wrongs* (Harvard UP 2016) 5; Jules Coleman, 'Tort Law and Tort Theory: Preliminary Reflections on Method' in Gerald J Postema (ed), *Philosophy and the Law of Torts* (CUP 2001) 184; John Gardner, 'What Is Tort Law For? Part 1. The Place of Corrective Justice' (2011) 30 Law and Philosophy 1, 9–11, 22–23; Robert Stevens, *Torts and Rights* (OUP 2007) 327–28; John CP Goldberg and Benjamin C Zipursky, *Recognizing Wrongs* (2020) 26–28, 234.

[2] Ripstein, *Private Wrongs* (n 1) 8; Scott Hershovitz, 'Treating Wrongs as Wrongs: An Expressive Argument for Tort Law' (2018) 10 Journal of Tort Law 405, 435.

Tort Liability in Warfare. Haim Abraham, Oxford University Press. © Haim Abraham 2024.
DOI: 10.1093/9780191997051.003.0001

The fact that states are immune from tort liability results in civilians becoming the default cost bearers. Consequently, in many instances, civilians have no redress for the losses they sustain through combat, neither from their own state nor from the state that inflicted the injuries on them. In other cases, civilians might be able to obtain partial redress through *ex gratia* or state-operated insurance-like schemes, or through peace treaty mechanisms. Yet, individuals do not have a right to claim that these mechanisms will be established, nor that they will be awarded payments that correspond with the actual costs of their losses once these mechanisms are constituted. Rather, these forms of redress are available largely at the discretion of the awarding state.

Moreover, there is a value in holding wrongdoers liable that is lost when a blanket immunity from liability is awarded. Scholarly views on the character and value of tort law diverge. For example, some maintain that through the imposition of tort liability, social welfare can be maximized and the cost of accidents, as well as their rate of occurrence, can be reduced.[3] Others hold that imposing liability on wrongdoers, towards the individuals whom they have injured, facilitates the restoration of their relationship to a rightful condition.[4] In the particular context of holding public actors liable, the value of an imposition of liability could lie, in addition, in the ability to curtail and redress misuse and abuse of public power.[5] No matter which stand one might take on the value of tort liability, identifying that it is of value suggests that a justification is required when an immunity from liability is granted.

Yet, legislatures, courts, and scholars have thus far failed to provide a robust justification for the existence and scope of states' immunity from tort liability. Arguments have been brief, mostly grounded in intuitions about warfare and the possible implications of availability of remedies in tort for the ability to engage in warfare. The shaky theoretical and doctrinal underpinnings of the justifications of immunity from tort liability are exacerbated by the courts'

[3] See, for example: Guido Calabresi, *The Costs of Accidents: A Legal and Economic Analysis* (Yale UP 1970) 26–31; Richard Posner, 'A Theory of Negligence' (1972) 1 Journal of Legal Studies 29, 32–33; Richard A Posner, 'Wealth Maximization and Tort Law: A Philosophical Inquiry' in David G Owen (ed), *The Philosophical Foundations of Tort Law* (OUP 1997) 99–103; John CP Goldberg, 'Twentieth-Century Tort Theory' (2003) 9 Georgetown Law Journal 513, 544.

[4] See, for instance: Beever (n 1) 19–21; Coleman (n 1) 184; Gardner (n 1) 9–11, 22–23; Andrew S Gold, *The Right of Redress* (OUP 2020) 31–33, 54–55; Goldberg and Zipursky, *Recognizing Wrongs* (n 1) 26, 275; Ripstein, *Private Wrongs* (n 1) 5; Weinrib, *The Idea of Private Law* (n 1) 104.

[5] TRS Allan, 'The Rule of Law as the Rule of Private Law' in Lisa M Austin and Dennis Klimchuk (eds), *Private Law and the Rule of Law* (OUP 2014) 72, 82; David Dyzenhaus, *The Constitution of Law: Legality in a Time of Emergency* (CUP 2006) 2; Hanoch Dagan, 'Private Law Pluralism and the Rule of Law' in Lisa M Austin and Dennis Klimchuk (eds), *Private Law and the Rule of Law* (OUP 2014) 159; Lorne Sossin, 'The Unfinished Project of Roncarelli v. Duplessis: Justiciability, Discretion, and the Limits of the Rule of Law' (2010) 55 McGill Law Journal 661, 672.

struggles to define the extent of states' immunity from tort liability and by the temptation for legislatures to expand the reach of this immunity. There is a considerable lack of clarity regarding the type of injuries that would or would not be barred from establishing a claim in tort, which further intensifies the precarious conditions of civilians living in conflict areas.

These issues have not been dealt with in a comprehensive way by existing scholarship. Indeed, some academics have argued that states have a moral obligation of compensation for wrongful injuries that they have inflicted, even in times of war.[6] Others have suggested legal reforms of international law and tort law in order to establish civilians' right to compensation.[7] Still, the moral arguments have not accounted for the legal impediments to liability, and the legal reform arguments have not properly considered the moral and legal norms that govern both the use of force in war and tort liability.

I address these shortcomings by offering a novel account of states' tortious liability that evaluates both the moral and legal considerations in relation to inflicting losses during belligerent activities. To this end, I rely on three frameworks. The first is the laws that regulate the conduct of belligerent activities, namely international humanitarian law and states' rules of engagement. Reference to these norms is required so that we may be able to identify the scope of states' authority to inflict losses on civilians through warfare and understand what happens to private law rights during combat. Second, I rely on a corrective justice approach to tort liability to elaborate on the moral and legal underpinnings of the idea that a wronged individual is entitled to a private law remedy from the person who wronged her, as well as the ability to articulate what constitutes a tortious wrong. Lastly, I employ a substantive rule of law approach to demonstrate the significance of tort remedies in safeguarding against abuse and misuse of public power and to assess the justifications for limiting these remedies.

My use of these three frameworks enables a comprehensive analysis of states and individuals' rights and obligations during war, and the applicability of tort liability in this context. I define what amounts to tortious wrongdoing in

[6] For instance, see: Gary J Bass, 'Jus Post Bellum' (2004) 32 Philosophy & Public Affairs 384; Frances M Kamm, 'Making War (and Its Continuation) Unjust' (2001) 9 European Journal of Philosophy 328; Larry May, *After War Ends: A Philosophical Perspective* (CUP 2012); Brian Orend, *The Morality of War* (Broadview Press 2006).

[7] Some of these include: Rebecca Crootof, 'War Torts' (2022) 97 New York University Law Review 1063, 1109; Emanuela-Chiara Gillard, 'Reparation for Violations of International Humanitarian Law' (2003) 85 International Review of the Red Cross 529; W Michael Reisman, 'The Lessons of Qana' (1997) 22 Yale Journal of International Law 381; Yaël Ronen, 'Avoid or Compensate? Liability for Incidental Injury to Civilians Inflicted during Armed Conflict' (2009) 42 Vanderbilt Journal of Transnational Law 181.

the course of combat, which I refer to as 'belligerent wrongdoing', and show that there are corrective justice duties to repair these wrongs. By establishing that private law rights remain relevant even during warfare, I argue that inflicting a loss on civilians is an ordinary *prima facie* wrong. However, if the loss is inflicted by states and combatants in compliance with international humanitarian law and the rules of engagement, the loss is justified and hence non-wrongful. Lacking this justification, ordinary moral corrective justice duties to repair arise. Furthermore, I argue that the current legal reality, in which states are immune from compensating civilians who suffer losses through combatant activities, is not legally or morally justified and show that tort liability could and should be an available form of redress for belligerent wrongs.

To clarify, my argument is not that violations of international humanitarian law and the rules of engagement generate (or should generate) new torts, nor is it that states' duties under international humanitarian law ought to be imported into tort law and become private law duties.[8] Rather, I maintain that in the context of warfare, identifying what should amount to a wrongful loss is informed by the availability of international humanitarian law and the rules of engagement as a justification. Without these justifications, bodily and property losses would be ordinary private law wrongs, which existing tort law doctrines could be used to address. Based on these conclusions, I argue that civilians who are injured through belligerent wrongdoing should be able to bring a claim in tort against the state that wronged them in that state's courts. Furthermore, I argue that despite the shortcomings of tort liability and litigation, it should be considered as the preferable means over its alternatives in this context.

My aims in this introductory chapter are threefold. First, I elaborate on the scope and character of two of the frameworks that I use—international humanitarian law and corrective justice—and show why they are relevant to the argument I am advancing in this book. Second, I demonstrate why the most appropriate forum to bring a claim in tort to is the state that inflicted the wrong or the state that is affiliated with the wrongdoer, and I offer a brief gloss on the relevance of choice of law rules to my main arguments. Third, I provide a roadmap of the structure and content of the arguments that I make in each of the subsequent chapters.

[8] Note, throughout this book, I use the terms 'violation' and 'infringement' of rights interchangeably. For a discussion on whether they should in fact be treated as such, see: John Oberdiek, 'Lost in Moral Space: On the Infringing/Violating Distinction and Its Place in the Theory of Rights' (2004) 23 Law and Philosophy 325.

II. The Relevant Law of War

To show that states could be held liable in tort for losses they inflict during combat, the basis for evaluating states' conduct must be attentive to the scope and character of rights and duties in times of warfare. Indeed, it is difficult to imagine that courts can, or ought to, evaluate states' peacetime and wartime conduct on the same basis. In peaceful everyday life, using and damaging another person's body and means is, generally, wrongful. In contrast, war is a state of affairs during which it is not necessarily wrongful to inflict such losses. War consists of a moral and legal state of affairs, that is distinct from a state of peace,[9] in which states can use force against one another, to include killing and injuring each other's population, damaging property, and crossing state lines.

Combatant activities are those actions that are taken by combatants against an enemy state, its forces or military assets, to achieve a military goal.[10] Put differently, these are acts done by agents of a state[11] for a public purpose other

[9] Stephen C Neff, *War and the Law of Nations: A General History* (CUP 2007) 102. Note, a state of war can exist even if no single combatant activity has been engaged in and even if war has not been officially declared.

[10] There are many possible military goals, from defeating the enemy, through destroying a specific asset or gaining control over a territory, to acquiring intelligence (Scott Sigmund Gartner, *Strategic Assessment in War* (Yale UP 1997) 14; Clayton R Newell, *The Framework of Operational Warfare* (Routledge 1991) 91). Furthermore, while military goals have a tactical significance, they could also at times be related to political goals.

[11] The term 'combatant' has been used in three distinct senses (see, for sources, the International Committee of the Red Cross, 'Customary IHL: Practice Relating to Rule 3. Definition of Combatants' <https://ihl-databases.icrc.org/customary-ihl/eng/docs/v2_rul_rule3> accessed 26 November 2019). First, 'combatant' has been used to describe anyone who engages in hostilities as part of an international armed conflict, subject to certain formalities to which they must adhere, such as a command structure, distinctive clothing, carrying weapons openly, and enforcing the laws of armed conflict (see, for example: Article 43(2) of Protocol Additional to the Geneva Conventions of 12 August 1949, and relating to the Protection of Victims of International Armed Conflicts 1977 (hereinafter: Additional Protocol I) and the military manuals of Australia, France, Israel, the United Kingdom, and the United States). Second, the term has been used to portray those individuals who have a right to engage in belligerent activities under international humanitarian law (for instance, in the military manuals of Canada and Germany). This definition seems to have been adopted by Israel's Supreme Court, which held that acts of terror cannot be considered combatant activities (CA 2144/13 *The Estate of Mantin v The Palestinian Authority* (Nevo, 6 December 2017) Justice Solberg, paragraph 55). Lastly, 'combatant' has been described as a status, which states can designate to members of their armed forces with full discretion (this is the approach in the Netherlands' military manual).

While the first definition does not require that a combatant will be an agent of the state, the second and third definitions do have such a requirement. However, as the sole legitimate grounds for engaging in combat is self-defence (a point that I will address in greater detail below), it seems that the combatant status should only be given to agents of a state. Considering that individuals who hold this status are authorized to use force in war and also become the direct subjects of such use of force, the bestowing of this status upon anyone who participates in hostilities means a potential expansion of the scope of hostilities. In contrast, limiting the combatant status to agents of states restricts who is entitled to use force, as well as who could be the target of an attack. Only those combatants who are posing a direct threat, either by taking part in an ongoing attack or by being a part of a potential future attack, can be targeted (Arthur Ripstein, 'Why It's Wrong to Target Civilians during War' (*Berkeley Talks: Tanner Lectures, day 2*, 22 May 2019) <https://news.berkeley.edu/2019/05/22/berkeley-talks-2019-tanner-lectures-02/> accessed 20 August 2020).

than policing or peacekeeping. These acts can be conducted even when there is no state of war.

It is clear that we cannot assess states' conduct in times of war and during combat by the same standards used in times of peace. Rather, actions done in these times should be judged in accordance with wartimes' own norms. But what are these norms? Scholars identify three distinct groups of norms that correlate with three distinct periods in the course of engaging in belligerent activities.

The first group of norms governs the decision to engage in belligerent activities (*jus ad bellum*) that is prior to any actual resort to military force. Theorists traditionally considered a decision to go into battle just if six criteria were met.[12] First, that the decision was made by a competent authority. Second, that there was a just cause to engage in combat. Third, that war was being conducted with the right intentions. Fourth, that there was a reasonable hope of success. Fifth, that all other measures had been exhausted and war was the only measure left. And lastly, that waging war was the proportionate response to the threat posed by another state. In the context of modern warfare, these criteria can assist states in determining whether they are acting in accordance with the sole justification to engage in combat: self-defence.

Jus ad bellum distinguishes between offensive and defensive warfare.[13] When the purpose of a war or a combatant activity is akin to law enforcement in the sense that it is conducted in order to punish another state, enforce rights, or acquire compensation, then it is an offensive form of warfare.[14] In contrast, when the purpose is to eliminate a threat, it is referred to as defensive.[15]

[12] See, for example: Francisco Suárez, *Selections from Three Works (1621)* (Gwladys L Williams tr, Liberty Fund 2014) 805; Endre Begby, Gregory M Reichberg, and Henrik Syse, 'The Ethics of War. Part II: Contemporary Authors and Issues' (2012) 7 Philosophy Compass 328, 328; Joseph C McKenna, 'Ethics and War: A Catholic View' (1960) 54 The American Political Science Review 647, 658.

[13] Note, the meaning of *offensive* wars in medieval and early modern Just War theory scholarship that I am describing here is different from the meaning of *aggressive* war post the Kellogg–Briand Pact and the United Nations Charter (hereinafter: the UN Charter). Offensive wars were seen as a form of law enforcement, whereas aggressive wars refer to those conflicts that violate the UN Charter (Article 8 *bis* of The Rome Statute of the International Criminal Court 2002).

[14] Emer de Vattel, *The Law of Nations (1758)* (Béla Kapossy and Richard Whatmore eds, Liberty Fund 2008) 471; Suárez (n 12) 816; Neff (n 9) 59–60.

[15] A further distinction can be drawn between a narrow and a broad interpretation of defensive wars. A narrow interpretation is analogous to an act of self-defence, that is, the defender state engaged in war to prevent an attack that was launched against it from succeeding. Just as an individual can repel any attempt to use her body or means against her wishes, so a state can do also (see: Neff (n 9) 126–28; Hugo Grotius, *On the Law of War and Peace (1625)* (Stephen C Neff ed, CUP 2012) 89). Conversely, a broad interpretation sees the war as defensive even when no attack has been launched, and the purpose of the war is to prevent such an attack from being launched to begin with (see: Alberico Gentili, *On the Law of War (1588)* (John C Rolfe tr, Oxford: Clarendon Press 1933) 58–61; Suárez (n 12) 804; Francisco de Vitoria, 'Relectiones: On the Law of War' (1557) §3; Vattel (n 14) 471; Grotius 82, 89–91; Neff (n 9) 127). This interpretation is less analogous to an individual acting in self-defence, as such actions

While in the past both offensive and defensive forms of warfare were perceived as legitimate, only the latter type remains lawful. Arguably, this change is attributable to two events of historical and normative significance. The first is the 1648 Peace of Westphalia, which established the horizontal relationship between European states by having all states recognize each other's exclusive sovereignty over their lands, people, and agents; and that they hold equal status.[16] However, it was not until the international community reacted to the horrors of World Wars I and II through the Kellogg–Briand Pact of 1928 and the United Nations Charter that the horizontal relationship between states became a firm legal norm. The Kellogg–Briand Pact was the first international treaty to ban offensive wars as an instrument of national policy[17] and was the precursor to Articles 2(4) and 51 of the UN Charter, which prohibit resort to armed conflict for any reason other than national self-defence.

The second group of norms regulates the actual conduct of hostilities (*jus in bello*). The main norms that are of relevance to my analysis are necessity, distinction, and proportionality.[18] The principle of necessity requires that the target of an attack, as well as the attack itself, will have some advantage to the war effort. The principle of distinction dictates that all combatants who are not ill or injured, who have not surrendered or been captured, as well as installations and infrastructures that either belong to the military or have a joint military–civilian character, can be directly targeted. However, all other individuals and objects can only sustain losses from combatant activities as an unintended side effect. Lastly, *in bello* proportionality means that only actions for

are only legitimate when they are a response to an actual and imminent threat, and not a potential future risk.

[16] Leo Gross, 'The Peace of Westphalia, 1648–1948' (1948) 42 American Journal of International Law 20, 26–28.

[17] Note that some view the Pact not so much as making aggressive war illegal, but merely as removing legal protections that individuals and states enjoyed from when such wars were viewed as legitimate (Oona A Hathaway and Scott Shapiro, *The Internationalists: How a Radical Plan to Outlaw War Remade the World* (Simon & Schuster 2017) 252–54).

[18] Michael Newton and Larry May, *Proportionality in International Law* (OUP 2014) 3, 68–69; Vitoria (n 15) 37; Vattel (n 14) 482, 510; Begby, Reichberg, and Syse (n 12) 333, 337; Thomas Hurka, 'Proportionality and Necessity' in Larry May and Emily Crookston (eds), *War: Essays in Political Philosophy* (CUP 2008) 130; Jeff McMahan, 'The Morality of War and the Law of War' in David Rodin and Henry Shue (eds), *Just and Unjust Warriors: The Moral and Legal Status of Soldiers* (OUP 2008) 22; Seth Lazar, 'The Morality and Law of War' in Andrei Marmor (ed), *The Routledge Companion to Philosophy of Law* (Routledge 2012) 377; Jeff McMahan, 'The Just Distribution of Harm between Combatants and Noncombatants' (2010) 38 Philosophy & Public Affairs 342; Michael Walzer, *Just and Unjust Wars: A Moral Argument with Historical Illustrations* (5th edn, Basic Books, a member of the Perseus Books Group 2015) 153–56; Michael Walzer and Avishai Margalit, 'Israel: Civilians & Combatants' (*The New York Review of Books*) <http://www.nybooks.com/articles/2009/05/14/israel-civilians-combatants/> accessed 8 March 2017.

which the anticipated military gain is proportionate to the foreseeable harms they inflict are justified.

The third group of norms directs states' rights and obligations at the conclusion of wars (*jus post bellum*). The character and scope of *jus post bellum* norms are less clear than those of *jus ad bellum* and *jus in bello*. Some criteria that have been raised, but have not been agreed upon, include restitution, reimbursement, punishment, rebuilding, reconciliation, reparation, and proportionality.[19] Furthermore, there is disagreement on whether these norms apply only to the just victor, to all parties regardless of guilt, or whether they are completely unnecessary for a fully coherent theory about just war.[20]

As the *in bello* principles are the only ones that govern the actual use of military force, one possible conclusion could be that they are the only relevant norms with which to evaluate the rights and obligations of states and individuals during armed conflicts for the purpose of establishing tort liability. Nevertheless, there is a disagreement between those theorists who are referred to as 'traditionalists' and those who are referred to as 'revisionists', concerning the possibility of disregarding belligerent activities' *ad bellum* moral character when determining the activities' *in bello* moral character. Traditionalists hold that there is a strict separation between the *ad bellum* and the *in bello* criteria, while the revisionists hold we can only understand the *in bello* criteria by inquiring into the cause of war and whether the war is just.[21] Put differently, traditionalists argue that a war could be *ad bellum* unjust and nonetheless the subsequent combatant activities could be *in bello* just, while the revisionists argue that if a war is *ad bellum* unjust, there is no way in which any actions could be *in bello* just.

While the disagreement between revisionists and traditionalists is framed in general terms, there are several difficulties with the revisionists' stand that arise in the particular context of an imposition of tort liability. First, the revisionists promote a binary understanding of warfare—either it is just and permitted, or unjust and prohibited. However, we can see how it could be possible to engage

[19] See: Vitoria (n 15) §50–56; Suárez (n 12) 839–51; May (n 6) 1; Brian Orend, '*Jus Post Bellum*: A Just War Theory Perspective' in Carsten Stahn and Jann K Kleffner (eds), *Jus Post Bellum: Towards a Law of Transition from Conflict to Peace* (CUP 2008) 40–41.

[20] Bass (n 6); Vitoria (n 15) §50; Orend (n 6) 162–63; Suárez (n 12) 839; May (n 6) 16; Seth Lazar, 'Skepticism about Jus Post Bellum' in Larry May and Andrew Forcehimes (eds), *Morality, Jus Post Bellum, and International Law* (CUP 2012) 218.

[21] Jeff McMahan, 'On the Moral Equality of Combatants' (2006) 14 Journal of Political Philosophy 377, 379; Thomas Hurka, 'Proportionality in the Morality of War' (2005) 33 Philosophy & Public Affairs 34, 44; Begby, Reichberg, and Syse (n 12) 336; Yitzhak Benbaji, 'The War Convention and the Moral Division of Labour' (2009) 59 The Philosophical Quarterly 593, 594; Lazar, 'The Morality and Law of War' (n 18) 377; Vattel (n 14) 542; Vitoria (n 15) §11; Suárez (n 12) 820; Walzer (n 18) 34–44.

in a wrongful activity in a non-wrongful way and to engage in a non-wrongful activity in a wrongful way. Take the following example that Arthur Ripstein has raised to convey the point about the distinctiveness of *jus ad bellum* and *jus in bello*.[22] Stealing a car is morally wrong, and driving a stolen car is legally wrongful in several ways. Still, the fact that the thief is driving the car she stole does not mean that there is no way in which she can abide by the speed limit. If the limit is no less than 60 km/h and no more than 100 km/h, and the thief is driving within these bounds, then she has not violated this legal norm despite the fact she has violated another norm. The opposite example is also valid. A person can drive her own car and drive above the speed limit or without a valid licence.

Nevertheless, revisionists seem to insist that war does not allow for this familiar distinction. This approach is not, however, reflected in international law. For instance, the Preamble to Additional Protocol I states that the *in bello* principles apply to all individuals regardless of the *ad bellum* character of the conflict, and that complying with the *in bello* principles does not absolve states from infringing their *ad bellum* duties.[23] Here, there is a clear choice to keep *ad bellum* criteria out of *in bello* calculus and vice versa. This choice recognizes that both the *ad bellum* unjust state and the *ad bellum* just state can act in a way that is *in bello* unjust. By relying on this understanding, I am able to offer a framework for holding states liable independently of the justice of their cause to engage in belligerent activities in the first place. Rather, according to my account, states would only be liable for losses that are wrongful in the *in bello* sense, not for all the losses that they inflict if they are *ad bellum* unjust.

By taking this stance, I am not holding that there cannot be other instances in which the revisionist account, or a middle ground between it and the traditionalist account, is appropriate. My argument is simply that in the particular context of an imposition of tort liability for wrongs committed during warfare, the traditionalist account is preferable as it results in a more coherent liability regime.

Second, the revisionist argument does not accurately capture the fact that the individuals who might decide to wage war unjustly are not likely to be the same individuals who would actually engage in belligerent activities. While both are agents of the state, they are separate moral and legal agents nonetheless. Indeed, the revisionist argument that opposes a separation between *ad*

[22] Arthur Ripstein, *Kant and the Law of War* (OUP 2021) 118; Arthur Ripstein, 'Rules for Wrongdoers' (*Berkeley Talks: Tanner Lectures, day 1*, 16 May 2019) <https://news.berkeley.edu/2019/05/16/berkeley-talks-transcript-2019-tanner-lectures-01/> accessed 4 November 2019.

[23] Paragraphs 4–5 of the Preamble to Additional Protocol I.

bellum and *in bello* principles seems convincing when the moral agent who decides to engage in unjust war is also the agent who conducts that war. Yet, assigning blame based on the actions of a different entity is difficult, as it conflates the different moral agents in war into a single entity. In this sense, the traditionalist argument that *ad bellum* and *in bello* principles should be evaluated separately seems to have greater force.

Lastly, the revisionist argument should also be rejected on instrumental grounds. If we do not separate *ad bellum* from *in bello*, then states that engage in unjust wars might be incentivized to act without any limits in order to achieve victory. If all actions done without a just cause are wrongful, then there is no difference between killing enemy combatants using conventional and non-conventional weapons; between killing combatants and non-combatants; and between inflicting losses on non-combatants in a way that abides by the *in bello* principles and a way that does not. If every action is wrongful, then states might rationalize that they might as well do anything in their power to ensure victory.[24] Wars of total annihilation could become standard practice. Alternatively, a sliding scale might be implemented, according to which the more a war is just, or the more injustice defeat will bring about, then the more rights could be violated and the less adherence to *jus in bello* would be required.[25] Consequently, *jus in bello* could become what David Dyzenhaus refers to as a 'grey hole', meaning that it would be nothing more than a façade with no actual legal substance.[26] A strict divide between *ad bellum* and *in bello* has the potential to incentivize states to restrict their belligerent activities and the losses they inflict, while maintaining the legal relevance and force of both bodies of law.

Still, there may be other external considerations that could influence how states conduct war. States might want to adhere to *in bello* rules for reciprocity, reputation, or high cost of waging a total war. Moreover, even if *ad bellum* and *in bello* principles are distinct, states still may not be incentivized to refrain from engaging in *ad bellum* unjust wars. Rather, they might simply be incentivized to wage them in accordance with the *in bello* principles. Yet, even if maintaining this divide fails to encourage states to refrain from waging wars altogether, its value lies in its ability to minimize civilian harms during combat.

[24] See: Gabriella Blum and John CP Goldberg, 'War for the Wrong Reasons: Lessons from Law' (2014) 11 Journal of Moral Philosophy 454, 474.

[25] Walzer (n 18) 229–30.

[26] David Dyzenhaus, 'Schmitt v. Dicey: Are States of Emergency inside or outside the Legal Order?' (2006) 27 Cardozo Law Review 2005, 2038.

As the discussion above demonstrates, it seems that the relevant norms for assessing states' conduct in times of war and during combat, for the purpose of determining tort liability, are those norms that regulate the actual engagement in belligerent activities. My analysis of the rights and duties of states and individuals in warfare shall therefore focus on, and be informed by, the *in bello* principles, as grounded in international humanitarian law and states' rules of engagement. In doing so, my analysis will be able to offer a nuanced account of tort liability that is based on the moral and legal fault of the relevant actors. In addition, it may provide incentives to contain the use of military force. Lastly, framing my analysis in this way will yield conclusions that coincide with the approach of the international legal order to separate between *ad bellum* and *in bello* issues of legality and justice.

III. The Relevant Tort Law Theory

The discussion thus far demonstrates that through reference to international humanitarian law and states' rules of engagement, we can determine the rights and duties of states and individuals during belligerent activities. Yet, these norms alone cannot provide the moral and legal underpinnings for the idea that a wronged individual is entitled to a private law remedy from the person who wronged her, nor do they articulate what constitutes a tortious wrong. For these purposes, we must turn to tort law theory, and I consider two of the leading approaches to it: an instrumentalist approach and a corrective justice approach.

As the discussion below shall demonstrate, in the particular context of liability for wrongful losses that are inflicted during combat, corrective justice seems to be more germane for two main reasons. First, as I show in greater detail below, a theoretical instrumentalist account analysis of tort liability during combatant activities results in the conclusion that state actors are likely to be systematically under-deterred from tort liability. Second, analysing tort liability for belligerent wrongs through a corrective justice approach offers a way to articulate which losses are wrongful, and why there is a duty to correct an infliction of wrongs, even during warfare.

To reach these conclusions, let me begin with an exposition of the instrumentalist account of liability that is based on an economic analysis of the law.[27]

[27] Gary T Schwartz, 'Mixed Theories of Tort Law: Affirming Both Deterrence and Corrective Justice' (1997) 75 Texas Law Review 1801, 1803.

According to this approach, actors are viewed as self-interested individuals, who consider only their own costs in choosing whether and how to engage in an activity,[28] causing them to act in ways that can reduce the overall social welfare. Proponents of this instrumentalist approach believe that a solution to this problem lies in tort, as it acts as a tool for the enhancement of social welfare by incentivizing actors to take into account the costs of wronging potential plaintiffs.[29] By imposing an objective standard of liability that is derived from a cost–benefit analysis, individuals are incentivized to take precautions that will reduce the cost of wrongful activities while not imposing excessive burdens.[30] Put differently, deterrence is viewed as a goal that ought to be achieved in order to maximize welfare, and liability is determined in reference to its deterring effects. An optimal level of deterrence would be achieved when the liability regime incentivizes individuals to act with care to avoid inflicting wrongful losses, avoiding a chilling effect on non-wrongful conduct and indifference to wrongful conduct.[31]

[28] W Jonathan Cardi, Randall D Penfield, and Albert H Yoon, 'Does Tort Law Deter Individuals? A Behavioral Science Study' (2012) 9 Journal of Empirical Legal Studies 567, 568.

[29] See, for example: Calabresi (n 3) 26–31; Posner, 'A Theory of Negligence' (n 3) 32–33; Posner, 'Wealth Maximization and Tort Law' (n 3) 99–103; Goldberg (n 3) 544. Note, deterrence is not the sole goal instrumentalists might seek to achieve through tort law. For example, they might wish to promote compensation, vindication of rights, economic efficiency, regulation and social policy, or equality (Mark A Geistfeld, 'Negligence, Compensation, and the Coherence of Tort Law' (2003) 91 Georgetown Law Journal 585; Jason Varuhas, 'The Concept of "Vindication" in the Law of Torts: Rights, Interests and Damages' (2014) 34 Oxford Journal of Legal Studies 253; Steven Shavell, *Economic Analysis of Accident Law* (Harvard UP 1987); George L Priest, 'The Invention of Enterprise Liability: A Critical History of the Intellectual Foundations of Modern Tort Law' (1985) 14 Journal of Legal Studies 461; Tsachi Keren-Paz, *Torts, Egalitarianism and Distributive Justice* (Ashgate 2007)).

[30] What is deemed as excessive could be understood by applying the Hand formula. If the marginal costs of avoiding an injury outweigh the marginal costs of the magnitude of loss times its probability of materializing, then the precautions taken are excessive (see, for example: Robert Cooter and Thomas Ulen, *Law & Economics* (5th edn, Pearson/Addison Wesley 2008) 349–53; Posner, 'A Theory of Negligence' (n 3) 32; Steven Shavell, *Foundations of Economic Analysis of Law* (Belknap Press of Harvard UP 2004) 182–89). For example, if preventing an accident between a car driver and a cyclist by installing better brakes will cost the driver $100, she will be liable if the probability of an accident is 50% and the magnitude of the loss is $202, as the cost associated with the risk of loss is $101 while the costs of prevention are $100.

[31] Calabresi (n 3) 26–31. One way to reduce the overall costs is to incentivize the least-cost avoider to act more carefully by holding her liable if the loss is realized (see: Posner, 'A Theory of Negligence' (n 3) 33). However, Calabresi and Hirschoff argue that optimal deterrence would be achieved by imposing liability on the individual who is in the best position to decide whether avoiding a loss is warranted (Guido Calabresi and Jon T Hirschoff, 'Towards a Test for Strict Liability in Torts' (1972) 81 Yale Law Journal 1055, 1060). For example, assume that the cost of the accident is $202. Further assume that we can reduce this cost to $0 by getting better car brakes, the cost of which is $100. Alternatively, we can also reduce the cost of the accident to $0 by having the cyclist wear a reflective vest, use bicycle lights, and wear a helmet, the costs of which are $90. Under this scenario, it would be best to have the cyclist shoulder the costs of the accident, as she is the least-cost avoider. For a critique of this approach in relation to cases in which parties fail to observe each other's costs of care at the time of the accident, see: G Dari-Mattiacci and N Garoupa, 'Least-Cost Avoidance: The Tragedy of Common Safety' (2007) 25 Journal of Law, Economics, and Organization 235.

Elsewhere, I have shown that an instrumentalist economic analysis approach and its conceptualization of tortious wrongdoing that is based on deterrence are ill-equipped to make sense of wrongdoing in the context of warfare and belligerent activities from both a theoretical and an empirical perspective.[32] Deterrence is commonly understood as the potential for tort liability to influence an actor's decision regarding whether and how to engage in a potentially injurious activity, considering the pecuniary costs and benefits that are associated with her various choices.

This understanding of deterrence is premised on three preconditions. First, it assumes that individuals have a choice about whether to participate in or refrain from an activity—or taking precautions in relation to that activity.[33] Without the ability to choose one course of action over another, deterrence plays no significant role in guiding individuals' behaviour. Second, it is assumed that individuals are capable of engaging in a cost–benefit analysis. This capability requires individuals to have accurate information about the costs and benefits associated with action and inaction; that individuals will have an opportunity to consider this information; and that they engage in a rational economic analysis in light of the possibility of incurring costs.[34] Partial information and lack of expertise in analysing its meaning result in erroneous determinations, which in turn could provide misguided *ex ante* incentives to individuals.[35] Third, it is also assumed that holding individuals liable for the cost of the wrongful losses they inflict will incentivize them to act more carefully, and that without this incentive individuals will not act with due care.[36]

Yet, it seems unlikely that the preconditions for the materialization of deterrence will be met by the relevant state actors who might be able to influence the decision on whether and how to engage in warfare—politicians, combatants, and government attorneys.[37] For instance, the ability to choose freely between courses of action varies between types of state actors, and for most it is limited. Whereas politicians have wide discretion, combatants' discretion is significantly more limited once politicians have ordered them to engage in, or refrain

[32] Haim Abraham, 'Tort Liability, Combatant Activities, and the Question of Over-Deterrence' (2022) 47 Law & Social Inquiry 885.

[33] Assaf Jacob, 'Immunity under Fire: State Immunity from Harm Caused due to "Combatant Activity"' (2003) 23 The Hebrew University Law Review 107, 127.

[34] However, a common criticism is that accurate information is rarely fully available to individuals prior to their actions, nor is it always fully available after the actions are completed and harm has been done (see: John G Fleming, 'Is There a Future for Tort?' (1984) 44 Louisiana Law Review 1193, 2000; Goldberg (n 3) 559).

[35] Goldberg (n 3) 552.

[36] Stephen D Sugerman, *Doing Away with Personal Injury Law* (Quorum Books 1989) 12–18.

[37] I refer to both commanding officers and their subordinates using the term 'combatants'.

from, a belligerent activity, and lower-ranking combatants' discretion is even more limited. In contrast, government attorneys seem to have no discretion over whether, and how, combatant activities will be engaged in, as their role is limited to advising politicians and combatants on the legal nature and implications that acts or omissions might have.

The ability to engage in a cost–benefit analysis is also limited. Combatants lack the time to make cost–benefit considerations in the heat of battle; or, they might not have a choice about their actions, for example if they are forced to act or act inadvertently. In both cases, it is hard to see how tort liability could incentivize combatants to act more carefully, as freedom of choice for combatants engaged in battle can be very limited.[38] Furthermore, it seems the relevant actors would probably not have full and accurate information about the various costs and benefits of combatant activities, given the uncertainties of warfare, and only government attorneys are likely to have an idea of the potential scope of liability.

Lastly, none of the relevant actors are likely to bear any of the costs personally, due to high litigation costs, low potential compensation, procedural hurdles discouraging potential plaintiffs from filing claims, and the fact that plaintiffs would prefer to sue states rather than individual state actors.[39] Consequently, state actors are unlikely to fully internalize the costs of wrongdoing, and states are likely to view the costs of potential tort liability as minor and give precedence to considerations that stem from security interests.[40]

Thus, it seems that politicians, combatants, and government attorneys are unlikely to be deterred by a potential imposition of tort liability given that the three preconditions for deterrence are not all met by any particular group of state actors. For the instrumentalist approach, these conclusions are a cause for concern, especially as means that could be used ordinarily to respond to under-deterrence, such as strict liability and punitive damages, do not seem

[38] Arguably, deterrence has little to no impact when we act with inadvertent carelessness. See: Bruce Feldthusen, 'If This Is Torts, Negligence Must Be Dead' in Ken Cooper-Stephenson and Elaine Gibson (eds), *Tort Theory* (Captus Press 1993) 409; Susan Randall, 'Corrective Justice and the Torts Process' (1993) 27 Indiana Law Review 1, 14. That said, commanders who are not present in the theatre of operations but are located in a shielded command post could potentially consider a cost–benefit analysis. In this context, the costs of compensating individuals could be relatively small in comparison to the costs of waging (let alone losing) a war. For example, a single Tomahawk cruise missile costs about $1.5m USD ('Rockets Galore' *The Economist* (29 September 2012) <https://www.economist.com/science-and-technology/2012/09/29/rockets-galore> accessed 29 March 2024).

[39] Abraham, 'Tort Liability, Combatant Activities, and the Question of Over-Deterrence' (n 32) 892, 911–13; Gilat Bachar, 'Access Denied—Using Procedure to Restrict Tort Litigation: The Israeli-Palestinian Experience' (2017) 92 Chicago-Kent Law Review 841, 849–51.

[40] Abraham, 'Tort Liability, Combatant Activities, and the Question of Over-Deterrence' (n 32) 897–903, 909–11.

to solve the issues at hand. When actors have no choice about if and how to act, have no ability to engage in a cost–benefit analysis, and generally do not shoulder the cost of wrongdoing, strict liability punitive damages are unlikely to have any effect. If deterrence is not, or could not be, achieved through tort law, tort liability is put into question and alternatives should be considered.

In contrast, for the corrective justice approach, deterrence is not an integral part of the process whereby the wrongful or non-wrongful character of a loss is determined.[41] Deterrence does not define which behaviour is wrongful, but rather it is an additional function of tort law after it has been determined and articulated as positive law.[42] Rather, for a corrective justice approach, the key concern is with wrongful violations of an individual's private rights, which must be rectified by holding the wrongdoer liable towards the injured individual for the wrongful loss she inflicted.[43] This notion is bipolar, relational, and formal, as it considers only the rights and entitlements of the individual who caused the wrong and the individual who suffered that same wrong.[44] External goals or policies do not affect the determination of whether a loss is wrongful and liability should be imposed.[45]

For the corrective justice approach, lack of deterrence in any particular instance does not undermine the value of tort law as such. Even if individuals were likely to be entirely undeterred by tort liability, tort law would still have value in its ability to articulate norms of conduct and to correct wrongful losses once they have been inflicted. The emphasis placed by corrective justice on tort law's formal structure means that it is less susceptible to empirical findings in relation to the preconditions for the materialization of deterrence. Therefore, the corrective justice approach seems to be more suitable in the particular context of liability for wrongful losses that are inflicted during combat. As the corrective justice approach is relevant even if the three above-mentioned preconditions cannot be realized during warfare, analysing tort law through the corrective justice lens enables us to articulate the norms of conduct even in the

41 Ernest J Weinrib, 'Deterrence and Corrective Justice' (2002) 50 University of California, Los Angeles Law Review 621, 624.

42 ibid 625.

43 Although the rights-based accounts I rely on throughout the book differ regarding several aspects of corrective justice and in their theories for tort liability, their views generally fit with the description above, and their differences do not affect my arguments here.

44 Weinrib, *The Idea of Private Law* (n 1) 73, 159–60; Weinrib, 'Deterrence and Corrective Justice' (n 41) 630–31; Carol Harlow, *State Liability: Tort Law and Beyond* (OUP 2004) 11; Ripstein, *Private Wrongs* (n 1) 167; John CP Goldberg and Benjamin C Zipursky, 'Tort Law and Responsibility' in John Oberdiek (ed), *Philosophical Foundations of the Law of Torts* (OUP 2014) 27; Martin Stone, 'The Significance of Doing and Suffering' in Gerald J Postema (ed), *Philosophy and the Law of Torts* (CUP 2001) 159.

45 Weinrib, *The Idea of Private Law* (n 1) 1–10; Goldberg (n 3) 571.

most extreme and difficult times. It is this ability that is key to understanding which losses are wrongful, and why there is a duty to correct the infliction of wrongs.

Furthermore, as my analysis of the rights and duties of states and individuals during war and combatant activities is informed by international humanitarian law and states' rules of engagement, it is clear why a corrective justice approach is more appropriate than a strict liability regime. Relying on the corrective justice approach to determine tort liability enables me to offer a nuanced account that is based on the moral and legal fault of the relevant actors, in a way that is coherent in terms of both private law and the laws of war. In contrast, a strict liability regime seems to be inconsistent with the fact that the laws of war only prohibit certain kinds of inflictions of losses since, under strict liability, liability would extend to all losses inflicted during war. As such, establishing a strict liability regime in this particular context would be less coherent than a regime that is based on corrective justice.

Still, it could be argued that the corrective justice approach to tort law is irrelevant in this context, since tort law should not apply at all because, by engaging in war, states are acting in a capacity to which there is no private analogy. This type of argument has been made more broadly in relation to all public officials' activities that have no private law analogue.[46] Indeed, when states impose taxes, expropriate lands, or wage war, they are inflicting losses in a public capacity. There is no legitimate private equivalent to inflicting such losses.

The problem this argument raises is that states are not equal to private individuals when they act in their public capacity. Our ability to use our bodies and means is limited. We can only pursue our purposes to the extent that our actions allow others to use their bodies and means to pursue their purposes.[47] We are constrained in this way as individuals who are free and equal agents and are in horizontal relationships with each other. We are all allowed to use our means and are constrained in the use of our means in the same way. Therefore, to a degree, the argument that states are not equal to private individuals holds true. Private individuals are in horizontal bipolar relationships with one another. In contrast, a state acting in a public capacity is not an equal agent to private individuals, as it is exercising its authority over all of the members of its community. The relationship in this context is vertical, not horizontal. Furthermore,

[46] Peter W Hogg, *Liability of the Crown* (2nd edn, Carswell Co 1989) 3; Ivor Jennings, *The Law and the Constitution* (5th edn, London UP 1959) 312; Wolfgang Friedmann, *Law in a Changing Society* (Penguin Books 1964) 277; Christopher Forsyth and William Wade, *Administrative Law* (11th edn, OUP 2014) 708.

[47] Ripstein, *Private Wrongs* (n 1) 167.

when a state is acting in a public capacity, it is not using the same rights that private individuals have, nor is it bound by the ability of private individuals to act in a similar way. Rather, it is bound by administrative and constitutional norms.[48] Thus, the basis for an imposition of tort liability appears to be missing when states inflict losses while acting in a public capacity.

Yet, the lack of equal rights and equal status between states and private individuals does not mean that tort law should not apply. The argument that states should not be held liable could be divided in the following ways. First, there is something in the public functions that states fulfil that has no private equivalent and should not be evaluated under the same normative system as private actions. Second, the position in which public officials are acting has no private equivalent and should not be subject to the same liability rules. Neither argument is sufficiently convincing to conclude that there should not be tort liability for belligerent wrongs, as they do not capture the relevant factor—the public or private nature of the loss that was inflicted.

As for the first argument, the issue with applicability of tort law cannot simply be derived from the fact that a public function has been pursued. The identity of service providers of various functions is contingent and varies over time. The public versus private divide is, consequently, more fluid than constant.[49] As history indicates, functions that were once fulfilled by public bodies, such as supplying water, electricity, or sewage services, are now commonly provided by private commercial entities. If we would hold private corporations liable for wrongs they inflict while providing public functions, it is difficult to justify not holding public bodies liable for providing the same functions based solely on the public nature of these functions. Put differently, it is not the identity of service providers that is relevant, it is whether a public function was carried out that is important. For example, a tax collector is carrying out a public function, but if she charges taxes without authority to do so then she is no longer acting in a public capacity.

The same issue is inherent in the second argument, that is, that the position public officials are acting in has no private equivalent and should not constitute liability under the same liability rules as private individuals. To clarify,

[48] Paul Miller and Jeffrey Pojanowski explain the basis for such inequality on the fact that states are artificial persons. See: Paul B Miller and Jeffrey A Pojanowski, 'Torts against the State' in Paul B Miller and John Oberdiek (eds), *Civil Wrongs and Justice in Private Law* (OUP 2020) 330. It is the fact that public power can be used only in the pursuit of public purposes, while private law is generally unconcerned with wrongdoers' motives, that led Donal Nolan to conclude that misfeasance in public office and exemplary damages should not be considered in private law terms but in public law ones. See: Donal Nolan, 'Tort and Public Law: Overlapping Categories?' (2019) 135 Law Quarterly Review 272, 282–83.

[49] Harlow (n 44) 31.

my argument is not that states' obligations towards one another under international humanitarian law should be imported into tort law and become obligations states owe to civilians. Instead, I argue that ordinary private law rights and obligations remain relevant during warfare, and that compliance with international humanitarian law and the rules of engagement provides a justification that makes violations of private law rights non-wrongful.

Holding public office does not mean it is not possible to commit a private wrong while wielding public power, or what could appear to be public power. Rather, we hold public officials and bodies liable because they have committed a private wrong. They have caused an injury to an individual's body or means in a way that 'triggers' corrective justice duties. These duties, as Aristotle explains them, are blind to the status of the injurer and injured. The only question is if one party has done a wrong and the other party has suffered it.[50] The reason for our indifference to the status of the state as such when it inflicts a wrongful loss is the same reason for our indifference to citizenship and residency status. It is not the status of parties that determines whether a corrective justice duty exists, but whether a wrongful private law loss was inflicted. The relevant question is whether a private or a public wrong has been inflicted. If it is private, then tort law should apply. The emphasis lies on the way in which states use the means at their disposal, rather than on their status as public bodies.[51]

Considering the conclusions of the discussion above, my analysis of the infliction of tortious wrongs during war and through combatant activities shall be based on a corrective justice approach. It will be bipolar, relational, and formal, as it shall only consider the rights and entitlements of the state and its agents who inflict wrongful losses, and the non-combatants who suffered those same wrongs. External goals and policies do not influence the classification of losses as wrongful or non-wrongful, as well as the determination of whether liability should be imposed.

IV. Forum and Choice of Law

In the context of international armed conflict, there are four possible avenues in which claims can be pursued: in the state where the wrongful loss was inflicted; in the state that either inflicted the wrong or is affiliated with the wrongdoer; in a state with universal jurisdiction; and in an international

[50] Aristotle, *Nicomachean Ethics* (Martin Ostwald tr, Bobbs-Merrill 1983) 120–21.
[51] Ripstein, *Private Wrongs* (n 1) 167–68.

forum. Below, I briefly illustrate why the most appropriate forum for such claims is in the courts of the state that inflicted the wrong or is affiliated with the wrongdoer. I also argue that the alternative choice of law rules do not impact the validity of my main arguments—that tort law could and should apply to redress belligerent wrongs.

The first issue to address is the question of which court has jurisdiction to hear tort claims in this context. One possibility is a finding that the most appropriate forum for a tort claim is within the state where the wrongful loss was inflicted.[52] When a claim is brought against a private individual in the jurisdiction in which the wrong was inflicted, no special issues arise in relation to the jurisdiction of the domestic courts over the dispute. Yet, when claims are brought against foreign states in the domestic jurisdiction where the wrong was inflicted, there could be some difficulties. As a general rule, states cannot be subjected to the jurisdiction of other states without their consent. This familiar principle in international law is known as the 'Sovereign Immunity Doctrine', and it is an expression of states' equal status and independence from one another.[53] The scope of the doctrine has been narrowed in many jurisdictions to exclude liability in tort for losses that a foreign state inflicts in the domestic state's jurisdiction while acting in a private capacity, as opposed to a public capacity.[54] Still, some might argue that inflicting losses through combatant activities should be considered as states acting in their 'sovereign capacity' and hence that the doctrine of sovereign immunity should remain in force.

Even if such an argument was rejected, three significant difficulties would remain in finding the courts of the place of the injury the most appropriate

[52] See, for example: *Haaretz.com v Goldhar* [2018] 2 SCR 3, Côte J paragraph 36; American Law Institute, *Restatement of the Law, Second: Conflict of Laws* (American Law Institute 1971) §27(1)A(h); Elizabeth T Lear, 'National Interests, Foreign Injuries, and Federal Forum Non Conveniens' (2007) 41 University of California, Davis Law Review 559, 569.

[53] See, for example: *The Parlement Belge* [1880] All ER Rep 104, 114; *Schreiber v Canada (Attorney General)* [2002] 3 SCR 269, 280–82; James Crawford, *Brownlie's Principles of Public International Law* (9th edn, OUP 2019) 470–92; Hazel Fox and Philippa Webb, *The Law of State Immunity* (3rd edn, OUP 2015) 38–39. Yet, other rationales for the sovereign immunity doctrine that focus on the need to maintain peaceful international relations or the inability to secure remedies have also been advanced (see, for instance: *Kazemi Estate v Islamic Republic of Iran* [2014] 3 SCR 176, 205; Craig Forcese, 'De-Immunizing Torture: Reconciling Human Rights and State Immunity' (2007) 52 McGill Law Journal 127, 133–35; Lee M Caplan, 'State Immunity, Human Rights, and *Jus Cogens*: A Critique of the Normative Hierarchy Theory' (2003) 97 American Journal of International Law 741, 748).

[54] For example: Section 6 of the State Immunity Act, RSC, 1985, c S-18 1985; Section 5 of the Foreign States Immunity Act 2008; 28 USC §1605(a)(5) 1976; Section 5 of the State Immunity Act 1978; Section 13 of the Foreign States Immunities Act 1985; *Al-Adsani v The United Kingdom* Judgment, 2001 ECHR, paragraph 54; *The Schooner Exch v McFaddon* 11 US 116 (2 March 1812) 136; *Verlinden BV v Cent Bank of Nigeria* 461 US 480 (23 May 1983) 486–89; *Opati v Republic of Sudan* 206 L Ed 2d 904 (18 May 2020) 909–10; *R v Hape* [2007] 2 SCR 292, paragraphs 40–43; Fox and Webb (n 53) 25–48; Forcese (n 53) 133–35; Caplan (n 53) 748.

forum. First, establishing that a belligerent wrong was committed will not be an easy task, as it is very likely that in most cases relevant information will be held by the state affiliated with the injurer and would not otherwise be available to plaintiffs.[55] Moreover, this information is very likely to be classified, and as such it will not be submitted to foreign courts for review. Consequently, and considering that 'war is the realm of uncertainty',[56] bringing a claim to the courts of the place of the injury is likely to be to the detriment of both plaintiffs and states, as these courts will be in an inferior position to ascertain the circumstances of an infliction of loss.

Second, enforcing judgments against the wrongdoer could be extremely difficult outside the jurisdiction of the state affiliated with the wrongdoer. The assumption here is that defendants and their assets will be present in the state that they are affiliated with. Assets in other states are likely to be less available, while legal, political, and financial hurdles to the enforceability of foreign courts' rulings are a common phenomenon.[57] Under such circumstances, the courts of the state affiliated with the wrongdoer are likely to be in a better position to provide an effective remedy.[58]

Third, by having the courts of the state that inflicted the wrong—or that is affiliated with the wrongdoer—review a claim for compensation, issues of comity and risk to peaceful international relations between states do not arise. These courts are domestic, and there is no significant difference between their

[55] Kathryn Lee Boyd, 'The Inconvenience of Victims: Abolishing Forum Non Conveniens in U.S. Human Rights Litigation' (1998) 39 Virginia Journal of International Law 41, 46.

[56] Carl von Clausewitz, *On War (1832)* (Michael Eliot Howard and Peter Paret eds, Princeton UP 2008) 101.

[57] Forcese (n 53) 133–35.

[58] While the courts of the affiliate state can have jurisdiction over tort claims for belligerent wrongs, there could nevertheless be other hurdles to litigation. These hurdles can be associated with the nature of post-conflict international litigation. The high costs of international litigation and the unfamiliar and inaccessible character of the jurisdiction's legal system to foreign plaintiffs can deter potential plaintiffs from pursuing their claims. In addition, those claims that will be brought despite these difficulties could be met with other procedural impediments. Combatants might have immunity from liability (for instance: Section 7A(a) of the Tort Ordinance 1968; John C Jr Jeffries, 'What's Wrong with Qualified Immunity' (2010) 62 Florida Law Review 851, 851–52; James E Pfander, 'Resolving the Qualified Immunity Dilemma: Constitutional Tort Claims for Nominal Damages' (2011) 111 Columbia Law Review 1601, 1602–3; Stephen R Reinhardt, 'The Demise of Habeas Corpus and the Rise of Qualified Immunity: The Court's Ever Increasing Limitations on the Development and Enforcement of Constitutional Rights and Some Particularly Unfortunate Consequences' (2015) 113 Michigan Law Review 1219, 1245–46). Likewise, private military companies might enjoy special immunities (see, for example: *Koohi v United States* 976 F2d 1328 (1992) 1336–37; *Boyle v United Techs Corp* 487 US 500 (27 June 1988) 510–12; *McKay v Rockwell International Corp* 704 F2d 444 (9th Cir Cal, 20 April 1983) 448–49). Additionally, states currently enjoy immunity from liability due to the combatant activities exception. In the next chapters, I articulate the justification for imposing liability on states for their belligerent wrongs, arguing in favour of restricting or even abolishing the combatant activities exception. Due to conceptual and space constraints, I will not address the issues surrounding immunities of combatants and private military companies here.

abilities to review the operation of their own wrongdoers in peacetime and in wartime for the purpose of determining tort liability. Moreover, they are in a better position to review evidence *in camera* and, as stated above, to enforce judgments in their own jurisdictions.

The same difficulties regarding the ability to obtain evidence, enforce judgments, and maintain comity between states also suggest that the courts that are affiliated with the wrongdoer are the more appropriate forum, as opposed to courts that assert universal jurisdiction, and international forums. Moreover, international forums suffer from an additional and unique issue that places them as an inferior forum for resolving tort claims for belligerent wrongs, as there are currently no institutions with compulsory universal jurisdiction that could adjudicate claims for compensation.

It follows that the most appropriate forum seems to be the civil courts of the state that inflicted the wrong or that is affiliated with the wrongdoer. That said, bringing claims to these courts does not mean that the jurisdiction in which the loss was inflicted is entirely irrelevant. In international tort cases, common law courts decide the governing substantive law according to one of three choice of law doctrines. The first is the doctrine of double actionability, which requires that an injury would be considered an actionable wrong in both the jurisdiction in which it was done and the jurisdiction in which the case was brought. However, this doctrine has been rejected to various extents.[59] The second is the doctrine of *lex loci delicti*, which holds that the substantive law that governs international tort claims is the law of the place in which the wrong was inflicted (*lex loci delicti*), while the procedural law is that of the place of adjudication (*lex fori*).[60] The third doctrine that is applied by many US states requires the

[59] For example, the Supreme Court of Canada and the High Court of Australia have both rejected this doctrine, though the Canadian court maintained an exception that allows for the applicability of the doctrine when not doing so will result in an injustice (see: *Regie Nationale des Usines Renault SA v Zhang* (2002) 187 ALR 1, 17; *Tolofson v Jensen* [1994] 3 SCR 1022, 49). Israel adopted a similar approach, rejecting the double accountability doctrine while creating a justice-based exception, according to which the *lex loci delicti* rule would be deviated from if the place in which the wrong occurred is entirely coincidental (CA 1432/03 *Yinon Manufacturing and Marketing Food Products Inc v Kraan* PD 59 (1) 345 (2004) 369–78; FH 4655/09 *Skalar v Uviner* PD 65(1) 735 (2011) 759). In contrast, in the United Kingdom, the double accountability doctrine was repealed through legislation, though it too has maintained several exceptions that allow for the application of the doctrine (Sections 10–13 of the Private International Law (Miscellaneous Provisions) Act 1995; *Kuwait Airways Corp v Iraqi Airways Co (No 3)* [2002] 3 All ER 209).

[60] In his book, Uglješa Grušić offers an extensive analysis of the way in which UK courts apply choice of law doctrines to torts committed by UK officials abroad while acting in their official capacity, noting that three different approaches to the relevant law have been used inconsistently. Grušić argues that there is greater justification to adopt English law as the choice of law basis on which claims relating to the tortious liability the UK government for its extraterritorial torts should be analysed. See: Uglješa Grušić, *Torts in UK Foreign Relations* (OUP 2023) 183–91, 267–78. For an argument of why a domestic state's courts could legitimately impose liability on their own state for its extraterritorial torts, see: Haim

courts to determine the applicable law according to the jurisdiction which has the most significant relationship to the occurrence of the wrong and the parties.[61] For all three doctrines, the jurisdiction of the state in which the wrong took place could remain relevant, as its positive laws could be considered in order to determine whether a certain loss is wrongful.

While the choice of law doctrine that will be in use ultimately depends on the particularities of each case, for the purpose of this book, there is no need to evaluate which of the doctrines should be adopted. Deciding on choice of law rules is a distinct question that does not impact the main argument I make—that there could and ought to be tort liability for belligerent wrongs, and that such wrongs could be actionable in any jurisdiction. The liability regime I advance in this book requires civilians to bring their claim to the courts of the state that wronged them or that is affiliated with their wrongdoer. The choice of law question does not sway the broader theoretical argument that the domestic state's courts can and should have the ordinary power to review the conduct of its state domestically and overseas.[62]

V. The Road Ahead

To advance my arguments, the book is structured as follows:

In Chapter 2, I develop an account of states' moral obligation to compensate civilians for inflicting what I define as 'belligerent wrongs', referring to violations of civilians' rights without proper justification. To establish my argument, I show that private law rights and duties exist and remain relevant during war. I argue that an infliction of a loss while engaging in belligerent activities is a violation of a private law right, and hence it is a *prima facie* private law wrong. Yet, such losses are justified and non-wrongful if they are imposed while complying with international humanitarian law and the rules of engagement. In instances in which a belligerent wrong cannot be justified, an ordinary corrective justice duty to redress the wrong arises. By conceptualizing belligerent wrongs and states' duty to correct them in this way, I lay the foundations to my argument that belligerent wrongs could and should be corrected through ordinary

Abraham, 'Myths and Misconceptions in Extraterritorial Torts' (forthcoming) University of Toronto Law Journal <https://dx.doi.org/10.2139/ssrn.4741760> accessed 12 March 2024.

[61] Restatement (Second) of Conflict of Laws §6, §145.
[62] See: Abraham, 'Myths and Misconceptions in Extraterritorial Torts' (n 60).

domestic tort law, while acknowledging the distinctive moral and legal norms that govern warfare.

In Chapter 3, I establish that a substantive rule of law approach also supports the argument that tort liability should be available to redress belligerent wrongs and argue that the main immunity that hinders the liability regime I advance—the combatant activities exception—should be abolished or narrowed. According to AV Dicey, tort law remedies are essential to rule of law–abiding regimes, as they enable individuals to enforce their rights and minimize the risk of arbitrary action and abuse of public powers. Civilians' right to obtain remedies in tort for the belligerent wrongs states inflict on them is a means through which states' use of power is constrained. I show that the combatant activities exception results in a regime in which the discretion of public officials and bodies is not properly governed by private law, and as such it deviates from the requirements of substantive rule of law.

I then turn to the writings of Trevor Allan and David Dyzenhaus, who suggest that when a public official or a public body diverges from the rule of law, they should only do so to attain a public purpose and have an adequate justification for doing so. My analysis demonstrates that the challenges the combatant activities exception raises—its ambiguous scope; public officials' unbounded discretion; the potential discriminatory application of the exception to certain populations; and the lack of access to legal remedies—are not properly justified according to substantive rule of law principles. Consequently, to be properly governed by the rule of law, the exception should either be abolished or alternatively it should be narrowed for it to be a justified divergence from the requirements of substantive rule of law.

In Chapters 4 to 6, I illustrate how the theoretical framework I suggest could operate through existing tort doctrines. Chapter 4 examines intentional torts that are inflicted in the process of engaging in actual combat. As losses are justified and non-wrongful if inflicted while adhering to international humanitarian law or the state's rules of engagement, if these norms are infringed intentionally by combatants or states, they constitute belligerent wrongs for which there is an ordinary duty of redress. However, acting with a relevant level of intent to breach these norms must be understood in context, meaning that awareness that the acts will be inconsistent with international humanitarian law or the rules of engagement is necessary for establishing an intentional belligerent tort. This articulation of intentional belligerent torts suggests that their infliction involves an element of misuse or abuse of public power, indicating that misfeasance in public office might be particularly relevant in this context.

In Chapter 5, I argue that combatants and states can be held liable in negligence for unintentional losses they inflict during warfare. While engaging in belligerent activities, combatants and states owe an ordinary duty of care to avoid wrongfully interfering with individuals' rights, that is, for inflicting a non-justified loss through acts that infringe international humanitarian law or the rules of engagement. I demonstrate that policy considerations that negate the existence of this ordinary duty of care are apparently unconvincing. I also suggest that the standard of care could be derived from the norms governing combatant activities, and thus would require states and combatants to act in compliance with international humanitarian law and the rules of engagement. Lastly, I show that combatant activities do not give rise to unique issues of causal uncertainty and that these issues could be addressed using ordinary doctrines.

The focus in Chapter 6 turns to assessing the viability of direct and vicarious impositions of liability on states for belligerent wrongs that are inflicted by their combatants, contractors, and citizens. I illustrate that there is nothing in the doctrine of vicarious liability that inherently rules out its applicability to belligerent wrongs, though its application would vary in accordance with doctrinal and theoretical variations between jurisdictions. Moreover, direct liability could be imposed for wrongful losses that are inflicted by third parties when a state's own failures have created the risk that materialized; when the state has had a non-delegable duty; or when it has ratified the wrongful conduct.

The upshot of my analysis is that even though tort liability *could* be imposed for belligerent wrongs, the applicability of negligence and intentional torts would be narrow. This narrow application of tort law is consistent with the narrow definition I have offered of belligerent wrongs, as the infliction of a loss that is done in breach of international humanitarian law or the rules of engagement. To demonstrate why tort liability should be available to redress belligerent wrongs, despite the narrow application of the regime I advance, in Chapter 7, I assess the comparative merits of tort law in relation to the two main relevant alternatives to it: *ex gratia* payments and state-operated insurance schemes. Examining these alternatives is vital. These payment schemes are currently the mechanisms through which states address the losses individuals sustain due to belligerent activities. Additionally, the tort liability scheme that I present would be rather narrow in scope, leaving room for arguments against the relevance or merit of relying on tort law to remedy belligerent wrongs, and in favour of these alternative schemes. The purpose of this chapter is to analyse whether indeed tort law is nevertheless the more appropriate avenue through which belligerent wrongs should be addressed.

I show that in some respects, the alternatives to tort liability schemes fall short of the benefits of tort liability, while in other respects, they prevail over it. Some factors, such as the length, cost, and location of the redress mechanism, appear to indicate that tort liability is inferior to its alternatives, to a certain extent. Other factors, for example the consistency and transparency of decisions, whether the payment amounts reflect the actual costs of the injuries, the identity of the administrating body, and the ability to correct wrongs, seem to result in the contrary conclusion.

However, in the particular context of infliction of losses during war, and considering the way in which the alternatives to tort liability are administered, there does not seem to be a strong reason to prefer *ex gratia* and state-operated insurance schemes over tort liability. Indeed, tort liability does have some shortcomings, and they can be significant. Yet, these shortcomings do not reach the degree that they rule out tort liability completely as a relevant mechanism of redress, and the benefits that arise from tort liability are substantial. Moreover, the inadequacies of *ex gratia* payments and state-operated insurance schemes are sufficiently weighty to question their desirability and effectiveness as mechanisms of redress, despite their current widespread adoption.

I believe that the deficiencies of the current form of providing redress for losses that are inflicted during battle indicate that choosing them over a tort liability regime comes at too high a cost. In doing away with tort liability, individuals lose the ability to turn to the courts' authoritative power to enforce their rights, vindicate their social standing, and restore their normative relationship with their wrongdoers. This cost, coupled with the deficiencies of the current mechanisms of redress, is sufficient to support the argument that revisions to the mechanisms of redress are needed, and that tort liability and litigation should be considered as the preferable means over its alternatives.

I conclude in Chapter 8 by demonstrating that the discussion conducted throughout this book elucidates why the current legal reality, in which states enjoy a blanket immunity from tort liability for losses they inflict during battle, should be altered. I show that the answer to the question that animated this book—could and should tort liability be imposed for losses inflicted during combat—is that states could be held liable in tort, and there are compelling reasons why they should be.

2
Defining Rights, Wrongs, and Duties

I. Introduction

Losses that are inflicted on civilians through armed activities are unique. Despite being able to articulate when imposing such losses might be intuitively, morally, and, legally wrongful, it is nevertheless commonly assumed that civilians lack a right to claim compensation for the losses they sustain directly from the state that wronged them. The main reasons for this assumption are twofold. First, under international law, states are not obligated to compensate private individuals for infliction of losses during war.[1] Second, proceedings that are ordinarily available for private individuals are frustrated in this context by immunities such as the 'Foreign Sovereign Immunity Doctrine', the 'Crown Act of State Doctrine', and the 'Combatant Activities Exception'. These immunities apply in a wide range of circumstances, barring tort liability for losses that are inflicted in the heat of battle and auxiliary operations, and extend to everything from minor property damage to loss of lives. Furthermore, these immunities remain in force even when states acknowledge that the losses were inflicted due to their errors in judgment.

The hardship of civilians who are left to shoulder the costs of losses that have been inflicted on them during war has led scholars to make pragmatic arguments for compensation. Yet, these arguments disregard norms of liability under international law and tort law. For instance, it has been suggested that compensation should be imposed whether international humanitarian law was infringed or not, as non-compensation makes little political sense,[2] results in injustice,[3] and

[1] *Jurisdictional Immunities of the State (Germany v Italy; Greece Intervening)* ICJ Judgment, 3 February 2012, Separate Opinion of Judge Koroma, paragraph 9; Andrea Gattini, 'To What Extent Are State Immunity and Non-Justiciability Major Hurdles to Individuals' Claims for War Damages?' (2003) 1 Journal of International Criminal Justice 348, 348. Note, a previous version of the arguments I am making in this chapter was published in: Haim Abraham, 'Tort Liability for Belligerent Wrongs' (2019) 39 Oxford Journal of Legal Studies 808.

[2] Dieter Fleck, 'Individual and State Responsibility for Violations of the Ius in Bello: An Imperfect Balance' in Wolff Heintschel von Heinegg and Volker Epping (eds), *International Humanitarian Law Facing New Challenges* (Springer 2007) 180.

[3] Emanuela-Chiara Gillard, 'Reparation for Violations of International Humanitarian Law' (2003) 85 International Review of the Red Cross 529, 551; W Michael Reisman, 'The Lessons of Qana' (1997) 22 Yale Journal of International Law 381, 397–98.

Tort Liability in Warfare. Haim Abraham, Oxford University Press. © Haim Abraham 2024.
DOI: 10.1093/9780191997051.003.0002

fails to provide proper incentives to avoid inflicting losses on civilians.[4] Similarly, it has been argued that liability should be imposed regardless of whether the loss was a tortious wrong since waging war is an ultra-hazardous activity.[5]

The conclusion that liability should be imposed regardless of whether international humanitarian law has been infringed or not, or whether a tortious wrong was inflicted or not, would be too hasty, however. Without reference to international humanitarian law, we cannot determine the rights and duties of states and individuals during belligerent activities. The very notions of 'war' and what it means to inflict a wrongful loss during war cannot be unpacked without reference to the theory and law of war. Furthermore, without reference to tortious wrongdoing and corrective justice, we lose the moral and legal underpinnings of the idea that a wronged individual is entitled to a private law remedy from the person who wronged her, as well as the ability to articulate what constitutes a tortious wrong.[6]

In this chapter, I tackle three preconditions that must be met to advance the claim that civilians could and should have a right in tort law to compensation for wrongs they sustain during battle, through the injuring state's domestic courts. The three preconditions are that there are rights during war; that there is a standard according to which mere

[4] Yaël Ronen, 'Avoid or Compensate? Liability for Incidental Injury to Civilians Inflicted during Armed Conflict' (2009) 42 Vanderbilt Journal of Transnational Law 181, 202–8.

[5] Rebecca Crootof, 'War Torts: Accountability for Autonomous Weapons' (2016) 164 University of Pennsylvania Law Review 1347, 1394–95; Marcus Schulzke and Amanda Carroll, 'Corrective Justice for the Civilian Victims of War: Compensation and the Right to Life' [2015] Journal of International Relations and Development 1, 3. Note, a third option has been raised by the international community, according to which states can be held liable for inflicting a loss while infringing international law (Draft Articles on the Responsibility of States for Internationally Wrongful Acts 2001). However, the draft articles suggest a compensation mechanism in which individuals have no standing. The parties to the conflict would be states, and therefore this mechanism is irrelevant for the purpose of this book, which is to articulate a direct action by private individuals in tort against states for inflicting belligerent wrongs.

[6] The conceptual difficulties for articulating rights, wrongs, and obligations without reference to both international humanitarian law and tort law and theory would arise whether liability was articulated through international law or tort law. In this book, I focus on articulating how liability could be imposed on states and combatants through domestic tort law. For an analysis on how international law of states' responsibility in armed conflicts could be developed more coherently, see: Haim Abraham, 'Frameworks for Accountability: How Domestic Tort Law Can Inform the Development of International Law of State Responsibility in Armed Conflicts' (2023) 64 Virginia Journal of International Law Online 1, 10–22. Note, Rebecca Crootof and I disagree on whether liability could be divorced from either body of law, and Crootof argues that strict liability could be imposed on states in the context of warfare as a matter of doctrine for policy reasons. See: Rebecca Crootof, 'Implementing War Torts' (2023) 63 Virginia Journal of International Law 319, 368–69. I agree that as a matter of positive law strict liability is possible, and indeed that are several instances in which domestic tort law does not follow the form or substance of corrective justice fully. But as I show throughout the book, I believe that in the context of armed conflicts, structuring liability without due regard to both tort law and international humanitarian law would be unwarranted for normative and policy-related reasons.

harms are distinguishable from wrongs, which I refer to as 'belligerent wrongs';[7] and that there is a duty to correct these wrongs.

I show that private law rights exist, and remain relevant, during war. Moreover, the way to distinguish between harms for which no liability arises and wrongs for which there can be tortious liability is unique in the context of belligerent activities. This evaluation requires gauging whether combatant activities have adhered to international humanitarian law and states' rules of engagement.[8] I argue that an infliction of a loss while engaging in belligerent activities is a violation of a private law right, and hence it is a *prima facie* private law wrong. Yet, such losses are justified and non-wrongful if they are imposed while adhering to international humanitarian law and the rules of engagement. When such a justification does not exist, an ordinary corrective justice duty to redress the wrongs arises, and as I show in Chapters 4 and 5, this duty could be discharged through ordinary domestic tort law.

By structuring tort liability in this way, I offer an account of the limits of liability in accordance with the distinctive features of war. Not all infringements of private rights are actionable, as engaging in combat would not be possible under such a liability regime. Likewise, not all violations of private law rights during combat are non-wrongful, as this regime fails to distinguish legitimate forms of warfare from illegitimate forms of violence. Rather, international humanitarian law and states' rules of engagement demarcate the boundaries of liability, as only losses that are inflicted in breach of these norms will give rise to liability.

To set the stage, I demonstrate in Section II of this chapter, the difficulty as well as promise that is entailed in the current international law regime. It does not provide civilians with a right to compensation, but it does provide the normative basis for distinguishing belligerent harms from belligerent wrongs. It is this normative basis that underlies my critique of the solutions that have been

[7] Some terminological and conceptual clarifications are in order. Rebecca Crootof coined the term 'war torts' in reference to a regime of states' international law liability towards civilians for losses inflicted through armed conflicts, to create a body of law and terminology similar to 'war crimes': Rebecca Crootof, 'War Torts' (2022) 97 New York University Law Review 1063, 1071, 1101. My articulation of 'belligerent wrongs' differs from Crootof's, as belligerent wrongs refer to the form and substance of the moral and legal wrongs that could be inflicted through combatant activities. Under my account, the relevant liability regime is ordinary tort law utilizing ordinary tort doctrines, and therefore wrongs would not be war torts, but simply torts. Belligerent wrongs are also distinguishable from Uglješa Grušić's articulation of 'Torts in External Exercise of Authority'. For Grušić, torts in external exercise of authority encompass issues that emerge under private international law when tort claims are brought to civil courts in the United Kingdom for losses inflicted by the state abroad, not just through armed activities. See: Uglješa Grušić, *Torts in UK Foreign Relations* (OUP 2023) 3–8. While Grušić's articulation also focuses on domestic tort law, it is broader in scope than my account as it aims to capture losses inflicted through a wider range of activities done abroad.

[8] Throughout the book, I use 'international humanitarian law' and '*jus in bello*' interchangeably.

suggested in the literature to the problem of remediless civilians—that these solutions do not properly capture what a wrong is, in the context of war.

In contrast to these proposed solutions, I argue that tort law is applicable to belligerent activities. To establish my claim, and the first precondition, I show in Section III that civilians' rights remain relevant during war. I do so by responding to the two main arguments to the contrary. First, I demonstrate that certain realist arguments about the lack of rights during war are inaccurate. Second, I establish that rights are relevant during belligerent activities as they are not overridden or suspended, nor do states and combatants have an immunity or excuse for infringing rights.

In Section IV, I turn to analyse the distinction between non-wrongful harms and wrongs. This distinction is familiar in the context of peacetime. 'Non-wrongful harms' refer to instances of causing a loss for which a person has no right to a remedy, whereas 'wrongs' refer to the infliction of a loss for which the wrongdoer has an obligation to provide the injured individual with a remedy. One example of non-wrongful harming is when a person uses her body and property in a *permissible way*, which changes the reality in which other people operate, without wronging them. If I open a restaurant near your café, and as a result you lose customers, it could be said that I have harmed you. You sustain a financial loss from the fact that I opened my restaurant, as diners come to have lunch at my business rather than yours. But I did not wrong you in the sense that you are entitled to demand compensation from me for that loss. You did not have a right that those customers go to your café and order your food. Nor have I used or damaged your café as a means of doing business. All I have done is changed the reality in which you operated.

Another example of non-wrongful harming is when a harm is *minor and ordinary*. When I inadvertently bump into your shoulder in a busy train station, I harm you but do not wrong you, as my bumping into you is a side effect of the ordinary and permissible use of our bodies. Even though we do not have permission to intentionally bump into other people, when such a harm is inflicted accidently, we accept it as part of what it means to live in a crowded urban environment.

A loss could also be harmful, but no liability would be imposed if there is an available affirmative defence. For instance, if you are trying to steal my bag, I can commit a battery by pushing you away, yet no liability would arise if by pushing you I am exercising my right to self-defence. In this sense, my actions are *justified* and by having this justification I have committed no wrong. Similarly, if I hit you while I am unconscious and convulsing, I will not be held liable because I was not in control of my actions and therefore they are *excused*. The excuse does not rule out the wrongful character of my conduct, but rather it is a defence against the ability to pursue a remedy for the wrong I caused.

I argue that while a state of war is a distinct moral and legal sphere from a state of peace,[9] differentiating non-wrongful harms from tortious wrongs is possible. Yet, it requires turning to the norms that govern warfare, otherwise tort liability would be divorced from the normative basis for evaluating wrongful actions in war and would contradict the basic structure of tort law: liability only arises when the inflicted loss is wrongful.[10] Seeing this argument through suggests that demarcating the line between non-wrongful harms and wrongs in warfare could only be done coherently by identifying which losses could be justified.[11] Accordingly, all losses that are inflicted on civilians through warfare are *prima facie* private law wrongs, but if they are inflicted while adhering to international humanitarian law and the rules of engagement, they are justified and non-wrongful.

Lastly, I address the third precondition by suggesting in Section V that wrongdoers have a corrective justice duty to remedy the belligerent wrongs they inflict. Corrective justice is the notion that a wrongful violation of an individual's private rights must be rectified by holding the wrongdoer liable towards the injured individual for the wrongful loss she inflicted.[12] This notion is bipolar, relational, and formal, as it only considers the rights and entitlements of the individual who caused the wrong and the individual who suffered that same wrong.[13] External goals or policies do not affect the determination of

[9] Immanuel Kant, 'Towards Perpetual Peace (1795)' in *Immanuel Kant: Practical Philosophy* (Mary J Gregor tr, CUP 1996) 320, 322; Stephen C Neff, *War and the Law of Nations: A General History* (CUP 2007) 58; Avishai Margalit, 'Decent Peace' (2005) 216 <http://tannerlectures.utah.edu/_documents/a-to-z/m/Margalit_2006.pdf> accessed 10 March 2017.

[10] Ernest J Weinrib, 'Corrective Justice in a Nutshell' (2002) 52 University of Toronto Law Journal 349, 349; Jules Coleman, 'Tort Law and Tort Theory: Preliminary Reflections on Method, Philosophy and the Law of Torts' in Gerald Postema (ed), *Philosophy and the Law of Torts* (CUP 2001) 184; John CP Goldberg and Benjamin C Zipursky, 'Tort Law and Responsibility' in John Oberdiek (ed), *Philosophical Foundations of the Law of Torts* (OUP 2014) 17; Martin Stone, 'The Significance of Doing and Suffering' in Gerald J Postema (ed), *Philosophy and the Law of Torts* (CUP 2001) 159–60.

[11] This argument does not mean that the law of war should not or cannot be used to evaluate the criminal or public law wrongfulness of belligerent activities as well. Nor is it the case that tort liability can only arise when the law of war supports a finding of criminal or public law wrongfulness. Rather, my claim is that international humanitarian law should not be understood only as a kind of criminal or public law set of norms. The mechanism through which wrongfulness is established in each body of laws is distinct, and the facts of a single case could support a finding of wrongfulness in tort law while at the same time not yielding a similar finding in criminal or public law.

[12] See, for instance: Allan Beever, *A Theory of Tort Liability* (Hart Publishing 2016) 19–21; Ernest J Weinrib, *The Idea of Private Law* (OUP 2012) 104; Arthur Ripstein, *Private Wrongs* (Harvard UP 2016) 5; Coleman, 'Tort Law and Tort Theory (n 10) 184; John Gardner, 'What Is Tort Law For? Part 1: The Place of Corrective Justice' (2011) 30 Law and Philosophy 1, 9–11, 22–23; Robert Stevens, *Torts and Rights* (OUP 2007) 327–28; John CP Goldberg and Benjamin C Zipursky, *Recognizing Wrongs* (2020) 26–28, 234. Although corrective justice scholars differ over several of its aspects, their views generally fit with the description above, and their differences do not affect my arguments in this book.

[13] Weinrib, *The Idea of Private Law* (n 12) 73, 159–60; Ernest J Weinrib, 'Deterrence and Corrective Justice' (2002) 50 University of California, Los Angeles Law Review 621, 630–31; Carol Harlow, *State*

whether a loss is wrongful or whether liability should be imposed.[14] As private law rights remain relevant in warfare, and losses are wrongful unless justified, a corrective justice duty to rectify belligerent wrong follows.

This ordinary duty could be discharged through ordinary domestic tort law doctrines.[15] That said, I do not argue that it could *only* be addressed through tort law. As I show in Chapter 7, it is possible to provide a kind of reparation through non-tort law means—indeed some states do so already. Unlike tort law, which can only compensate civilians for wrongful losses, non-tort law means do not require a finding that an action was wrongful, in order to provide payment. Payment could even be made whether international humanitarian law has been breached or not. For example, many states, including Canada, Israel, and the United States, employ *ex gratia* payment schemes to address some of the losses they inflict. These are ad hoc payments, over which states have complete discretion. They are not meant to repair a wrong or assign blame but only provide partial payment to the individual who has suffered the loss. Additionally, the award of an *ex gratia* payment is not dependent on a breach of international humanitarian law or any other law. Similarly, payments made via domestic social insurance, statutory entitlements, or international compensation funds are not dependent on a breach of international humanitarian law. Rather, they depend on conformity to certain factual and legal criteria.

Yet, while these non-tort law means address losses, they do not correct wrongs. This feature is exactly why there is no need to establish that a wrongful loss has been inflicted before providing a payment. In contrast, when tort law is the mechanism through which compensation is obtained, the link between the factual infliction of a loss and its normative nature as a wrong is crucial. When tort litigation is complete, and the wrongdoer compensates the plaintiff, the former corrects the wrong it inflicted. Therefore, the normative significance of awarding compensation through tort law makes it the ideal mechanism through which corrective justice can be attained. Still, it might be that tort law should be abandoned in favour of other solutions if tort law, as the ideal mechanism for obtaining corrective justice, is empirically inferior in some particular yet significant way.[16] I engage in this evaluation in greater detail in Chapter 7 and show that the alternatives to tort liability that are currently used are not

Liability: Tort Law and Beyond (OUP 2004) 11; Ripstein, *Private Wrongs* (n 12) 167; Goldberg and Zipursky, 'Tort Law and Responsibility' (n 10) 27; Stone (n 10) 159.

[14] Weinrib, *The Idea of Private Law* (n 12) 1–10; John CP Goldberg, 'Twentieth-Century Tort Theory' (2003) 9 Georgetown Law Journal 513, 571.

[15] For an analysis of how particular tort doctrines could apply to belligerent wrongs, see Chapters 4–6.

[16] Arthur Ripstein, *Equality, Responsibility, and the Law* (CUP 1998) 20–21.

superior to it. However, my focus in this chapter is much narrower, as I only aim to demonstrate that tort law can correct belligerent wrongs.

II. No Redress for the Misfortunes of War

Under international law, there is no obligation for states to compensate civilians whom they injure in the process of belligerent activities. Nevertheless, international law duties to compensate other states do exist. Arguably, Article 3 of the Hague Regulations and Article 91 of Additional Protocol I ground such duties, as they hold that a state which inflicts a loss on another nation while infringing the law of war is liable to pay compensation for it.[17] This obligation is more explicit in the Draft Articles on the Responsibility of States for Internationally Wrongful Acts.[18] The obligation to pay compensation for such infringements lies between the states which were parties to the conflict. Put differently, the Hague Regulations, Additional Protocol I, and the Draft Articles do not establish a private law duty of compensation towards individuals, nor do they provide recourse for individuals against states.[19]

There are two main issues that arise from this regime. First, civilians who sustain a loss might be the ultimate beneficiaries of compensation made between states, but it is generally viewed that they cannot themselves bring claims for compensation for the infringement of international law.[20] This lack of standing

[17] Protocol Additional to the Geneva Conventions of 12 August 1949, and relating to the Protection of Victims of International Armed Conflicts 1977; Convention (IV) Respecting the Laws and Customs of War on Land and its annex: Regulations concerning the Laws and Customs of War on Land 1907; International Committee of the Red Cross, 'Commentary on the Additional Protocols of 8 June 1977 to the Geneva Conventions of 12 August 1949' 1053–57 <https://ihl-databases.icrc.org/applic/ihl/ihl.nsf/Comment.xsp?action=openDocument&documentId = 1066AF25ED669409C12563CD00438071> accessed 29 June 2018.

[18] Draft Articles on the Responsibility of States for Internationally Wrongful Acts (n 5) 31.

[19] An articulation of the lack of a creation of a private law duty by the above-mentioned international law sources can be found in Article 2(b) of the United Nations General Assembly Resolution 60/147 on the Basic Principles and Guidelines on the Right to a Remedy and Reparation for Victims of Gross Violations of International Human Rights Law and Serious Violations of International Humanitarian Law 2005. This Article requires states to ensure compliance with their international law obligations through domestic law, which suggests that international law operates strictly between states.

[20] Gillard (n 3) 532; Ben Saul, 'Compensation for Unlawful Death in International Law: A Focus on the Inter-American Court of Human Rights' (2004) 19 American University International Law Review 523, 531–32; Rainer Hofmann and Frank Riemann, 'Compensation for Victims of War: Background Report' (International Law Association Committee on Compensation for Victims of War 2004) 8 <https://www.ila-hq.org/en_GB/documents/background-report-berlin-2004>. That said, there have been other sources of international law, namely multilateral treaties, that have been interpreted as giving standing to civilians to bring claims directly against states for wrongful belligerent action. For example, the European Court of Human Rights interpreted Article 41 of the Convention for the Protection of Human Rights and Fundamental Freedoms 1950 as the source through which it can impose compensation on state parties for infringing rights that are protected by the Convention in cases of belligerent activities (*Isayeva v Russia* (App no 57950/00) (24 February 2005) (European Court

means that civilians are unable to vindicate their rights to life, bodily integrity, and property through the judiciary. Furthermore, as these types of disputes are settled between states, civilians might not be fully compensated for the losses they sustained. This is clear in the case of civilians being indirect beneficiaries. For instance, if the payment owed by state A is directed at rebuilding infrastructure, the individual civilians are not directly compensated for their losses.

The second main issue that arises from the current regime is that many of the misfortunes of war are left without adequate redress. One way in which losses are not properly redressed is that collateral damage is generally permitted during war, resulting in civilians shouldering many of the costs of belligerent activities while the injuring state bears no responsibility to ameliorate them. Another way in which losses are not properly redressed, at least from a corrective justice viewpoint, is that even if the individuals have a private or social insurance against belligerent losses, the wrong is not corrected by the wrongdoer.[21]

There have been several attempts to solve these issues. Some of these suggestions seem to be grounded in duties that are completely external to tort law. For example, Dieter Fleck argues that 'as a matter of sound policy' states should be under an international law duty of compensation for gross infringements of human rights or international humanitarian law.[22] In contrast, Emanuela-Chiara Gillard claims that the duty of compensation under international law should be expanded much further. She argues that insistence on violation of international law as the basis on which compensation is made will result in injustice, whereby civilians who suffered similar losses will be treated differently.[23] Gillard suggests that compensation should be awarded either for all losses inflicted in the process of belligerent activities that are *jus ad bellum* unjust or even for all losses without any restrictions.[24] Gillard is not alone

of Human Rights) 231–45; *Tagayeva and others v Russia* (Application no 26562/07 and 6 other applications) (13 April 2017) (European Court of Human Rights) 642–58).

[21] Ripstein, *Equality, Responsibility, and the Law* (n 16) 20–21.

[22] Fleck (n 2) 707–8.

[23] Gillard (n 3) 551. Gillard invites us to imagine a situation in which the houses of two neighbours were destroyed during belligerent activities, but one house was intentionally targeted while the other was unintentionally damaged. She argues that the former type of loss is a violation of international humanitarian law and hence compensation will be granted, while the latter is permitted collateral damage and compensation will not be justified.

[24] Gillard (n 3) 551. Note, international humanitarian law encompasses actions that relate to the conduct of belligerency itself, or *jus in bello*. In this sense, the law is indifferent to the a priori just or unjust nature of the decision to engage in belligerent action, or *jus ad bellum*. However, Gillard seems to be suggesting that the law should not be ignorant of *ad bellum* considerations, at least for the purpose of awarding compensation.

in arguing that liability for collateral damage should be divorced from international humanitarian law. Michael Reisman holds that civilians should be compensated for any loss states inflict on them in the process of belligerent activities, regardless of whether international law has been violated.[25] His argument is based on notions of distributive justice that drive administrative no fault compensation schemes.[26]

Other suggestions seem either to be rooted in tort law or fall completely under its domain. For instance, Yaël Ronen argues that compensation for collateral damage should follow a strict liability rule, as it would be more effective than a negligence rule at incentivizing states to minimize the harm they inflict on civilians.[27] Marcus Schulzke and Amanda Carroll also propose adopting a strict liability rule, but their approach is different to Ronen's. Unlike Ronen, who analyses liability from an economic perspective, Schulzke and Carroll argue that liability follows from a corrective justice duty.[28] They hold that liability should be strict, as waging war is an ultra-hazardous activity and any harm caused to civilians during belligerent activities is an infringement of their rights that could only be vindicated by holding states strictly liable.[29] In this sense, Schulzke and Carroll's suggestion goes further than Ronen's, as they hold that any loss caused in combat establishes a duty of compensation, even if neither *jus ad bellum* (the law governing resort to military force) nor *jus in bello* (the law governing the conduct of hostilities) has been breached. Rebecca Crootof similarly holds that an ideal liability regime under international law would be one in which states would owe a duty to compensate

[25] W Michael Reisman, 'Compensating Collateral Damage in Elective International Conflict' (2013) 8 Intercultural Human Rights Law Review 1, 10.

[26] In these schemes, the state will be liable for compensating individuals whom it injured if the state (and hence the general public) benefited from the injuring activity (ibid 4–8; L Neville Brown and John Bell, *French Administrative Law* (5th edn, Clarendon Press; OUP 1998) 193–94; Cees van Dam, *European Tort Law* (OUP 2006) 478–79). This is a distributive justice notion, as by holding the state liable for such injuries all members of a political community share the burden of an injurious action equally, rather than only a single individual (Brown and Bell 184). Reisman believes that holding states liable for losses that do not violate international law will have two additional benefits. First, he claims that by internalizing the costs of lawful losses, states will be incentivized to take more precautions and collateral damage will be reduced. Second, Reisman argues that compensation is a basic human right duty, yet states discriminate in discharging this duty between their own nationals and foreign nationals. Providing compensation in the context of belligerent activities will, according to Reisman, strengthen states' commitment to the rule of law, as it will eliminate unjustified discrimination between national and foreign civilians. See: Reisman, 'Compensating Collateral Damage' (n 25) 11–12.

[27] In her view, it is possible to divorce liability from culpability, as strict liability does not require proof of fault in the conduct of the injuring state. Still, her argument does not divorce liability from international humanitarian law completely, as she suggests that liability would be imposed only when *jus ad bellum* is infringed. See: Ronen (n 4) 195–98, 205.

[28] Schulzke and Carroll (n 5) 13. On the incoherence of strict liability rules from a corrective justice perspective, see: Weinrib, *The Idea of Private Law* (n 12) 179–80.

[29] Schulzke and Carroll (n 5) 15–19.

civilians regardless of whether the loss was inflicted while adhering to the law of war.[30] Yet, she does not take a stand on whether liability should be strict or fault based; which institution should award compensation; or whether individuals should have a direct right to claim compensation.[31]

All of these suggestions share a common flaw: the liability regimes they offer are divorced, to varying degrees, from international humanitarian law. While this detachment solves the problem of civilians' lack of remedy for losses they sustain during battle, other moral and legal problems arise. Without reference to international humanitarian law, we cannot determine the rights and duties of states and individuals during belligerent activities. Both 'war' and 'wrongful losses during war' cannot be understood without relying on the theory and law of war.[32]

Several additional difficulties arise from the suggestions that are not based on tort law in particular. First, they might require the establishment of procedures and institutions that do not exist. Currently, there are no institutions with international jurisdiction that could adjudicate claims for compensation for belligerent wrongs. Indeed, there are some permanent institutions with multinational jurisdiction, such as the European Court of Justice, the European Court of Human Rights, the Inter-American Court of Human Rights, the International Court of Justice, and the International Criminal Court. But these courts' jurisdictions are limited since they are voluntary; consequently, their reach is not global because the courts have jurisdiction only over those states that surrender to their jurisdiction.[33] Furthermore, while there have been some ad hoc institutions established for the purpose of awarding compensation to civilians in the aftermath of violent conflicts—for instance, the United Nations Compensation Commission and the Eritrea–Ethiopia Claims Commission—these institutions are exceptional. They represent the convergence of the political interests of states, and as such it is doubtful they could be viewed as a proper template for compensation, given that they are not likely to be established and their jurisdiction is limited to specific violations at specific times and in specific states.[34] However, the difficulties posed by international bodies

[30] Crootof, 'War Torts' (n 7) 1109.

[31] ibid 1118–20; 1140–41.

[32] On the problematic nature of treating responsibility without proper account of the nature of war, see: Michael Walzer, 'Response to McMahan's Paper' (2006) 34 Philosophia 43.

[33] *Italy v France, United Kingdom of Great Britain and Northern Ireland, and United States of America (Preliminary Question)* [1954] ICJ Rep 19, at 32; Lindsey Cameron and Vincent Chetail, *Privatizing War: Private Military and Security Companies under Public International Law* (CUP 2013) 540; Ronen (n 4) 197.

[34] Ronen (n 4) 205.

with universal jurisdiction could be overcome, at least in part, by turning to domestic courts for the enforcement of international law.

Second, even if these procedures and institutions are established, non-tort law liability regimes could address losses, but they cannot correct wrongs in the normative sense. In non-tort law regimes, there is no need to establish that a particular person or entity wronged you. Nor is the wrongdoer necessarily compelled to compensate you for your losses. Instead, all harms—whether wrongful or not—could serve as the basis for payment. In addition, it might not be the wrongdoer who is compelled to pay the person who suffered the loss. Rather, it could be an insurer or the state.

In contrast, when tort law is the mechanism through which compensation is obtained, the link between the factual infliction of a loss and its normative nature as a wrong is key. When the tort litigation ends, and the wrongdoer compensates the plaintiff, the former corrects the wrong it inflicted. This is the basic obligation that arises from corrective justice—a person who wrongfully infringed the rights of another is under a duty to correct the wrong she created.[35] There is normative significance to awarding compensation through tort law that is lacking in a non-tort law regime, and the two cannot be said to be alternative mechanisms for securing the exact same result.[36]

III. Civilians' Rights Remain in War

To claim that a person has a duty to compensate another for an injury she caused assumes, among other things, that the injured party has a right to her body and her property, and that other people do not have the right to use or damage her body and property. It is the infringement of one's rights that constitutes a wrong, which in turn gives rise to an obligation to correct it.[37] If there are no rights, there are no infringements of rights; no legal wrongs; and no grounds to claim compensation in tort. This is the first of three preconditions that needs to be established in order to show that civilians have a right to compensation for belligerent wrongs.

[35] Ripstein, *Private Wrongs* (n 12) 167–68; Arthur Ripstein, *Force and Freedom: Kant's Legal and Political Philosophy* (Harvard UP 2009) 82–83. For an account that divorces liability from causation, see: Ehud Guttel, Alon Harel, and Shay Lavie, 'Torts for Non-Victims: The Case for Third-Party Litigation' (2018) 2018 University of Illinois Law Review 1049. However, this account is not based on a corrective justice conception of tort law but an instrumentalist one.

[36] See Arthur Ripstein's similar position on tort law versus mandatory public participation schemes: Ripstein, *Private Wrongs* (n 12) 294.

[37] Weinrib, 'Corrective Justice in a Nutshell' (n 10) 349; Coleman, 'Tort Law and Tort Theory' (n 10) 184; Goldberg and Zipursky, 'Tort Law and Responsibility' (n 10) 17; Stone (n 10) 159–60.

In the context of war, there are three main arguments regarding the existence of rights of private citizens: a realist argument that there are no rights during war; an argument that there are rights, but they are irrelevant; and lastly, an argument that rights remain and are relevant during war.[38] In the discussion below, I demonstrate that the latter approach is the most coherent and compelling. By negating the realist argument, I show that there are rights during war, and that they remain relevant during belligerent activities. In doing so, the first precondition will be established.

A. There Are Rights during War

The argument that there are no rights during war is often grounded either on the lack of proper legal structure whereby rights could exist or on the special character of war as an extra-legal domain, though these two explanations can overlap. Political realists' depictions of rights during war offer a good example of such overlapping accounts.[39] They hold that war is a situation in which human society falls apart. It is an extreme time of hellish consequences. As such, they argue that there are no laws and no rights during war. In this sense, they seem to be basing their argument on the nature of war as a special legal and moral sphere rather than on the structure of international relations.

To establish their claim, realists often refer not only to the writings of Cicero, who coined the famous maxim that 'in times of war, the law falls silent' (*inter arma enim silent legēs*),[40] but also to Hobbes' structuralist account. He argued that individuals are in a horizontal relationship with one another, but that members of a political community are in a vertical relationship with their sovereign. Put differently, individuals hold the same status in relation to one another and are not in a position of power over one another, whereas they are all

[38] Some of these options have been suggested by: Michael Walzer, *Just and Unjust Wars: A Moral Argument with Historical Illustrations* (5th edn, Basic Books, a member of the Perseus Books Group 2015) 135–36; Yitzhak Benbaji, 'The War Convention and the Moral Division of Labour' (2009) 59 The Philosophical Quarterly 593, 613; Ronen (n 4) 188–92.

[39] For a discussion on this depiction, see, for example: Walzer, *Just and Unjust Wars* (n 38) 4; Jeff McMahan, 'Killing in War: A Reply to Walzer' (2006) 34 Philosophia 47, 47; Jeff McMahan, 'The Morality of War and the Law of War' in David Rodin and Henry Shue (eds), *Just and Unjust Warriors: The Moral and Legal Status of Soldiers* (OUP 2008) 33; Nick Fotion, Bruno Coppieters, and Ruben Apressyan, 'Introduction' in Bruno Coppieters and Nick Fotion (eds), *Moral Constraints on War: Principles and Cases* (Lexington Books 2002) 1–7; Theodore Christov, *Before Anarchy: Hobbes and His Critics in Modern International Thought* (CUP 2015) 107–9; Kenneth N Waltz, 'Realist Thought and Neorealist Theory' (1990) 44 Journal of International Affairs 21, 34–37.

[40] Marcus Tullius Cicero, *The Speeches of M Tullius Cicero against Catiline and Antony and for Murena and Milo* (Herbert ED Blakiston tr, Methuen and Co 1894) 150.

the subjects of the state that has power over them. Furthermore, Hobbes argued that the relationship between states is akin to that among private individuals—namely that it is horizontal. Yet, unlike individuals, who are in a shared vertical relationship with their state, there is no authority to which all states are subject and they are not a part of a single political community. Thus, nations exist in a state of nature in which there is no law. As Hobbes puts it:

> Where there is no common power, there is no law, and where there is no law, there is no injustice . . . Justice and injustice are qualities that relate to men in society, not in solitude. It also follows that in this same condition, there is no propriety, no dominion, and no distinct mine or thine. All that is a man's is what he can get, and as long as he can keep it.[41]

As there is no vertical relationship with a sovereign who can adjudicate disputes in a state of nature, such a state entails a condition of constant war as parties will use force to obtain things and maintain their hold of them. In this condition, peace is the exception.[42] Individuals left the lawless state of nature only by entering into a shared vertical relationship with a state. Yet, according to the realist account of Hobbes, there is no similar structure for states' relationships with each other, which means that they have never left the state of nature.[43]

Nevertheless, the realist argument that the lack of a vertical relationship means that there are no laws or rights is puzzling for several reasons. First, even if nations have no rights against each other in a state of nature,[44] this does not show that there are no rights for private individuals. Indeed, the idea that there are no rights for private individuals during war seems to take Hobbes' argument a step too far. Hobbes held that prior to the existence of a shared vertical relationship, individuals were in a state of nature.[45] But the fact that states engage in wars does not return *individuals* to a state of nature. If this were the case, then individuals would never have rights beyond those that exist in a state of nature, as, according to the realist Hobbesian account, nations never left this state and are in a constant state of war. As the onset of war does not revert

[41] Thomas Hobbes, *Leviathan (1651)* (Routledge 2006), Book I, ch XIII, 84.
[42] Neff (n 9) 131–32.
[43] Hedley Bull, *The Anarchical Society: A Study of Order in World Politics* (Columbia UP 1977) 46.
[44] An alternative way of framing the issue is not to view the state of nature as a condition in which nations have no rights, but rather as a state in which rights cannot be secured although they can be understood (see: Arthur Ripstein, 'Political Independence, Territorial Integrity, and Private Law Analogies' (2019) 24 Kantian Review 573, 590).
[45] Hobbes (n 41), Book I, ch XIII, 84.

individuals back to a state of nature, it cannot be that during war the rights of private individuals expire.[46] As the status of these rights is not dependent on the normative condition that exists between states, individuals can hold those who wrongfully infringed their rights—including states—accountable.

Second, in order to establish that there are no laws during war, realists need to repudiate familiar legal doctrines and instruments. The law of war is just one example. States are bound to comply with them, and many military codes adopt them and use them in their rules of engagement. Moreover, when states do not adhere to the law of war, they can be sanctioned by other states and international organizations such as the Security Council, which may even issue a resolution permitting engagement in belligerent activities to enforce the law of war.[47] These doctrines and institutions do not cease to exist in war. In fact, their very purpose is to deter states from engaging in combatant activities, as well as regulating these activities if they take place. They would not make sense if they did not have any force in war.

Indeed, there is no international institution with universal jurisdiction to settle disputes and oblige states to comply with its resolutions. The lack of such an institution does not mean, however, that there is no law and there are no rights during war; rather there is less effective law enforcement on the international level. The law of war can be enforced by domestic courts and institutions, even if these courts and institutions are sometimes unwilling to do so.[48] Furthermore, the lack of a common power to adjudicate claims and enforce the law between states on the international level is less problematic when it comes to enforcing the rights of private individuals against states that violated them. If state A inflicts a loss on a citizen of state B, this citizen could bring a claim in tort against state A in its own courts. In this scenario, both state A and the citizen of state B are subject to the power of state A's courts, and the realist Hobbesian problem does not arise. Even if the claim against state A is brought before the courts of state B, state A would only be bound insofar as it willingly subjects itself to the jurisdiction of state B's courts.[49] Thus, it is difficult to maintain the realist Hobbesian argument that there are no laws or enforcement mechanisms

[46] For a critique of the political realist reading of Hobbes, see: Christov (n 39) 104–35. Christov criticizes the particular argument that derives individuals' rights from state rights, holding that this move is illogical considering that states are artificial individuals (ibid 114).

[47] Take for example the Security Council's Resolution 1973 (2011). This resolution was adopted in response to the gross violations of international law by the Libyan government, against the forces that were attempting to oust it and against the civilian population.

[48] See, for instance: *HCJ 69/81 Abu Ita v Judea and Samaria Commander* PD 37(2) 197 (1983); *HCJ 201/09 Doctors for Human Rights v The Prime Minister* PD 63(1) 521 (2009).

[49] Still, if state A is not willing to subject itself to the jurisdiction of the courts of state B, the realist Hobbesian difficulty remains.

during war, as to a certain degree there is a common power on the international level to adjudicate disputes and enforce rights.[50]

B. Rights Are Relevant during War

If the existence of rights during war is not necessarily negated, how can we explain the fact that states are able to inflict losses on civilians? This puzzle would be resolved if the argument that during war private law rights are irrelevant could be sustained. By irrelevant I do not mean that rights will have no moral, political, or legal significance. Rather, I mean that the enforceability of rights and duties will be impaired to the degree that states will have a legal right to commit a legal wrong.[51] This would be the case if during war, rights were overridden or temporarily suspended, or if states could not be held liable for any infringement of private law rights.

Overriding rights and duties implies the use of one's authority against another. A city can expropriate a parcel of land from a private individual to expand a highway. The police can block streets to cars in order to allow a parade to take place. Parents can ground their children. Furthermore, an override means that rights and duties remain in full force until they are overridden. The override can take one of two forms: either an overridden right expires permanently or it is set aside in a certain context as other rights and duties take precedence. I shall refer to the first kind of consequence as the 'override-expiry

[50] Political and legal realists would reply to this argument that although laws and legal institutions exist, they are only a reflection of the interests of the stronger world powers, who make and break the laws with impunity while using the laws to keep weaker nations in check (see, for example: Michael J Glennon, 'The UN Security Council in a Unipolar World' (2003) 44 Virginia Journal of International Law 91, 105–8; Martti Koskenniemi, *The Gentle Civilizer of Nations: The Rise and Fall of International Law 1870–1960* (CUP 2001) 459–80; John R Bolton, 'Is There Really "Law" in International Affairs?' (2000) 10 Transnational Law and Contemporary Problems 1). However, this view has been criticized. International law and international institutions are more than just power masked as legitimate legal processes. (See, generally: Jutta Brunnée and Stephen J Toope, *Legitimacy and Legality in International Law: An Interactional Account* (CUP 2010) 40–47; Jutta Brunnée and Stephen J Toope, 'The Rule of Law in an Agnostic World: The Prohibition on the Use of Force and Humanitarian Exceptions' in Wouter Werner, Marieke De Hoon, and Alexis Galan (eds), *The Law of International Lawyers* (CUP 2017) 155–61; Eden Sarid, 'International Underwater Cultural Heritage Governance: Past Doubts and Current Challenges' (2017) 35 Berkeley Journal of International Law 219, 249–54). Moreover, the fact that laws are broken or changed does not negate their normative power and significance. If someone robs me, my right to my property remains. It does not dissolve with the act of my robbing me. Similarly, if the legislature changes laws regulating electoral ridings, for example, it does not mean that the Elections Act has no normative force.

[51] For an analysis of the legal right to do a legal wrong, see: Ori Herstein, 'A Legal Right to Do Legal Wrong' (2014) 34 Oxford Journal of Legal Studies 21, 27. For an opposing view which holds that there can be no legal right to infringe a legal duty if the latter is categorically enforceable, see: David Enoch, 'A Right to Violate One's Duty' (2002) 21 Law and Philosophy 355, 383–84.

account' and the second as the 'override-precedence account'. After a city expropriates a parcel of land from an individual, she no longer has a right to that land. Once a claim-right expires, it can no longer be breached. In contrast, when the police block several streets for a parade to take place, or when parents ground their children, one right or interest is held to be superior to another. The superior right or interest takes precedence, but the inferior right does not expire. It simply has lesser force in this particular context.[52]

An alternative description would be that during war, private law rights and duties are suspended, in which case they cannot be breached or overridden. They are temporarily 'out of commission', and anything that would violate them in other circumstances could be done while the suspension is in force.[53] Unlike the override-precedence account, in which one claim-right or duty is suppressed by another specific claim-right or duty, suspension could have either an *in rem* or *in personam* effect, depending on the type of right that is suspended. For instance, if one person's right over her bicycle is suspended, then anyone else can use or damage it without infringing the owner's rights. As property rights are *in rem*, their suspension means that anyone can use or damage the property without wronging the owner. In contrast, if a person had a lease on a bicycle, which gave her the right to ride it, and that right was suspended, no one would have a right to use or damage the bicycle. The bicycle owner's property right remains in force, while the lessee's *in personam* right is suspended.

As rights and duties are equally suspended for all parties to a conflict, no state is acting in a position of authority over another state. They are all acting equally in liberty, and consequently there is a conceptual fit with the horizontal relationship of states. The suspension account also sheds light on why certain actions are rightful during war and wrongful at its conclusion. Given that rights and duties are only suspended for the duration of the belligerent activities, it is clear why, once those activities have ended, the rights and duties regain their full force.

52 Joseph Raz, 'Legal Rights' (1984) 4 Oxford Journal of Legal Studies 1, 19.

53 Some scholars' arguments that view warfare as a realm beyond the rule of law could be understood in this way (see, for example: Carl Schmitt, *Political Theology: Four Chapters on the Concept of Sovereignty (1922)* (University of Chicago Press 2005) 5–13; John Ferejohn and Pasquale Pasquino, 'The Law of the Exception: A Typology of Emergency Powers' (2004) 2 International Journal of Constitutional Law 210, 210; Cass R Sunstein, 'Minimalism at War' (2004) 2004 Supreme Court Review 47, 108; Richard A Posner, *Not a Suicide Pact: The Constitution in a Time of National Emergency* (OUP 2006) 93; Eric A Posner and Adrian Vermeule, *Terror in the Balance* (OUP 2007) 11–14). That said, there may still be other limitations which remain in force while rights and duties are suspended. These limitations could explain why certain weapons and tactics cannot be used despite the fact that force could generally be applied.

Both the override and suspension accounts focus on the status of the rights of non-combatants. Another way of thinking about how states might have a legal right to do legal wrong focuses on the state and its combatants, rather than on the civilian population. In this context, it could be argued that private law rights are irrelevant during war when combatants and states are either immune to or excused from liability for infringing the rights of civilians—or if inflicting such losses is permitted to them. For an immunity to render private law rights irrelevant, it would need to apply whether the combatants inflicted a wrongful loss or not,[54] and would need to extend to all sides of a conflict.[55] In contrast, an excuse means that while a breach of rights is a wrong, there could be an affirmative defence to liability. While the breach of a norm is wrongful, no liability arises.[56] The rationale behind this defence is that under certain conditions, the prospect of liability could not guide behaviour, such as in cases of mistake, duress, and temporary insanity.[57] Lastly, according to the permissible harms account, while private law rights and duties remain in force, their breach is nonetheless permissible when they are inflicted as a side effect of the ordinary use of our body and property. They are simply the harms we accept as part of what it means to be able to take these kinds of actions and pursue our purposes while ensuring that others are able to do the same.[58] However, we cannot use other people's body and property without proper authority, as doing so inhibits their ability to use their body and property.[59]

[54] Adil Ahmad Haque, *Law and Morality at War* (OUP 2017) 27.

[55] Note, Haque argues that, as all states have an interest that they and their own combatants are not criminally liable for their actions, they agreed to grant each other immunity. While Haque only refers to immunity from criminal liability, it seems that this model could also apply to civil liability (ibid 25–28).

[56] Weinrib, *The Idea of Private Law* (n 12) 54; Kent Greenawalt, 'The Perplexing Borders of Justification and Excuse' (1984) 84 Columbia Law Review 1897, 1900; George P Fletcher, *Rethinking Criminal Law* (OUP 2000) 759; Heidi M Hurd, 'Justification and Excuse, Wrongdoing and Culpability' (1999) 74 Notre Dame Law Review 1551, 1558; John Gardner, *Offences and Defences: Selected Essays in the Philosophy of Criminal Law* (OUP 2007) 82–83; John CP Goldberg, 'Tort Law's Missing Excuses' in Andrew Dyson, James Goudkamp, and Frederick Wilmot-Smith (eds), *Defences in Tort* (Hart Publishing 2015) 54.

[57] Arthur Ripstein, 'In Extremis' (2005) 2 Ohio State Journal of Criminal Law 415, 423–24; Gardner, *Offences and Defences* (n 56) 86; George P Fletcher, 'The Right and the Reasonable' (1985) 98 Harvard Law Review 949, 955.

[58] Note, there is disagreement amongst scholars as to whether all justified actions are part of an account of permissible harms and vice versa (see: RA Duff, 'Rethinking Justifications' (2004) 39 Tulsa Law Review 829, 831; Malcolm Thorburn, 'Justifications, Powers, and Authority' (2008) 117 Yale Law Journal 1070, 1090; Fletcher, 'The Right and the Reasonable' (n 57) 977–78). However, I find these two categories to be sufficiently distinct for the following reason: inflicting a permissible harm means acting in a way that is intrinsically not wrongful, whereas having a justification means that the infliction of harm would be wrongful without the extrinsic influence of the justification.

[59] Ripstein, *Private Wrongs* (n 12) 167. The element of use without authority operates on a horizontal and a vertical level. The relationship between private individuals is horizontal in the sense that all individuals are equally their own masters and are thus free from the will of others. As such, they can agree that their means will be used by others. When such agreement is reached, individuals have horizontal authority to use the rights of others. In this sense, consent negates the possibility of inconsistent use of

That said, each of the override, suspension, immunity, excuse, and permissible harms models is inadequate in capturing the status of private law rights during war, as they either fail to account for the horizontal relationship between states or they result in conclusions that cannot and ought not to be supported. For instance, the override account is not apt to describe what happens to rights and duties during war for two reasons. First, as the loss of the binding force of rights and duties is only temporary and limited to the duration and engagement in belligerency, the override-expiry account cannot be the right fit. When a claim-right or duty is overridden, it expires. It cannot be revived. Seeing the override-expiry account through, if combatants of one state take control over a house in the heat of battle, it becomes a property with no owners. Hence, either the combatants or their state can take ownership of the house. However, this is not how we understand the legal implications of that takeover. When the fighting is done, the combatants must return the house to its owner. The override-expiry account does not explain what happens to rights and duties at the conclusion of belligerent activities such as this.

Second, as the relationship between states is horizontal, the override account more generally is ill-suited to describe what happens to rights and duties during war. The horizontal relationship between states means that in any engagement with each other, states do not exert authority over one another as they hold equal status.[60] The conduct of belligerent activities does not change the nature of the relationship of states from horizontal to vertical. Nonetheless,

another person's rights (Ernest J Weinrib, 'The Monsanto Lectures: Understanding Tort Law' (1989) 23 Valparaiso University Law Review 485, 514–15). In contrast, the relationship between the state and its subjects is vertical in the sense that the state and its agents can interfere with individuals' rights unilaterally under certain circumstances. Taxes can be collected. Lands can be expropriated. Freedom of movement could be limited. These are all examples of the state acting in a way that is inconsistent with the rights of private individuals without requiring their consent. Yet, by acting in these ways, no wrong is committed when the state and its agents are acting in accordance with their public powers, as they are exercising their vertical authority over private individuals.

[60] Ripstein, 'Political Independence, Territorial Integrity, and Private Law Analogies' (n 44) 585. Ripstein develops a Kantian account of warfare, through which the legality of warfare is assessed and which, if followed, would ultimately support my argument that individuals' private rights remain relevant during warfare. According to Ripstein, Kant views states as moral persons that are normatively equal to one another, and due to this equality states are entitled to be independent from one another. Consequently, engaging in war is permitted only to the extent that it is done in self-defence to enforce the right to independence. Moreover, states cannot unilaterally make, apply, and enforce laws for and upon other states, and they are under a duty to refrain from interfering with individuals and states' abilities to interact with one another through their legal orders. Ripstein then articulates the structure of cosmopolitan right, part of which is the requirement that the right to bodily integrity and property does not expire when individuals travel between states. See: Arthur Ripstein, *Kant and the Law of War* (OUP 2021) 57–58, 101–2, 250–51. Taken together, it is possible to deduce from Ripstein's account that individuals' private law rights remain relevant during warfare. The ability to engage in war for self-defence does not provide states with the authority or normative power to change other nations' laws and those nations' subjects' private law rights. Furthermore, given that individuals' private law rights to life and

an override implies that one state is exercising its authority over another state and its citizens. If the override account were applicable, one possible conclusion would be that all states are simultaneously in a position of authority over their rival state, meaning that the rights and duties of each party could be simultaneously overridden by, and could override, the other's. This conclusion is starkly opposed to the horizontal relationship of states. As no state is in a position of authority over another, no state's rights and duties can override those of a rival state.

The suspension account is also insufficient, as it does not properly explain why parties to a conflict remain under a duty to comply with international humanitarian law. A suspension of private law rights in the context of war would only apply between states that are parties to the conflict, and it would be conditional because only certain kinds of losses are justified. If rights and duties are suspended, then combatants and states should be at liberty to inflict losses on civilians. Yet, this liberty is qualified, as losses can only be imposed as long as they abide by international humanitarian law.

Two conclusions follow from this qualification. First, combatants and states are always under a public law duty to refrain from acting in a way that violates international humanitarian law. Put differently, international humanitarian law does not provide states with permission or liberty to inflict certain losses. Rather, it is a set of prohibitions on states' conduct that is constantly in force.[61] Second, under the suspension account, private law rights can be simultaneously relevant and irrelevant. The right to property, for example, would be considered as suspended and irrelevant in relation to a combatant who shot a civilian's car while adhering to international humanitarian law, and as effective and relevant in relation to a combatant who violated these principles. As property is an *in rem* right, to hold that it is relevant and irrelevant at the same time in this context is incoherent. Thus, the suspension account does not seem to aptly capture what happens to rights and duties during war.

property do not expire when they leave their own state, there is no reason to reach the opposite conclusion when they remain in their own state and are harmed by a foreign sovereign.

[61] The debate about the nature of international humanitarian law as permissive or restrictive goes beyond the scope of this chapter. For an account of this debate, see: Jeff McMahan, *Killing in War* (OUP 2009) 52–53; Jeff McMahan, 'On the Moral Equality of Combatants' (2006) 14 Journal of Political Philosophy 377, 389–90; Thomas Hurka, 'Liability and Just Cause' (2007) 20 Ethics and International Affairs 199, 210; Haque (n 54) 34; Walzer, *Just and Unjust Wars* (n 38); Arthur Ripstein, 'Rules for Wrongdoers' (Berkeley Talks: Tanner Lectures, day 1, 16 May 2019) <https://news.berkeley.edu/2019/05/16/berkeley-talks-transcript-2019-tanner-lectures-01/> accessed 4 November 2019; Evan J Criddle and Evan Fox-Decent, *Fiduciaries of Humanity: How International Law Constitutes Authority* (OUP 2016) 174–75.

Likewise, the immunity model is similarly deficient, and it could be understood in two ways. A broad interpretation of the model would extend immunity for any losses inflicted during battle: immunity would extend not only to actions that adhere to international humanitarian law but also to actions that are done in breach of it. In this sense, there would be no private law repercussions for war crimes, while it would be possible to impose criminal liability for violating them, as current domestic and international criminal law demonstrate. This result is unwarranted and unjust.

In contrast, a narrow interpretation of the model would grant immunity only for certain losses that were inflicted during battle. For instance, Adil Haque argues that the immunity under international humanitarian law only extends to combatants whose actions do not violate *jus in bello* but do violate the enemy state's domestic criminal law.[62] As long as *jus in bello* is not infringed, states and combatants will be immune from liability. This does not deem these actions wrongful or not but simply means that they follow certain constraints on the use of force. However, by extending immunity only to combatant activities undertaken in accordance with *jus in bello*, Haque's immunity model seems to be going back on its own premise. Remember, the immunity model is supposedly agnostic on the question of whether a loss was inflicted wrongfully or not. The only issue relevant to determining whether immunity should be extended or not is the question of whether the baseline criterion that was set for the immunity is met. Yet, by referring to adherence to *jus in bello* as the criterion for immunity, the narrow interpretation is not agnostic to the nature of the loss as wrongful or not, as immunity is only extended when losses are not wrongful. Consequently, the narrow interpretation fails to do what it is purported to be doing, which is providing an immunity regardless of the nature of the loss. Instead, the narrow interpretation of the immunity model appears to be operating more akin to an affirmative defence, in which case rights remain relevant.

Regarding the inapplicability of the excuse model, it is commonly viewed that excuses are not an available defence to tort liability.[63] Following this view

[62] As I stated above, while Haque only refers to immunity from criminal liability, it seems that this model could also apply to civil liability. See: Haque (n 54) 25–26.

[63] James Goudkamp, *Tort Law Defences* (Hart Publishing 2013) 82–83; John Gardner, 'Justification under Authority' (2010) 23 Canadian Journal of Law and Jurisprudence 71, 92; Jules Coleman, *Risks and Wrongs* (OUP 2002) 224; Goldberg, 'Tort Law's Missing Excuses' (n 56) 54; Joseph Raz, 'Responsibility and the Negligence Standard' (2010) 30 Oxford Journal of Legal Studies 1, 9–10; Ripstein, *Equality, Responsibility, and the Law* (n 16) 138–39. The exception to this widely accepted view is held by George Fletcher, who, without offering an exhaustive account, claims that excuses may be available in tort law (George P Fletcher, 'Fairness and Utility in Tort Theory' (1972) 85 Harvard Law Review 537, 551–53).

results in the conclusion that excuses would not properly capture the reason for lack of tortious liability to compensate wrongful interference with rights in war. Nevertheless, there are two additional reasons for which the excuse model is poorly fitted to capture what happens to rights and duties during belligerent activities. First, the basic assumption of the excuse account is that the infliction of wrongs was committed without authority, which is why losses are wrongful. Applying this assumption to combatant activities results in a puzzle. When combatants are acting within the confinements of international humanitarian law, they are exercising their public powers properly, as combatants are authorized to inflict losses that are consistent with international humanitarian law. However, if they act within the scope of their powers, then the excuse model does not seem to be the reason why no liability arises, as this defence is only relevant when the actions are done either without authority or outside its scope. Even if we oppose the common belief and assume that the excuse model could apply to tort liability, it seems that this model is nevertheless an inappropriate way of thinking about defences to tort liability in the context of war.

Second, an excuse operates to exclude liability on the basis that a wrong was committed, but considering the particular circumstances of the case, there is a reason to refrain from an imposition of liability as the wrongdoing is understandable.[64] Applying this rationale to combatant activities would mean that all injuries that are inflicted during battle are wrongful, but complying with international humanitarian law makes the infliction understandable considering the circumstances. Admittedly, there could be some appeal to this view, as it does not dismiss the losses and tragedies that befall civilians during armed conflicts. Nevertheless, it would be a mistake to think about losses that are inflicted during war in this way, as it conceives of war as a peacetime activity.[65] This view does not properly account for the nature of warfare and the moral and legal norms that guide it. Combatants who killed civilians while adhering to international humanitarian law are not murderers who are excused from liability. They have not committed murder. It is not that the deaths of civilians in these circumstances are not regrettable, but rather that combatants have not acted in an inappropriate way.[66] Hence, it is clear that the excuse model cannot properly capture rights and duties in the context of belligerent activities.

[64] Goldberg, 'Tort Law's Missing Excuses' (n 56) 62.

[65] Michael Walzer attributed this flaw to Jeff McMahan's account of individual responsibility in war. See: Walzer, 'Response to McMahan's Paper' (n 32) 43.

[66] John Goldberg argues that in relation to excuses, the wrongs are regrettable not only because they occurred as a matter of fact but also because they were brought about by acting in a deficient way: John CP Goldberg, 'Inexcusable Wrongs' (2015) 103 California Law Review 467, 472.

Lastly, the permissible harms model also seems to offer an inadequate way of thinking about rights during war. In the context of war, I argue that the key to articulating the types of conduct and losses that would be considered ordinary lies in international humanitarian law and states' rules of engagement.[67] These principles require that combatant activities adhere to three criteria: necessity, distinction, and proportionality. It is not that these principles themselves are a source that grants states and combatants with authority and permission to act in certain ways. Rather, I view them as restrictions on the power to engage in belligerent activities. Still, by restricting certain forms of conduct, other forms remain permitted. Applying the permissible harms model in this context would mean that losses that were inflicted during battle while adhering to these three criteria would be viewed as permissible harms that we accept as part of what it means to be able to engage in combat lawfully. Yet, when these criteria are breached, the subsequent losses are no longer in the range of permissible harms. Directly targeting civilians or inflicting disproportionate loss, for instance, are the kinds of losses that are wrongful.

Nonetheless, there is some difficulty in holding that the permissible harms model applies in times of war in the same way it applies in times of peace. The underlying assumptions of the permissible harms model are that either the harms themselves or the chances of their realization are fairly minor.[68] In the context of war neither of these seem to be the case, even when international humanitarian law is adhered to. Bumping into someone's shoulder on a busy train station is hardly the same as incidentally shooting a civilian. Therefore this model, also, does not seem to properly capture what happens to private law rights and duties during war.

Thus, I have established the first of the three preconditions that are required in order to claim that civilians have a private law right to compensation for belligerent losses: that rights exist and are relevant during war. By negating the realist Hobbesian argument, I demonstrated that there are rights during war. Through this discussion, I have also shown that none of the override, suspension, immunity, excuse, and permissible harms accounts constitutes the proper way of articulating what happens to rights and duties during war, and that private law rights remain relevant in this context.

The next key precondition, which I address in the following section, is whether there is a standard that applies while belligerent activities take place,

[67] For a full discussion that demonstrates why the argument that a breach of *jus ad bellum* means that any subsequent infliction of loss is wrongful, see Chapter 1.

[68] Weinrib, *The Idea of Private Law* (n 12) 148–50.

according to which certain losses could be considered merely harmful while others constitute wrongs. I argue that in the context of belligerent activities, this standard is informed by international humanitarian law and the rules of engagement. Accordingly, when states interfere with individuals' rights during combat, the interference is harmful but not wrongful as long as it occurred while adhering to these norms.

IV. Harmful and Wrongful Losses

The justification model provides the conceptual basis for distinguishing between non-wrongful belligerent harms and belligerent wrongs. According to this model, while an infringement of rights is *prima facie* wrongful, the existence of a justification rules out the wrongful nature of the breach.[69] For instance, murder is the commission of a wrongful act of taking another person's life. However, if this outcome is brought about while acting in self-defence, then not only is the act not wrongful, it is no longer considered to be murder.

In the context of belligerent activities, individuals do not lose their rights. Therefore, while combatants can wrongfully interfere with these rights, they are under the ordinary private law duty to refrain from doing so. Such interferences would be deemed wrongful when they are brought about in a defective way.[70] My argument is that belligerent activities that interfere with individuals' rights are *prima facie* defective and wrongful, but by complying with international humanitarian law and the state's rules of engagement, an affirmative defence is extended—making the infringement of rights merely harmful. Inflicting losses under these conditions is justified since it is within the scope of a state's authority to inflict these kinds of belligerent losses. International humanitarian law and the rules of engagement are, in this sense, restrictions on states' authority to engage in acts of war. When losses are inflicted while in

[69] Greenawalt (n 56) 1900; Fletcher, *Rethinking Criminal Law* (n 56) 759; Hurd (n 56) 1558; Ripstein, 'In Extremis' (n 57) 424–25; Coleman, *Risks and Wrongs* (n 63) 217; Goldberg, 'Tort Law's Missing Excuses' (n 56) 54. This view of the nature of justification is most common. For an opposing view, according to which justifications do not rule out the wrongful nature of the act but only provide for a defence from liability, see: Goudkamp (n 63) 78–82. The permissible harms model is distinguishable from the common view of the justification model in the sense that according to the former some harms are simply not wrongful, whereas according to the latter some wrongful actions could be redeemed if a proper justification is established. This difference suggests that the two models also differ in the burdens they place. The permissible harms model places the burden on the plaintiff to show that the defendant has actually acted in an impermissible way. In contrast, the justification account assumes that the defendant acted wrongfully, and the burden is placed on her to establish that an affirmative defence can redeem the nature of her injurious action.

[70] Ripstein, *Private Wrongs* (n 12) 167.

breach of these norms, these losses are outside the legitimate scope of states' authority and could not be justified. The violation of international humanitarian law and the rules of engagement renders the justification defence unavailable, and combatants' interference with individuals' private rights would be deemed defective and wrongful. Put differently, violations of the law of war do not generate new torts. Rather, existing tort law doctrines can be used to address the infliction of wrongful losses, and identifying what amounts to a wrongful loss in the context of warfare is informed by the law of war.

The justification model provides a way to distinguish between harms and wrongs by evaluating whether international humanitarian law and the rules of engagement were breached or adhered to. This evaluation could be done in one of two ways. First, it is possible to assess to what degree the combatant activities align with international humanitarian law. When the activities adhere to the principles of international humanitarian law, then the losses they inflict are justified. States have the authority to engage in combatant activities that adhere to international humanitarian law, as well as to inflict the losses that are a product of engaging in such activities. In contrast, when these principles are infringed, no such justification exists, as, in these instances, the activities are done without proper authority.

Given the important role that the principles of international humanitarian law have in charting the scope and character of tort liability during warfare, it is crucial to have an accurate account of them. While the principles are vaguely framed, generally speaking they require that a combatant activity will be necessary to obtaining a military goal, will refrain from directly targeting non-combatants, and the losses it inflicts will be proportionate to the military advantages it secures. These definitions are clear enough to offer guidance, but they leave a wide margin of discretion regarding the interpretation of their scope.

An example could help illustrate this point. Combatants may fire at enemy forces for the purpose of eliminating the threat they pose, as taking this action is within the scope of their public authority. In doing so, the combatant activity meets both the necessity requirement, as a military goal can be obtained from this engagement, and the distinction requirement, given that the target of the attack is enemy forces and not civilians. Furthermore, the activities are justified even if some of the bullets ricochet and hit civilians, as long as the resulting injuries are not disproportionate to the military gain in neutralizing the risk the enemy forces pose. The reason that no wrong has been inflicted under these circumstances is that by acting in adherence to international humanitarian law, the combatant activities are justified and non-wrongful. In contrast, if civilians were the subject of an attack, or if they suffer losses that vastly outweigh the military gains, the combatant activities cannot be justified and are wrongful.

To clarify, violating the requirements of 'necessity', 'distinction', and 'proportionality' does not generate tort liability in and of itself, and I am not arguing that there is, or should be, independent torts of 'unnecessary, 'non-discriminatory', or 'disproportionate' belligerent losses.[71] Nor do these principles generate new private law duties or confer new private law rights. Rather, international humanitarian law defines the scope of states' and combatants' authority to engage in warfare and informs their rights and duties in this context. Through this process, the applicability of ordinary tort doctrines could be derived, considering that rights remain relevant during warfare, as does the familiar duty to avoid inflicting a wrongful loss on other individuals.

It is also important to note in this context that assessing whether international humanitarian law has been infringed is done using an objective standard[72] and generally requires taking into account the impact a belligerent activity has had on a group of individuals collectively, not individually. For example, according to the principle of proportionality, more indirect civilian injuries are permissible as more combatants and military installations are targeted for greater military advantage.[73] Suppose that for a certain belligerent activity the deaths of ten civilians would be proportionate. However, an attack that would kill 100 civilians was planned. All 100 deaths would be wrongful and in breach of international humanitarian law, not just the extra ninety, since the breach of the principle of proportionality is not associated with inflicting

[71] In this book, I do not examine whether a new tort ought to be established. This argument, that a new cause of action in tort might be needed to address wrongs that are inflicted through acts that constitute severe violations of customary international law, was raised by the Supreme Court of Canada the majority's opinion in *Nevsun v Araya*, and was critiqued by Brown and Rowe JJ dissent. See: *Nevsun Resources Ltd v Araya* [2020] SCJ No 5, Abella J paragraph 126; Brown and Rowe JJ paragraphs 215–23. To establish that ordinary tort law could apply to address belligerent wrongs, I do not need to examine whether a new tort should be recognized, nor do I attempt to answer this question.

[72] In this sense, courts do not examine the individual combatants' actual beliefs, but the view of a reasonable combatant in those particular circumstances (see, for example: *Prosecutor v Galić* ICTY IT-98-29, Trial Chamber Judgment of 5 December 2003, paragraph 58). Thus, the principles of international humanitarian law can be violated even when combatants believe they are complying with them, and in fact intend to do so.

[73] Yuval Shany, *The Principle of Proportionality under International Law* (The Israeli Democracy Institute 2009) 59. Article 51(5)(b) of Additional Protocol I states that 'among others, the following types of attacks are to be considered as indiscriminate: . . . (b) An attack which may be expected to cause incidental loss of civilian life, injury to civilians, damage to civilian objects, or a combination thereof, which would be excessive in relation to the concrete and direct military advantage anticipated.' (Additional Protocol I). Similarly, Article 8(2)(b)(iv) of the Rome Statute holds that 'intentionally launching an attack in the knowledge that such attack will cause incidental loss of life or injury to civilians or damage to civilian objects . . . which would be clearly excessive in relation to the concrete and direct overall military advantage anticipated' constitutes a war crime in international armed conflicts (The Rome Statute of the International Criminal Court 2002).

a loss on a particular individual. Rather, it is the estimated aggregate losses and aggregate gains that determine whether the principle is violated or not. If the principle of *in bello* proportionality is infringed, there can be no justification for an infliction of loss on any of the members of that group individually. Consequently, each individual who sustained this wrongful loss has a private claim against the state that caused it.

The second means of evaluating whether an infliction of a loss on civilians through warfare is justified is by examining states' and combatants' compliance with the rules of engagement. The rules of engagement are a concretized and detailed version of international humanitarian law in the sense that they are a specification of its principles requiring combatants to take only certain actions in response to specific events.[74] They inform combatants of the type of force they can use, against whom, and under what circumstances.[75] However, the rules of engagement do not explain to combatants *why* they allow the use of force. Rather, the rules only clarify to combatants the conditions under which the use of force is permitted. While states have a wide discretion regarding their interpretation of the principles of international humanitarian law, the rules of engagement can be restrictive, to various degrees, but they cannot authorize conduct that is inconsistent with international humanitarian law.

My argument is that if states and combatants adhere to the conditions that are set out in the rules of engagement, then the action complies with the requirements of international humanitarian law. Hence, all belligerent activities that are conducted in breach of these rules will create risks that, if they materialize, will constitute wrongs. Conversely, all losses that are inflicted while the rules of engagement are observed will only constitute non-wrongful harms.

[74] Note, international humanitarian law does not inform combatants about which actions they may do. Rather, they inform them about which actions are prohibited. See: Detlev F Vagts and Theodor Meron, 'So-Called "Unprivileged Belligerency": Spies, Guerrillas, and Saboteurs' in Detlev F Vagts and others (eds), Richard Baxter, *Humanizing the Laws of War: Selected Writings of Richard Baxter* (OUP 2013) 38; Derek Jinks, 'International Human Rights Law in Time of Armed Conflict' in Andrew Clapham and Paola Gaeta (eds), *The Oxford Handbook of International Law in Armed Conflict* (OUP 2014) 666. In contrast, rules of engagement do specify to combatants which actions they may or may not take.

[75] See, for example: Rules of Engagement for US Military Forces in Iraq as cited in: Human Rights Watch, 'Off Target: The Conduct of the War and Civilian Casualties in Iraq' (Human Rights Watch 2003) 138–39 <https://www.hrw.org/reports/2003/usa1203/usa1203.pdf> accessed 26 March 2024. Also see the Rules of Engagement for the Israel Defense Forces, as cited in 'The Security Forces Open Fire in the Territories' (*B'tselem*, July 1990).

V. There Is a Duty to Compensate

The discussion above illustrates that the first two preconditions that are required in order to establish a right to compensation in tort apply. Rights and duties do not expire during war, nor are they overridden or suspended. Moreover, the justification model provides us with a way of distinguishing between harms and wrongs. Once we have reached the conclusion that rights remain relevant during war, and we have identified what would constitute their wrongful breach, corrective justice duties— including the tort law duty of compensation—exist. This duty of compensation exists because the effects of wrongs must be corrected in order to maintain civilians' status as free and equal agents.[76] This reasoning is true whether the losses were inflicted in times of peace, or in times of war.

My argument is further clarified by examining the structure of corrective justice: (1) I have a right to my body and property; (2) other individuals cannot use or damage my body and property without my consent or proper use of authority; (3) if someone uses or damages my body or means without my consent or proper authority, then she has wronged me; and (4) all wrongs must be corrected by the wrongdoer.[77] This structure is not blind to the circumstances in which a loss has been inflicted. Still, once what is understood to be a wrong has been committed, the circumstances no longer have an effect on the existence of a corrective justice duty. Put differently, what matters is whether someone suffered a wrong, and someone inflicted a wrong.[78] When a wrong is inflicted, and no defence is available to the wrongdoer, a duty of compensation must be discharged.

In the context of war, the only defence that should be available is that of a justification when a loss is inflicted while adhering to international humanitarian law and the rules of engagement. It is not the violation of these norms that constitutes a private law wrong. Rather, adherence to these norms simply

[76] Ripstein, *Force and Freedom* (n 35) 82. Positioning corrective justice within Kant's philosophy of right, Ernest Weinrib states that 'since the vindication of right includes the prevention or reversal of violations of right, the freedom of all is immediately joined with a reciprocal universal coercion' (Weinrib, *The Idea of Private Law* (n 12) 107).

[77] See, for example: Aristotle, *Nicomachean Ethics* (Martin Ostwald tr, Bobbs-Merrill 1983) 1132; Beever (n 12) 19–21; Coleman, *Risks and Wrongs* (n 63) 331–32; Fletcher, 'Fairness and Utility in Tort Theory' (n 63) 543–57, 580; Gardner, 'What Is Tort Law For?' (n 12) 30–33; Goldberg and Zipursky, *Recognizing Wrongs* (n 12) 26–28, 234; Gregory C Keating, 'Reasonableness and Rationality in Negligence Theory' (1996) 48 Stanford Law Review 311, 318–25, 382–83; Stephen Perry, 'The Moral Foundations of Tort Law' (1992) 77 Iowa Law Review 449, 497–507; Ripstein, *Private Wrongs* (n 12) 167–68; Ripstein, *Force and Freedom* (n 35) 82–83; Stevens (n 12) 327–28; Weinrib, *The Idea of Private Law* (n 12) 26–28, 57–61, 75–76.

[78] Aristotle (n 77) 1132.

provides a justification that turns what would otherwise be a wrongful infringement of ordinary private law rights to person and property, into mere harms for which there is no corrective justice duty. Still, when international humanitarian law and the rules of engagement are violated, tort liability could and should be imposed.

Nevertheless, some have argued that there is something unique about combatant activities that suggests that there should not be a duty to correct losses that were inflicted during war, generally and not in relation to a specific body of law. For instance, Seth Lazar contends that there should not be a *post bellum* duty of compensation for four reasons.[79] First, it would impose what he defines as 'crippling burdens' on all parties to a conflict, as they would have to compensate for the vast losses inflicted during war. Second, compensation would be awarded to the holders of property, who are likely not those most in need. Third, the cost of compensation would be passed on to all of the state's citizens so that those who are morally liable would not be held legally liable, and the cost would also be borne by faultless individuals. Finally, the process of adjudicating claims could revive or deepen the animosity between parties to a conflict instead of letting bygones be bygones. Lazar is therefore not only opposed to the idea of having a tort law duty of compensation for belligerent wrongs but is also opposed to the notion of compensation for losses that are inflicted during war more generally.

Others have argued against a duty of compensation under tort law in particular. For example, in the US *Koohi* case, Judge Reinhardt holds that an imposition of liability will over-deter combatants, making it less likely that they will take all measures needed for securing victory.[80] He also holds that compensation in these circumstances would be unjust, as it would necessarily discriminate between individuals who sustained losses and would punish the combatants for fulfilling their duties.[81] Relying on the *Koohi* case, Chief Justice Barak of the Supreme Court of Israel held that tort law is ill-equipped to deal with the special risks that are created during belligerent activities, and hence it should not be applicable.[82] It has also been argued that tort law should not be available to enemy civilians who have been injured during battle, as, if it were

[79] Seth Lazar, 'Skepticism about Jus Post Bellum' in Larry May and Andrew Forcehimes (eds), *Morality, Jus Post Bellum, and International Law* (CUP 2012) 207—11.
[80] *Koohi v United States* 976 F2d 1328 (1992) 1334–35.
[81] ibid.
[82] CA 5964/92 *Jamal Kasam Bani Uda v Israel* 57(4) PD 1 (2002) 7–8.

available, filing claims in tort would become another means by which warfare is conducted.[83]

While I address the arguments against the availability of a right to remedy under tort liability in greater detail in Chapter 7, my analysis of private law rights in warfare and my articulation of belligerent wrongs demonstrate how the arguments against a duty of compensation fall short. My account of tort liability for belligerent wrongs is both narrow and ordinary. It is narrow in the sense that not all harms that are inflicted in the course of conducting belligerent activities give rise to tortious liability. Only wrongful losses do. This is not to say that Lazar's concern about crippling liability could never materialize under my account of liability, despite the fact that it is a narrow liability model. Lazar's claim is empirical, and there might be some circumstances under which liability could in fact be overwhelming for states. However, the narrow scope of liability that arises from the liability model I offer is not likely to result in states being required to pay significantly larger amounts of compensation than the *ex gratia*, insurance, and settlement payments that are currently used. These sums do not appear to be a burden that states could not carry. The liability model I offer would simply mean that states would be under a duty to provide compensation, rather than payments being a matter subject to their discretion.

Furthermore, the liability model I propose is narrow also because it is based on a formal account of corrective justice. Liability will be pursued through the injuring state's civil courts, which will award a remedy when a wrong has been inflicted and wrongdoer identified. It is this formality that minimizes the risk that enemy states will use tort law as a means of warfare, maintaining tort liability within the realm of right, and not within the realm of might. In fact, it is immunity from tort liability, as well as tort liability regimes that do not adhere to the formal structure of corrective justice, that seems to increase the risk of liability reviving or enhancing animosity between states. Both of these approaches can be used in a way that discriminates between potential plaintiffs and defines what amounts to a tortious wrong by taking into account factors that are external to the relationship between the wrongdoer and the wronged

[83] CC (Be'er Sheva) 45043-05-16 *A v Israel* (Nevo, 4 November 2018) 79–80. While discussing the amendment of the Israeli combatant activities exception, the Minister of Justice stated that: 'The Bill that was tabled is meant to prevent false claims against Israel. There is almost no country in the world that pays compensation during armed conflict, or even opens the door to those people who might be injured in such a conflict to file a claim against it . . . the 260 million ILS that were paid were deducted from the Ministry of Defense' budget' ('Protocol 405, Constitution, Law, and Justice Committee, 25 December 2001, 12:00' 4). In a later session, the Minister of Justice was even more explicit: 'there is no country in the world, only a foolish country, that provides its enemies with the option of suing it and getting compensation. We are the only stupid country that allows such a thing' ('Protocol 493, Constitution, Law, and Justice Committee, 24 June 2002, 11:30' 493).

individual. Consequently, tort liability can be used as a means of restricting enemy civilians' access to justice and effective remedies whilst broadening the scope of the enemy state's potential liability to the domestic state's civilians.[84]

The narrow scope of liability also undermines the arguments that it will result in over-deterrence or will inappropriately 'punish' public officials.[85] As liability would only be imposed for infringing the international humanitarian law and the rules of engagement, rational combatants should not be over-deterred from taking actions that adhere to these principles. Liability for violating these norms would be appropriate, as inflicting a loss under these circumstances is a wrong that cannot be justified.

My account is also ordinary, which helps to elucidate why some of the arguments against a duty of compensation are mistaken while others are not unique to the context of belligerent activities. The claim that only holders of property rights will obtain compensation, rather than those who are most in need, is mistaken. Corrective justice applies to individuals who have property and to those who do not. It is not extended based on any standard of worthiness other than the fact that a right has been wrongly violated. While empirically the possibility that liability to compensate might be greater for individuals who own property than for those who do not, all would have a right to compensation. As Ernest Weinrib suggests, tort law is a means through which individuals' private law rights and status as free and equal moral agents can be guaranteed and enforced by an independent public body against everyone else.[86]

Moreover, and as I argued in further detail in Chapter 1, the process to obtain a remedy in tort that I suggest is ordinary in two main ways. First, the forum in which a claim for compensation should be made against a state, for inflicting a belligerent wrong, should be that of the alleged wrongdoer. States' own courts routinely review the conduct of public officials through tort claims. Second, the litigation is not between two states but between an individual who sustained a wrongful loss and the state that inflicted it. It is unlikely that tort

[84] For examples of such uses in Israel and the United States, see: Haim Abraham, 'Discrimination in the Fight against Terror: Israeli Court Applies Jewish Nation-State Law' (*Just Security*, 21 September 2018) <https://www.justsecurity.org/60803/discrimination-fight-terror/> accessed 12 April 2020; Haim Abraham, 'Awarding Punitive Damages against Foreign States Is Dangerous and Counterproductive' (*Lawfare*, 1 March 2019) <https://www.lawfareblog.com/awarding-punitive-damages-against-foreign-states-dangerous-and-counterproductive> accessed 12 April 2020.

[85] The results of an indicative empirical study I conducted suggest that tort liability is likely to under-deter state actors from engaging in belligerent activities, though it could create incentives for state actors to exercise an appropriate level of care. See: Haim Abraham, 'Tort Liability, Combatant Activities, and the Question of Over-Deterrence' (2022) 47 Law & Social Inquiry 885, 914–15.

[86] Ernest J Weinrib, *Reciprocal Freedom, Private Law, and Public Right* (OUP 2022) 72–73, 81.

litigation will escalate relationships between states to the degree that they will once more engage in belligerent activities against one another.

In addition, the claim that there is an issue with holding states liable as they will pass the costs of compensation onto their citizens and consequently the wrongdoer will not bear the costs of the wrong is relevant even in the context of peacetime. As the resources of the state are the resources of its public, the passing of costs of compensation for state liability onto citizens is unavoidable. This is true for liability that is imposed for a belligerent wrong or a peacetime wrong, and there are no relevant differences, in terms of the costs the public bears, between holding a state liable for negligent police shooting and negligent combatant shooting. This issue may suggest that tort law should be abandoned in favour of other second-best solutions. Yet, insofar as tort law remains as a possible recourse, it should be available for both belligerent and peacetime wrongs. I analyse this point further in Chapter 7.

VI. Conclusions

In this chapter, I established that the necessary preconditions for tort liability to be available to address these wrongs can be met. I argued that the key to understanding the operation of tort law in the context of warfare is to evaluate combatant activities according to the norms which govern them, namely international humanitarian law and the rules of engagement. By doing so, I was able to demonstrate that rights remain relevant in times of violent conflict. I articulated 'belligerent wrongs' as violations of ordinary private law rights that are inflicted while infringing international humanitarian law and the rules of engagement, ruling out a justification that would make the losses non-wrongful. Furthermore, I showed that when a belligerent wrong is committed, an ordinary corrective justice duty to redress the wrong arises.

My analysis in this chapter demonstrates how some arguments that resist the availability of civilians' right to compensation could be explained away by articulating an account of liability that is properly informed by both tort law and theory, and theory and law of war. In Chapter 3, I turn to tackle additional critiques that have been used as justifications for providing states with near blanket immunity from tort liability. I show that these justifications are incompatible with the requirements of a substantive rule of law approach, offering additional reasons to support the argument that tort liability should be available to address belligerent wrongs.

3
The Combatant Activities Exception and the Rule of Law

I. Introduction

In Chapter 2, I demonstrated that the three preconditions for the existence of corrective justice duties are met when losses are inflicted during war. First, I established that there are private rights during war. Second, I argued that the distinction between wrongful and non-wrongful losses should be based on adherence to the law of war and the rules of engagement, and that only those losses that are inflicted while adhering to these norms are justified and non-wrongful. Third, and consequently, states are under an obligation to redress these 'belligerent wrongs' because the effects of wrongs must be corrected to maintain civilians' status as free and equal agents. In doing so, I showed that the moral underpinnings for the imposition of tort liability for belligerent wrongs exist.

In this chapter, I examine a particular immunity that many common law states enjoy for any losses they inflict during warfare, which prevents individuals from being able to obtain a remedy through tort law for the injuries they sustain. I refer to this immunity as the 'combatant activities exception'.[1] In Canada, Israel, and the United States, the combatant activities exception is grounded in legislation and acts as a defence to liability.[2] In contrast, in

[1] There are other immunities that could be used in the context of belligerent activities, such as the Domestic Crown Act of State doctrine in England and the Foreign Country exception in the United States (*Rahmatullah v Ministry of Defence* [2017] AC 649, 799; 28 USC §2680(k) 1948). However, these exceptions are not unique to losses that are inflicted during warfare, and some of them are *sui generis* to a particular jurisdiction. For these reasons, as well as for brevity, I address some of these immunities in other chapters where their operation and implications are relevant, while focusing solely on the combatant activities exception in this chapter.

[2] The Canadian exception has the widest scope, as it applies in times of peace and of war, for actual engagement in battle as well as training and auxiliary activities. See: Section 8 of the Crown Liability and Proceedings Act (RSC, 1985, C. C-50) 1985. Contrastingly, in Israel, the exception clarifies that 'the state is not liable in tort for any action done as a combatant activity by the Israel Defense Forces' (hereinafter: 'IDF'). See: Section 5(a) of the Civil Wrongs (Liability of the State) Act 1952. Similarly, the US exception states that no liability would be imposed in 'any claim arising out of the combatant activities of the military or naval forces, or the Coast Guard, during time of war.' (28 USC §2680(j) 1948). Note, unlike the Israeli and US combatant activities exceptions, Section 8 of the Crown Liability and Proceedings Act is not dedicated solely to combatant activities. Rather, it also provides immunity to

Tort Liability in Warfare. Haim Abraham, Oxford University Press. © Haim Abraham 2024.
DOI: 10.1093/9780191997051.003.0003

Australia and the United Kingdom, the exception was established through case law as courts held that states and combatants do not owe a duty of care in tort while engaging in belligerent activities.[3] In all of these jurisdictions, the exception raises four main difficulties: its scope is ambiguous, its application is potentially discriminatory, it frustrates access to legal remedies, and it creates a sphere in which public officials' discretion is unbounded.

I argue that due to these substantive and procedural difficulties, the combatant activities exception results in a situation in which public officials and bodies are not properly governed by private law. They enjoy a special immunity that means that they are not subject to the same rules as private individuals or, put differently, they are not entirely subject to the rule of law. This immunity contradicts a basic feature of a rule of law–abiding legal regime, according to which officials and private individuals alike are subject to the same common law rules, even while pursuing a public function, and if their actions wrongfully infringe an individual's rights, liability can and ought to be imposed.[4] The bar on tort remedies for wrongful losses inflicted during combat eliminates a mechanism by which individuals may stand on their rights and hold public officials accountable.

Moreover, the combatant activities exception stands in stark contrast to a general trend of eliminating states' special immunities from tort liability, which began in the mid-twentieth century and was motivated by the aim to minimize the risk of arbitrary action and abuse of public powers. As such, the continuing existence of the combatant activities exception begs the question of whether it is, or could be, properly justified in the present day.[5]

non-combatant activities. Still, across all jurisdictions, the exception provides the state with immunity from liability for belligerent activities, but its precise scope within each jurisdiction is a matter of significant debate.

[3] *Shaw Savill & Albion Co v Commonwealth* (1940) 66 CLR 344; *Mulcahy v Ministry of Defence* [1996] QB 732. In the United Kingdom an additional, but narrow, version of the combatant activities exception was enacted in relation to property damage in the War Damage Act (1965). However, UK courts have mainly relied on the broader common law combatant activities exception.

[4] Albert Venn Dicey, *Introduction to the Study of the Law of the Constitution* (10th edn, Macmillan [ua] 1959) 369–70, citing Lord Bowen in the Report of the Committee Appointed to Inquire into the Circumstances Connected with the Disturbances at Featherstone on 7 September 1893; Erwin Chemerinsky, *Closing the Courthouse Door: How Your Constitutional Rights Became Unenforceable* (Yale UP 2017) 22.

[5] My aim is not to examine the exception's validity or compliance with principles of justice, but to assess whether the creation and application of the combatant activities exception goes beyond a legitimate use of authority by the state according to substantive rule of law. (On the distinction between justice, authority, and the rule of law, see: Jacob Weinrib, *Dimensions of Dignity: The Theory and Practice of Modern Constitutional Law* (CUP 2016) 67–71). Nor am I questioning all immunities from tort liability. Although a substantive rule of law approach could be used to examine other immunities from liability, engaging in such analysis goes beyond the scope of this book and is not required to establish my argument. Hence, I will not pursue this line of inquiry.

This need for a proper justification is amplified by the fact that divergences from the rule of law, and consequently from the basic principle that an infliction of a private law wrong warrants a private law remedy, require an adequate justification. If a state suppresses individuals' private law right to a remedy without appropriate justification, its use of authority is defective. It is using its legislative or regulative powers beyond what it can do normatively, and so it is using wrongful means in the pursuit of its ends. My argument here is that the combatant activities exception is an example of states' defective use of authority in pursuit of their ends, as the justifications that have been articulated for this divergence do not stand up to scrutiny.

My analysis in this chapter is based on a substantive rule of law approach,[6] which has played a significant role in limiting the scope of states' immunity from liability and enabling the pursuit of private law remedies for wrongs committed by states. I establish that the combatant activities exception grounds principles that deviate from the requirement of substantive rule of law, and that it does so without proper justification.

The origins of the substantive rule of law approach are often traced to the work of A. V. Dicey. For Dicey, personal freedom and private rights are the basis for the English constitutional system. He articulates three rule of law principles as means for guaranteeing individuals' rights: The most relevant one for the purposes of this book is that the same ordinary law should apply to private individuals and public officials alike. However, public officials may be granted special powers to pursue a public purpose, in which case they must act within the scope of their authority or otherwise be held accountable for overstepping their authority.[7] Dicey argues that the three rule of law principles are enforced through private law remedies, namely compensation, and the writ of *habeas corpus*.[8] My analysis proceeds with Dicey's arguments in mind—the

[6] For the reasons stated in Chapter 1, my analysis throughout the book is based on a rights-based approach to tort law and theory, in which morality and equality have significant roles. Given this theoretical orientation, I will not address the formal approach to the rule of law in this chapter, since this approach does not consider matters of morality and equality as necessary requirements and demands that law should remain a separate matter. As such, the gap between rights-based approaches and the formal rule of law approach is too wide to allow for a relevant discussion. While such an analysis is beyond the scope of this book, it is possible to evaluate whether the combatant activities exception aligns with the various legislative and executive desiderata put forward by scholars such as Fuller, Hart, and Raz. See: Lon L Fuller, *The Morality of Law* (Yale UP 1964) 122; HLA Hart, *The Concept of Law* (Penelope A Bulloch and Joseph Raz eds, 3rd edn, OUP 2012) 114; Joseph Raz, *The Authority of Law: Essays on Law and Morality* (2nd edn, OUP 2011) 214–18.

[7] The other two principles are: that punishment could only be imposed by courts on an individual if he or she breached an established and ordinary legal norm, and not by an arbitrary decision of a public official; and that the constitution is the result of judicial decisions about individuals' private rights (Dicey (n 4) 188, 193, 195, 289).

[8] ibid 124–28.

basic starting point for a rule of law–abiding regime is to provide compensation to individuals as a matter of right. Compensation enables individuals to enforce their rights and hold officials accountable.

I then turn to two contemporary scholars—TRS Allan and David Dyzenhaus—who build on Dicey's arguments, whose writings offer means of determining which deviations from the rule of law could be justified. Both Allan and Dyzenhaus suggest that three core principles animate the requirements of substantive rule of law: freedom as independence, dignity, and equality of citizenship.[9] By freedom as independence, Allan and Dyzenhaus each suggest that the rule of law should be understood as constituting liberty by enabling individuals to pursue their ends without being subject to the arbitrary whims of others.[10] Dignity and equality of citizenship are, hence, an integral part of freedom as independence, as dignity signifies each person's status as an independent agent who is free to use her means to pursue her goals, and equality of citizenship means substantive equality within the political community.[11]

Allan and Dyzenhaus argue that the purpose of the legal system is to ensure and maintain these three core principles and that without the legal system these principles cannot be guaranteed. Infringement and restriction of rights are divergences from the substantive rule of law principles, which place an onus of justification on public actors to show that they are pursuing good

[9] Allan's rule of law account is more substantive and liberal, arguing that the rule of law should be preserved to the highest degree possible while noting that a breach of the rule of law might result in something that is not law at all. See: TRS Allan, *The Sovereignty of Law: Freedom, Constitution and Common Law* (OUP 2013) 91; TRS Allan, 'The Rule of Law' in David Dyzenhaus and Malcolm Thorburn (eds), *Philosophical Foundations of Constitutional Law* (OUP 2016) 216–17. In this sense, Allan's account is clearly distinguishable from a formal rule of law approach. In contrast, Dyzenhaus sees his view as a midway between a thick substantive conception and a formal account, holding that the substantive rule of law principles are in fact embedded in Lon Fuller's eight desiderata. Like Fuller, Dyzenhaus argues that only extreme cases of infringement of the rule of law will actually result in something that is not law at all. Yet, in all other cases—which is to say, in most cases—a breach of the rule of law results in bad law rather than no law at all. See: David Dyzenhaus, 'Process and Substance as Aspects of the Public Law Form' (2015) 74 Cambridge Law Journal 284, 284; David Dyzenhaus, 'Liberty and Legal Form' in Lisa M Austin and Dennis Klimchuk (eds), *Private Law and the Rule of Law* (OUP 2014) 96; David Dyzenhaus, *The Constitution of Law: Legality in a Time of Emergency* (CUP 2006) 42, 203–4; David Dyzenhaus, 'Form and Substance in the Rule of Law: A Democratic Justification for Judicial Review' in Christopher F Forsyth (ed), *Judicial Review and the Constitution* (Hart Publishing 2000) 168–69; Fuller (n 6) 39.

[10] Allan, 'The Rule of Law' (n 9) 204; Dyzenhaus, 'Liberty and Legal Form' (n 9) 92–93; Dyzenhaus, *The Constitution of Law* (n 9) 2; TRS Allan, 'The Rule of Law as the Rule of Private Law' in Lisa M Austin and Dennis Klimchuk (eds), *Private Law and the Rule of Law* (OUP 2014) 72.

[11] Dyzenhaus, 'Liberty and Legal Form' (n 9) 95; Dyzenhaus, 'Form and Substance' (n 9) 172; Dyzenhaus, *The Constitution of Law* (n 9) 12–13; Allan, 'The Rule of Law' (n 9) 203–4; Allan, 'The Rule of Private Law' (n 10) 86; Allan, *The Sovereignty of Law* (n 9) 90. Compare to Peter Hogg's understanding of Dicey's idea of equality in: Peter W Hogg, *Liability of the Crown* (2nd edn, Carswell Co 1989) 1.

public ends by using the right kind of means.[12] Public actors' pursuit of good ends cannot justify the use of wrongful means, nor can the use of good means justify the pursuit of wrongful or private ends.

The structure of this chapter is as follows. I begin by placing the combatant activities exception in the wider context of the history of state liability in tort, highlighting that it is in juxtaposition to the general trend of allowing tort claims to be brought against the state. In Section II, I turn to identify and analyse the four main concerns that the combatant activities exception raises from a substantive rule of law perspective. In Section III, I examine the four justifications that have been offered for the combatant activities exception and show that they do not meet the rational connection and necessity requirements for divergence from the rule of law. I shall conclude by offering an account of the possible implications required by the substantive approaches to rule of law. I argue that not only does the substantive approach to the rule of law indicate that there ought to be liability for belligerent wrongs, but it also suggests that the exception should either be interpreted narrowly or abolished.

II. From Sovereign Immunity to Qualified State Liability

The combatant activities exception is intrinsically linked to the erosion of states' domestic blanket immunity from tort liability. Indeed, it was not always possible for individuals to bring a claim in tort against a state in that state's own courts.[13] For example, in England, between the fourteenth and twentieth centuries, there was no available legal recourse against the Crown in tort due to the feudal principle 'the king can do no wrong', that provided the Crown with *de facto* immunity.[14] In the eighteenth century, a practice emerged for bypassing

[12] Allan, *The Sovereignty of Law* (n 9) 92; Allan, 'The Rule of Law' (n 9) 219; Dyzenhaus, *The Constitution of Law* (n 9) 12–13, 139. As Jacob Weinrib puts it: 'An adequate justification must establish that public authority is consistent with the right and the duty of each person to interact with every other on terms of equal freedom' (Weinrib (n 5) 48).

[13] My inquiry centres on states' liability in their own courts under domestic tort law. I will, therefore, not consider similar questions and immunities that arise when tort claims are brought against states outside of their own jurisdictions, such as the Foreign Sovereign Immunity Doctrine and the Foreign Act of State Doctrine. For an overview and analysis of these doctrines, see: Hazel Fox and Philippa Webb, *The Law of State Immunity* (3rd edn, OUP 2015) 25–49, 468–83; Uglješa Grušić, *Torts in UK Foreign Relations* (OUP 2023) 77–114. I will also not discuss the Crown Act of State Doctrine in this chapter, though I do in Chapter 6, since its application is not unique to warfare; its existence has not influenced the scope, character, or justifications of the combatant activities exception in a meaningful way; and, unlike the combatant activities exception, it does not exist in many common law jurisdictions.

[14] During the middle ages, the 'king can do no wrong' maxim did not mean that the king was above the law, even though claims could be brought only in contracts and restitution and were subject to his consent. The maxim was misinterpreted as stating that nothing the king does could constitute a tort or an authorization to commit a tort, despite its original meaning that the king has no privilege to

this immunity and providing a remedy to injured individuals. Accordingly, the Crown would name a defendant in tort actions, against whom damages could be awarded, but it would subrogate the defendant if compensation was awarded.[15]

The United States also had a doctrine to provide the federal government with immunity from tort liability, which was akin to the English 'the king can do no wrong' maxim, holding that immunity from liability is derived from sovereignty.[16] According to the American doctrine, the federal government was immune from any suit against it, unless it consented to be sued.[17] Compensation for injuries caused by public officials was awarded through private bills in Congress, in ever growing numbers.[18]

By the mid-twentieth century, many common law jurisdictions enacted laws that rendered states liable in tort for certain actions. As early as 1903, Australia enacted Part IX of the Judiciary Act, which gave a limited right to sue the Commonwealth both in contract and in tort without petition of right (and was later extended). In the late 1940s, and following several court cases that resulted in intensive political pressure on the legislatures, both the United Kingdom and the United States enacted legislative reforms that allowed the state to be sued in tort.[19] Many jurisdictions followed the British and American examples, including Canada, Israel, and New Zealand, making it possible for the state to be held liable in tort.[20]

commit illegal acts, even if he acts illegally. Consequently, fault could not be attributed to the Crown, and liability was imposed on public officials if they could be identified as the wrongdoers. See: TT Arvind, 'Restraining the State through Tort? The Crown Proceedings Act in Retrospect' in TT Arvind and Jenny Steele (eds), *Tort Law and the Legislature: Common Law, Statute and the Dynamics of Legal Change* (Hart Publishing 2013) 406; Peter W Hogg, Patrick Monahan, and Wade K Wright, *Liability of the Crown* (4th edn, Carswell 2011) 4–6; Joseph M Jacob, 'The Debates behind an Act: Crown Proceedings Reform, 1920–1947' (1992) 92 Public Law 452, 455; Guy I Seidman, 'The Origins of Accountability: Everything I Know about the Sovereign's Immunity, I Learned from King Henry III' (2005) 49 St Louis University Law Journal 393, 430, 434–36, 477; Harry Street, *Governmental Liability: A Comparative Study* (Archon Books 1975) 2.

15 Arvind (n 14) 419.

16 *United States v Lee* 106 US 196 (1882) 205–8; *Feres v United States* 340 US 135 (1950) 139. For an argument that the state immunity doctrine cannot justifiably be a part of US law, see: Chemerinsky (n 4) 21–24.

17 This point was made in several key cases relating to the tort liability of the federal government, for example: *Feres* (n 16) 139; *Nevada v Hall* [1979] 440 US 410, 442.

18 *Feres* (n 16) 140; *Skeels v United States* 72 F Supp 372 (WD La, 1947) 373. In 1942, President Roosevelt reported that the number of private bills reached 2,000 per congress (see: Irvin M Gottlieb, 'The Federal Tort Claims Act: A Statutory Interpretation' (1946) 35 Georgetown Law Journal 1, 4).

19 28 USC §1346, 1948; 28 USC §2674, 1948; Crown Proceedings Act 1947; Joe Richman, 'The Day a Bomber Hit the Empire State Building' *NPR* (28 July 2008) <https://www.npr.org/2008/07/28/92987873/the-day-a-bomber-hit-the-empire-state-building> accessed 18 August 2016; Hogg (n 11) 83.

20 Crown Liability Act, RSC, c. 30, 1953; Crown Proceedings Act 1950; Civil Wrongs (Liability of the State) Act; Hogg (n 11) 84. Note, in Canada, it was possible to sue the Crown in tort since the enactment of the Exchequer Court Act of 1887, but liability was limited in two ways. First, it arose

Since then, there has been an overall trend in common law jurisdictions of eliminating state immunities,[21] motivated mainly by political and commercial interests. As the modern state began to fulfil and regulate an increasing number of functions, unrest over its immunity from liability began to grow.[22] The legal and business communities viewed the immunities as granting the state an unfair advantage because remedies against it were scarce and insufficient.[23]

While political and commercial interests drove legislative amendments, the justification for revoking state immunity from tort liability was framed in substantive rule of law terms, namely as a growing concern for due process and equality under the law.[24] Having a special immunity is concerning to a substantive rule of law approach because liability articulates and enforces the limits of legitimate discretion that states and officials possess, thus reducing the potential for arbitrary action.[25]

Alongside enabling tort claims against the state, several immunities from liability were created, including the combatant activities exception. The reasons

only for wrongful losses that were inflicted by servants of the Crown while acting within the scope of their public power. Second, liability could only be imposed after a fiat was granted through a Petition of Right. See: 'Canada, Parliament, House of Commons Debates, 21st Parliament, 7th Session, Vol. 2, 1470 (January 21, 1953)' 1471 <http://parl.canadiana.ca/view/oop.debates_HOC2107_02/373?r = 0&s = 3>.

[21] Anthony Bradley and John Bell, 'Governmental Liability: A Preliminary Assessment' in Harry Street (ed), *Governmental Liability: A Comparative Study* (Archon Books 1991) 15; Carol Harlow, *State Liability: Tort Law and Beyond* (OUP 2004) 23. Erwin Chemerinsky notes in relation to US local and state immunity, as opposed to federal immunity, that it is possible to identify an objectionable opposite trend of expanding immunity from tort liability (Chemerinsky (n 4) 23–24).

[22] Harold G Aron, 'Federal Tort Claims Act: Comments and Questions for Practicing Lawyers' (1947) 33 American Bar Association 226, 228; D Park Jamieson, 'Proceedings by and against the Crown' (1948) 26 Canadian Bar Review 373, 373; Fox and Webb (n 13) 32–33. In the United States, for example, the volume of private bills, through which compensation for losses inflicted by states were granted, the inadequacy of Congress as an institution for the determination of facts, and the capricious results of the private bills process, all led to a strong demand that claims for compensation should be submitted to and determined by the courts. See: *Feres* (n 16) 140; *Skeels* (n 18) 373; Edwin Borchard, 'Government Liability in Tort' (1948) 26 The Canadian Bar Review 399, 399–400.

[23] Arvind (n 14) 407–11. In the United Kingdom, unions and business owners, mainly the Liverpool Shipowners Association, pushed for the reform through their close political relations in order to promote their financial interests. See: Jacob (n 14) 455–65; Sir Thomas Barnes, 'The Crown Proceedings Act, 1947' (1948) 38 Canadian Bar Review 387, 389. Lord Chancellor William Jowitt remarked that amending the law so that the Crown could be sued in tort 'would bring considerable credit to [the Labour] Party' [Jacob (n 14) 477)]. However, it was not until the House of Lords' decision in *Adams v Naylor* and the Court of Appeals' decision in *Royster v Cavey* that pressure resulted in legislative amendments. See: *Adams v Naylor* [1946] AC 543; *Royster v Cavey* [1947] KB 204; Harry Street, 'Crown Proceedings Act, 1947' (1948) 11 Modern Law Review 129, 129.

[24] Hogg (n 11) 1–2; Margaret Helen Kerr, Laurence M Olivo, and JoAnn Kurtz, *Canadian Tort Law in a Nutshell* (Carswell 2014) 74; Aron (n 22) 227.

[25] *Aleksic v Canada (Attorney General)* [2002] OJ No 2754, Wright J, paragraph 11; *Bici v Ministry of Defence* [2004] EWHC 786 (QB), paragraph 86; Dicey (n 4) 202–3; Lorne Sossin, 'The Unfinished Project of Roncarelli v Duplessis: Justiciability, Discretion, and the Limits of the Rule of Law' (2010) 55 McGill Law Journal 661, 672.

for the creation of this exception are yet to be traced in some jurisdictions, such as Canada and the United States, where a lack of legislative history makes it particularly challenging to identify such reasons.[26] In other jurisdictions, the rationale for the establishment of the combatant activities exception varies. For instance, when the combatant activities exception was first introduced into legislation in Israel, it was due to a concern with the possibility that tort liability for military activities could over-deter combatants or that Israel would be unable to withstand the financial burdens of liability.[27] In contrast, in Australia and the United Kingdom, the courts grounded the motivations for a combatant activities exception in what they viewed to be a matter of sound reason and policy, as the notion of combatants taking reasonable care and courts reviewing their actions seemed improper.[28]

Two key questions emerge. First, in what ways does the existence of the combatant activities exception raise concerns over divergence from substantive rule of law principles, which were the basis for holding states liable in tort? Second, can this divergence be justified by rule of law standards? As I show below, while the exception is a divergence from substantive rule of law principles, justifications for its existence and scope are questionable.

III. Substantive Rule of Law Concerns

The assertion that the combatant activities exception is an instance of divergence from substantive rule of law principles is uncontroversial. The exception provides states with a special immunity, and in doing so, they are not subject to the same ordinary rules as private individuals. However, a comprehensive appreciation of the scope of divergence from substantive rule of law requires further analysis. As I show below, such an analysis reveals that the combatant

[26] 'Canada, Parliament, House of Commons Debates, 21st Parliament, 7th Session, Vol. 4, 3326 (March 26, 1953)' 3332 <http://parl.canadiana.ca/view/oop.debates_HOC2107_04/36?r=0&s=3>; *Johnson v United States* 170 F2d 767 (9th Cir, 1948) 769.

[27] For instance, Knesset member Jacob Shapira stated that: 'the State's security interests necessitate that during belligerent activities combatants' hands shall not be tied by potential compensation that will be required, but that their thoughts would be solely focused on those actions that are essential for the protection of the state. In addition, there is a financial difficulty. It is not enough to sign a promissory note, as the state will be obliged to pay it off. No state can take such a financial obligation upon itself' ('Protocol 49, Constitution, Law, and Justice Committee, August 13, 1952' 49). However, these considerations of over-deterrence and financial inability were never discussed again, and instead the rationales for the combatant activities exception related to limiting a perceived enemy's access to court, limiting courts' power to hold that the State has inflicted a wrong, and a belief that tort liability is incoherent in the context of warfare. See: Haim Abraham, 'Tort Liability, Combatant Activities, and the Question of Over-Deterrence' (2022) 47 Law & Social Inquiry 885.

[28] *Shaw Savill* (n 3) 361; *Mulcahy* (n 3) 748–49.

activities exception raises four main difficulties. First, its scope and character are ambiguous. Second, it has the potential to discriminate between certain populations, namely between nationals and non-nationals. Third, the exception seems to be in opposition to the requirement that public officials' discretion will be bounded. Fourth, individuals are left without means of obtaining legal remedies.

A. Ambiguity

According to the substantive rule of law approach, the purpose of the rule of law is to constitute liberty and protect individuals from being subjected to others' arbitrary ends.[29] The clearer the legal regime, the more it can assist in promoting these rule of law principles.[30] In contrast, ambiguity in the law could undermine these principles by illegitimately limiting the rights of private individuals in three distinct, though related, ways. First, limitation of rights could lack a legitimate public end or could go beyond the minimal necessary degree for attaining public ends.[31] Second, ambiguities in legal norms could produce a mandate for public officials to act with unbounded discretion.[32] Third, ambiguities could result in inadequate clarity regarding officials' scope of permissible action and subsequently lead to wrongful infringement of individuals' dignity, equality, and freedom as independence.[33]

Different degrees of ambiguity pose different levels of difficulty to substantive rule of law. Ideal legal norms are entirely clear, whereas defective legal norms are entirely opaque. The more opaque a norm that regulates the application of public power is, the less protection the norm offers against public power being used arbitrarily or without authority.

The combatant activities exception, in its various iterations across jurisdictions, is an example of an ambiguous norm that is inconsistent with substantive rule of law. While courts seem to be in agreement about the applicability of

[29] Allan, 'The Rule of Private Law' (n 10) 72; Dyzenhaus, 'Liberty and Legal Form' (n 9) 92–93; Dyzenhaus, *The Constitution of Law* (n 9) 2.

[30] Allan, *The Sovereignty of Law* (n 9) 91; Weinrib (n 5) 75. For a view that laws should be stated as clearly as possible to provide proper guidance to individuals' behaviour, see: Hart, *The Concept of Law* (n 6) 155; HLA Hart, *Essays in Jurisprudence and Philosophy* (OUP 1983) 114–15; Raz (n 6) 213.

[31] Allan, *The Sovereignty of Law* (n 9) 91–92; Dyzenhaus, *The Constitution of Law* (n 9) 12–13.

[32] Unbounded discretion of public officials stands in opposition to the principles of freedom as independence, dignity, and equality, and hence it is unwarranted (see: Hanoch Dagan, 'Private Law Pluralism and the Rule of Law' in Lisa M Austin and Dennis Klimchuk (eds), *Private Law and the Rule of Law* (OUP 2014) 159; Sossin (n 25) 672).

[33] Weinrib (n 5) 52–53.

the exception when combatants are actually engaging in battle,[34] they struggle to identify which activities would qualify as 'combatant' under the exception when they fall short of actual engagement in belligerent action.

For instance, how should courts classify activities, such as delivering supplies or building infrastructure, that do not consist of actual engagements with the enemy but are auxiliary to warfare? Currently, it appears that only in the United Kingdom is there a definitive stance on this point, as the Supreme Court held that the exception should not apply to auxiliary activities at all.[35]

In other jurisdictions, the applicability of the exception to auxiliary activities is less clear. For instance, while Australian courts held that the exception applies to activities that are auxiliary to actual or imminent combat,[36] it remains unclear whether the Australian exception applies to post-warfare auxiliary activities or training.[37]

In Canada, the text of Section 8 of the Crown Liability and Proceedings Act seems to suggest that the exception applies to any acts or omissions, including auxiliary activities, that are done for the defence of Canada or to maintain the country's combat ability.[38] Nevertheless, courts are conflicted about the question of whether the exception should only apply to non-negligent activities[39] or

[34] See, for example: CA 1459/11 *The Estate of Hardan v Israel* (Nevo, 16 June 2003) (regarding the shooting of four unarmed farmers who were mistakenly identified as armed terrorists during Operation 'Defensive Shield'—a large-scale military operation conducted by the IDF in 2002 in the West Bank); *Koohi v United States* 976 F2d 1328 (1992) (regarding the shooting down of a civilian aircraft by a US warship in the midst of the 'tanker war' between Iran and Iraq); *Aleksic* (n 25) (regarding losses incurred by plaintiffs due to the participation of Canada in NATO's missile and aerial bombardment of parts of Yugoslavia in the spring of 1999); *Shaw Savill* (n 3) (regarding damage occasioned by a collision between the plaintiff's ship *Coptic* and His Majesty's Australian ship *Adelaide* in September 1940, while engaging in active naval operations against the enemy in the present state of war); *Smith v Ministry of Defence* [2013] 4 All ER 794 (regarding the deaths of three soldiers and the injuries of another two, while serving in the British Army in Iraq between 2003 and 2006, due to friendly fire and a detonation of an improvised explosive device).

[35] As is inferred from the leading precedent of *Smith* (n 34) 830–31.

[36] *Shaw Savill* (n 3) 362; *Parker v Commonwealth* (1965) 112 CLR 295, 302; *Groves v Commonwealth* (1982) 150 CLR 113, 117.

[37] *Groves* (n 36) 119.

[38] 'Anything done or omitted in the exercise of any power or authority exercisable by the Crown, whether in time of peace or of war, for the purpose of the defence of Canada or of training, or maintaining the efficiency of, the Canadian Forces.' (Section 8 of the Crown Liability and Proceedings Act).

[39] The courts are split in regard to the meaning of non-negligent activities. In some cases, the exception is said to apply to policy and management decisions, while operations based on these decisions do not fall under its scope (see: *Swanson Estate v Canada* [1992] 1 FC 408 (Fed CA) paragraphs 28–31; *Ring v Canada (Attorney General)* 2007 NLTD 146 (NL TD) paragraph 107; *Parrish & Heimbecker Ltd v Canada (Minister of Agriculture & Agri-Food)* 2008 FCA 362 (FCA) paragraphs 20–21; *Comeau's Sea Foods Ltd v Canada (Minister of Fisheries and Oceans) (CA)* [1995] 2 FC 467 paragraph 48). In other cases, the exception is interpreted as an expression of the defence of statutory authority, meaning that non-negligent losses that were inflicted while acting in accordance with a power granted by law are immune from liability (see: *Robitaille v R* [1981] 1 FC 90 (Fed TD) paragraph 6; *K & L Land Partnership v Canada* 2014 BCSC 1701 paragraph 102). Nevertheless, both interpretations are declaratory in the sense that Section 8 is grounding in legislation common law principles of determination of liability.

should include negligent activities as well.[40] Similar confusion exists in relation to the interpretation of what constitutes actions done 'in defence of Canada',[41] and one court even found the exception so perplexing that it refused to decide whether the exception applies.[42]

The ambiguity of the exception regarding its applicability to auxiliary activities is more evident in Israel and the United States. In both jurisdictions, the applicability of the exception to auxiliary activities is contested, with some courts interpreting the exception broadly while others interpreting it more narrowly. For example, in some cases, the exception was held to be inapplicable for losses caused by units and vessels aimed at supplying ammunition that were standing by, away from the theatre of battle—but the exception might apply if the ammunition was supplied on the battlefield, to forces actively engaging in battle.[43]

[40] *Hainsworth v Canada* [2003] OJ No 6162 (Ont SCJ) paragraph 32; *Prentice v Canada (FCA)* [2006] 3 FCR 135, 165.

[41] *Aleksic* (n 25) 32.

[42] *Morton v Canada (Attorney General)* [2005] 75 OR (3d) 63, 68. In this case, the plaintiff, a structural engineer with the Maryland National Guard, was injured while playing basketball in a gym at a Canadian Forces Base. Canada argued that it should not be held liable for the faulty construction and maintenance of the gym, as these activities fall under Section 8 of the Crown Liability and Proceedings Act. Quinn J held that 'Legislation can be humbling. I do not know what s 8 means. I have read it several times. I am embarrassed to say that my comprehension did not improve with repetition. Consequently, I am unable to say whether it is an impediment to the action of the plaintiffs.'

[43] See: *Johnson* (n 26) 770; CA 623/83 *Levi v Israel* [1986] PD 4(1) 447, 479–80. In the United States, there is still no conclusive authority on the application of the exception to auxiliary activities. The exception provides immunity from liability to: 'Any claim arising out of the combatant activities of the military or naval forces, or the Coast Guard, during time of war' (28 USC. §2680(j)). The exception was interpreted in the *Johnson* case as applying to activities auxiliary to actual or imminent battle as well as training activities (*Johnson* (n 26) 770). In contrast, in the *Skeels* case, it was held that no auxiliary activities should enjoy the exception's protection (*Skeels* (n 18) 374). For a general review of the exception that highlights its many conflicting interpretations, see: James Lockhart, 'Construction and Application of Combatant Activities Exception to Federal Tort Claims Act, 28 USCA §2680(j)' (2007) 23 American Law Reports 489. In Israel the situation is similarly complex. The Israeli legislature has expanded the definition of 'combatant activities' to include 'any action of fighting terror, insurgency, or uprising, as well as actions aimed at the prevention of terror, insurgency, or uprising, which are of a belligerent nature considering the overall circumstances' (Section 1 of the Civil Wrongs (Liability of the State) Act). Still, there are many contradictory court rulings about its application. For example, the exception was held to apply in some auxiliary activities to actual or imminent combat, such as ambush and intelligence gathering—see, for example: CA 542/75 *Atallah v Israel* PD 31(2) 552 (1997); CA 1864/09 *The Estate of Skafi v Israel* (Nevo, 07 September 2011); PCA 3866/07 *Israel v Almakoosi*; *Hardan* (n 34). Contrastingly, the exception was held to be inapplicable for other auxiliary activities, such as driving to the battlefield and taking over structures for imminent battle. See: CC (Tel Aviv) 5859/67 *Ben-Ya'acov v Ben-Hananya* PD 71 197 (1970); ReqCivC (Jerusalem) 6396/07 *Israel v Kasad Investment and Trade Co* (Nevo, 29 November 2007); CC (Jerusalem) 13578/07 *Nelbandiyan v The Armenian Patriarchate of Jerusalem* (Nevo, 01 August 2013). That said, the overall trend in Israel is to expand the range of activities to which the exception would apply (Abraham (n 27) 904–13; Haim Abraham, Gilat Bachar, and Ceasefire Centre for Civilian Rights, 'Mapping Civilian Harm Claims against Israel and the Palestinian Authority' (2023) <https://civilian-harm-map.ceasefire.org/en/civilian-harm> accessed 4 October 2023).

The ambiguous character of the combatant activities exception goes beyond the matter of which activities fall within its purview, extending to the question of whose activities are immune from liability. There is a wide array of individuals who may be engaged in belligerent activities in the contemporary theatre of battle, including soldiers, mercenaries, guerrilla fighters, terrorists, civil war fighters, contracted civilian service providers, private individuals, and even automated weapons. Does the exception apply to all combatant activities, regardless of the 'status' of the actor? Once more, it is possible to identify inconsistency across jurisdictions, as well as ambiguities within jurisdictions.

Take Canada, for example. Its combatant activities exception stipulates that no tort liability could be imposed for 'anything done or omitted in the exercise of any power or authority exercisable by the Crown, whether in time of peace or of war, for the purpose of the defence of Canada or of training, or maintaining the efficiency of, the Canadian Forces'.[44] The exception does not limit its applicability to a particular class of individuals, beyond requiring an exercise of power or authority of the Crown. As such, a plain reading of the Act suggests that the exception applies to acts and omissions by any servant of the Crown, which includes agents but excluding independent contractors.[45] Put differently, the exception could apply to wrongs inflicted by combatants, but also to those inflicted by the Bank of Canada, Canada Post, and VIA Rail employees, for instance, as these are Crown corporations with Agent status.[46] However, as Canadian courts remarked repeatedly, the character and scope of the exception is an unsettled matter,[47] and as such it is unclear whether it indeed applies to all of these actors or just some of them.

A similar ambiguity exists in the United States, even though its combatant activities exception seems to apply only to losses inflicted by military, naval, and Coast Guard forces.[48] The cause of ambiguity in this context is not open-textured language. Rather, it is due to the Supreme Court ruling in *Boyle v United Technologies Corp*, which extended the 'discretionary function' exception to private military contractors.[49] Several Circuit Courts have relied on *Boyle* to extend the applicability of the combatant activities exception to

[44] Section 8 of the Crown Liability and Proceedings Act.
[45] ibid, Sections 2 and 3(b).
[46] Treasury Board of Canada Secretariat, 'List of Crown Corporations' (15 May 2007) <https://www.canada.ca/en/treasury-board-secretariat/services/guidance-crown-corporations/list-crown-corporations.html> accessed 4 October 2023.
[47] *10565 Nfld Inc v Canada (Attorney General)* [2017] NLTD(g) 84, paragraph 202; *K & L* (n 39), paragraph 100.
[48] 28 USC §2680(j).
[49] 28 USC §2680(a) 1948; *Boyle v United Techs Corp* 487 US 500 (27 June 1988) 509–13.

private military contractors, but there is no uniform approach to when such extension is warranted.

In *Koohi*, the Ninth Circuit held a narrow view, holding that the combatant activities exception would extend to immunize contractors from liability in relation to actual use of force through 'authorized military action'.[50] In *Saleh*, a broader approach was taken by the DC Circuit, which held that the exception can be extended to the degree that it eliminates tort from the battlefield, even in relation to the liability of contractors.[51] The Second, Third, and Fourth Circuits articulated an approach that falls somewhere in between. According to this approach, the combatant activities exception could be extended when a contractor was involved in the military's combatant activities, and the military 'specifically authorized or directed' the contractor's action.[52] As this point is yet to be settled through legislation or the Supreme Court, we are currently left with contradicting meanings of an exception that should apply uniformly in all federal courts.

This discussion demonstrates that, to various degrees, the ambiguity of the combatant activities exception hinders courts' abilities to review the application of public power and safeguard against it being used arbitrarily or without authority. In addition to courts' lack of means to prevent abuses of public power, the exception's ambiguity creates the background conditions for it to be discriminatory, prevent access to remedies, and result in public officials' unbounded discretion.

B. Discriminatory Character

An additional potential difficulty lies in the fact that the exception could be designed to target certain populations, mainly non-citizens. From a substantive rule of law perspective, while laws can discriminate between individuals, doing so must be justified by furthering a legitimate public purpose while upholding the principle of equality of citizenship.[53] Arbitrary discrimination between individuals cannot be justified as it undermines equality by implying that certain groups have an inferior status in relation to others.[54]

[50] *Koohi* (n 34) 1336–37.

[51] *Saleh v Titan Corp* 580 F3d 1 (CADC, 2009) 7–9.

[52] *Badilla v Midwest Air Traffic Control Service, Inc* 8 F4th 105 (2021) 127–29; *In re KBR, Inc, Burn Pit Litigation* 744 F3d 326 (4th Cir, 2014) 348–51; *Harris v Kellogg Brown & Root Services, Inc* 724 F3d 458 (3rd Cir, 2013) 480–81.

[53] Allan, 'The Rule of Private Law' (n 10) 80; Allan, 'The Rule of Law' (n 9) 211; Dyzenhaus, *The Constitution of Law* (n 9) 12–13; Dyzenhaus, 'Form and Substance' (n 9) 172.

[54] Allan, 'The Rule of Private Law' (n 10) 86.

Two questions follow. First, does the exception apply only to certain individuals, based on particular characteristics? If so, and secondly, is this an instance of arbitrary discrimination or is there something in the circumstances of losses inflicted during warfare that requires differentiating between individuals? The answers to both questions depend on whether the exception is examined in isolation of other mechanisms of redress.

If we were to focus on the operation of the combatant activities exception as a single legal norm and leave out other norms that regulate compensation and payments for losses that are inflicted during warfare, the exception does not seem to be discriminatory. In Australia, the United Kingdom, and the United States, the wording of the exception and the way it has been applied by the courts bar claims of nationals and non-nationals alike.[55] Even in Israel, where legislative amendments of the exception were aimed at discriminating between nationals and non-nationals,[56] the application of the exception by the courts does not seem to discriminate on these grounds.[57]

However, examining the operation of the exception alongside other mechanisms of redress that are made available, namely *ex gratia* payments and

[55] See, for instance: *Parker* (n 36); *Groves* (n 36); *Shaw Savill* (n 3); *Mulcahy* (n 3); *Multiple Claimants v Ministry of Defence* [2003] EWHC 1134 (QB); *Smith* (n 34); *Bici* (n 25); *Skeels* (n 18); *Johnson* (n 26); *Rotko v Abrams* 338 FSupp 46 (D Conn, 1971); *Vogelaar v US* 665 FSupp 1295 (1987); *Koohi* (n 34); *Ibrahim v Titan Corp* 391 F Supp 2d 10 (DDC, 2005); *Saleh* (n 51). In Canada, there is currently no case that examines the application of the combatant activities exception to non-nationals.

[56] The exception was amended to include unique procedural requirements and statutory limitations for losses inflicted in the West Bank and Gaza Strip, and excludes liability of residents of enemy states or territories, which was interpreted by the Supreme Court to include all civilians in the Gaza Strip (Sections 5A–5B of the Civil Wrongs (Liability of the State) Act; CA 993-19 *Ploni v Israel* (Nevo, 05 July 2022), Judge Sohlberg, paragraphs 67, 89–90; Judge Grosskopf, paragraphs 4–16). In the explanatory notes to Amendments 4 and 7, the legislature stated that 'during armed conflict between peoples, each party bears the costs of its injured, and is responsible for them' (Draft Bill 2645 Handling Lawsuits against the Operations of the Security Forces in Judea and Samaria and Gaza (Amendment 4) 1997; Draft Bill 3173 Civil Wrongs (State Liability) (Amendment 7) 2005). When Amendment 4 was in deliberation in the Knesset's Constitution, Law, and Justice Committee, the Minister of Justice was even more explicit about the purpose of the exception to bar non-nationals from securing compensation: 'There is no country in the world, only a foolish country, that provides its enemies with the option of suing it and get compensation. We are the only foolish country that allows such a thing.' ('Protocol 493, Constitution, Law, and Justice Committee, June 24, 2002, 11:30').

[57] See, for example: CC (Jerusalem) 317/93 *Abu Jabar v Israel*, TK-District 94(3) 6; CA 311/59 *Mifal Takhanot Hatraktorim Ltd v Hayat* [1960] PD 14, 1609; CC (Jerusalem) 22938/00 *Noodle v Israel* (Nevo, 03 November 2005); *Levi* (n 43); PCA (Tel Aviv) 2086/07 *The Council of Elkana v Israel* (Nevo, 22 December 2008); FTCC (Tel Aviv) 58222-03-11 *Eldan Transportation Inc v Israel* (Nevo, 10 January 2013); CC (Ashdod) 3781/05 *Etgar v Israel* (Nevo, 27 August 2013); CC (Jerusalem) 8538-08-10 *Get v Israel* (Nevo, 12 May 2015); CA 2144/13 *The Estate of Mantin v The Palestinian Authority* (Nevo, 06 December 2017); CA 5964/92 *Jamal Kasam Bani Uda v Israel* 57(4) PD 1 (2002); CA (Jerusalem) 32/93 *Tabenja v Israel* (Nevo, 10 January 1994); CA 4112/09 *Zayger v Judea and Samaria Military Commander* (Nevo, 01 January 2012); CC (Jerusalem) 17071/01 *The Estate of Fisher v Israel* (Nevo, 28 May 2007); CA 6982/12 *The Estate of Corrie v Israel* (Nevo, 12 February 2015); *Nelbandiyan* (n 43); CC (Jerusalem) 1625/02 *The Estate of Shakhatit v The Megido Prison Commander* (Nevo, 7 December 2008); *Skafi* (n 43).

state-operated insurance schemes, suggests that, in fact, there is discrimination between nationals and non-nationals. Generally speaking, nationals have access to reparations for the losses they sustain through various statutory schemes as a matter of right, whereas non-nationals might have access to discretionary *ex gratia* or settlement schemes.[58] More broadly, there is an argument that states categorize harms which are caused by their own militaries to their own nationals as policing activities, for which tort liability can be imposed. Meanwhile, injuries caused under similar circumstances to foreign nationals are considered combatant activities, for which there is no liability.[59]

In the particular case of Israel, it is possible to map the application of the combatant activities exception over time and within a geographical context to uncover the discriminatory dimensions of its application. An examination of over 470 rulings from 1959 to 2023 reveals that even though the combatant activities exception can apply regardless of nationality, in reality, it has been found to be applicable mostly to claims by Palestinian plaintiffs.[60] In fact, 90% of all cases in which the applicability of the combatant activities exception has been considered by courts were cases brought by Palestinian plaintiffs, and in eight out of ten of those cases, the exception was found to be applicable. For Israeli plaintiffs, the exception was held to apply in only two out of ten cases. These figures, alongside a sharp decline in the number of tort claims Palestinians file against Israel for losses inflicted by its military forces, indicate that the express aims of the legislator—to limit Palestinian access to remedies—have been achieved.[61]

[58] Some examples of statutory schemes for nationals include: Compensation for Victims of Hostile Activities Act 1970; Property Tax and Compensation Fund Act 1961; Department of Defense, 'Wounded, Ill, and/or Injured Compensation and Benefits Handbook' 31–36 <https://warriorcare.dodlive.mil/files/2019/06/DoD_Compensation_and_Benefits_Handbook.pdf> accessed 26 November 2019; 34 USC §20144(c)(1-2) 2015. In contrast, Australia, Canada, Germany, Israel, Italy, Norway, the United States, and the United Kingdom have also made *ex gratia* payments for losses inflicted on foreign nationals. For a fuller discussion, see: Yaël Ronen, 'Avoid or Compensate? Liability for Incidental Injury to Civilians Inflicted during Armed Conflict' (2009) 42 Vanderbilt Journal of Transnational Law 181, 214–15; Michael Friscolanti, 'Canadian Military Payments for Death and Destruction in Afghanistan', *Maclean's - The Canadian Encyclopedia* (2013) <http://www.thecanadianencyclopedia.ca/en/article/canadian-military-payments-for-death-and-destruction-in-afghanistan/> accessed 20 December 2018; Center for Civilians in Conflict, 'United States Military Compensation to Civilians in Armed Conflict' (2010) <https://civiliansinconflict.org/wp-content/uploads/2017/09/CENTER_Condolence_White_Paper_2010.pdf>; Headquarters Department of the Army, 'The Commanders' Emergency Response Program (CERP)' (2013) <armypubs.army.mil/doctrine/DR_pubs/dr_a/pdf/atp1 + 062x2.pdf>; John Fabian Witt, 'Form and Substance in the Law of Counterinsurgency Damages' (2008) 41 Loyola of Los Angeles Law Review 1455, 1458.

[59] W Michael Reisman, 'Compensating Collateral Damage in Elective International Conflict' (2013) 8 Intercultural Human Rights Law Review 1, 12.

[60] Abraham, Bachar, and Ceasefire Centre for Civilian Rights (n 43).

[61] See also: Abraham (n 27) 903–11; Gilat Bachar, 'Access Denied—Using Procedure to Restrict Tort Litigation: The Israeli-Palestinian Experience' (2017) 92 Chicago-Kent Law Review 841, 849–51.

The discussion thus far suggests that the answer to the first question—whether the exception discriminates between groups based on particular characteristics—is negative when considered in isolation. However, when the broader context of the operation of compensation and payment schemes is taken into account, it is clear that different groups are subject to different legal regimes. Furthermore, in jurisdictions where there is sufficient empirical data to evaluate the application of the combatant activities exception, it appears to discriminate between groups.

We must therefore consider whether there is something in the circumstances of losses that are inflicted during warfare that justifies differentiating between groups. At this point, some might argue that the combatant activities exception merely captures the relevant differences between times of peace and war as well, as the materialization of extraterritorial losses, and as such this is not an instance of arbitrary discrimination but a required distinction. For example, because war is morally and legally distinct from peace,[62] what amounts to wrongful and non-wrongful losses differs across these contexts.[63] Losses that would be wrongful in peacetime will be non-wrongful during belligerent activities. In peacetime, pointing a gun towards a person while saying 'I am going to kill you' constitutes the wrong of assault.[64] However, the same words might be at most a non-wrongful harm when spoken by combatants of opposing states during belligerent activities. Accordingly, a distinction between losses that are inflicted through ordinary peacetime activities and those inflicted through warfare could appear fundamental.

Moreover, in some jurisdictions, there is a view that domestic courts could not and should not impose liability on their own state and its agents for extraterritorial wrongs, as in doing so courts will assert illegitimate state authority over foreign states.[65] According to this view, limiting tort liability for

[62] Immanuel Kant, 'Towards Perpetual Peace (1795)' in Mary J Gregor (tr), *Immanuel Kant: Practical Philosophy* (CUP 1996) 320, 322; Stephen C Neff, *War and the Law of Nations: A General History* (CUP 2007) 58; Avishai Margalit, 'Decent Peace' (2005) 216 <https://tannerlectures.utah.edu/_resources/documents/a-to-z/m/Margalit_2006.pdf> accessed 10 March 2017.

[63] This distinction does not mean that these categories are mutually exclusive. Rather, it is an assertion that in some instances harms are not wrongs and vice versa. See: Arthur Ripstein, 'In Extremis' (2005) 2 Ohio State Journal of Criminal Law 415, 417. For convenience, I refer to non-wrongful losses as harms, and wrongful losses as wrongs.

[64] Sections 21, 24, and 33 of the American Law Institute, *Restatement of the Law (Second)* (American Law Institute 1965); Philip H Osborne, *The Law of Torts* (5th edn, Irwin Law 2015) 269–70.

[65] This position was clearly articulated in the United States in 28 USC §2680(k); *Hernandez v Mesa* 140 S Ct 735 (US, 25 February 2020) 748. Similarly, in *R v Hape* the majority of the Supreme Court of Canada held that 'Canadian law, whether statutory or constitutional, cannot be enforced in another state's territory without the other state's consent' (*R v Hape* [2007] 2 SCR 292, paragraphs 69, 115–16). For a critique of this view and an analysis of when and why it would be legitimate for states to impose tort liability on one another for extraterritorial torts, see: Haim Abraham, 'Myths and Misconceptions

extraterritorial torts is justified even if doing so would impact nationals and non-nationals differently, as such limitation would be required to avoid illegitimate use of authority.

Neither of these arguments seem particularly convincing. The fact that there could be a relevant difference between losses inflicted in times of peace and times of war does not mean that there are always relevant differences. For instance, directly targeting non-combatants in battle is as much of a wrong as randomly murdering individuals during peacetime is. Once what amounts to a wrong during warfare is articulated and the applicability of tort doctrines is clarified, it is challenging to reject the possibility of imposing tort liability on the grounds of moral and legal differences between war and peace. All individuals hold the same basic *universal* status and rights as free and equal agents. The right to life, bodily integrity, and property are some of the components of this basic universal status.[66] If states inflict a belligerent wrong on individuals, they owe a corrective justice duty to them regardless of nationality.

Additionally, the view that an imposition of liability by a court on its own state for extraterritorial losses would be an illegitimate assertion of authority over the foreign state in which the loss materialized appears to be incorrect. A court that reviews the actions of its own state might be exercising the authority of the state, but there is nothing in this use of authority that is extraterritorial. The location in which the loss materialized could affect the relevant applicable law, and a foreign state's tort law could be considered to determine whether a certain loss is wrongful.[67] Yet, this is not the same as asserting authority over a foreign state.

in Extraterritorial Torts' (forthcoming) University of Toronto Law Journal <https://dx.doi.org/10.2139/ssrn.4741760> accessed 12 March 2024.

[66] Sections 1, 3, and 17 of the Universal Declaration of Human Rights 1948.

[67] In international tort cases, common law courts decide the governing substantive law according to one of three doctrines. The first is the doctrine of double actionability, which requires that an injury would be considered an actionable wrong in both the jurisdiction in which it was done and the jurisdiction in which the case was brought. However, this doctrine has been rejected to various extents. For example, the Supreme Court of Canada and the High Court of Australia have both rejected this doctrine, though the Canadian court maintained an exception that allows for the applicability of the doctrine when not doing so will result in an injustice (see: *Regie Nationale des Usines Renault SA v Zhang* (2002) 187 ALR 1, 17; *Tolofson v Jensen* [1994] 3 SCR 1022, 49). Israel adopted a similar approach, rejecting the double accountability doctrine while creating a justice-based exception, according to which the *lex loci delicti* rule would be deviated from if the place in which the wrong occurred were entirely coincidental (*CA 1432/03 Yinon Manufacturing and Marketing Food Products Inc v Kraan* PD 59 (1) 345 (2004) 369–78; *FH 4655/09 Skalar v Uviner* PD 65(1) 735 (2011) 759). In contrast, in the United Kingdom, the double accountability doctrine was repealed through legislation, though it too has maintained several exceptions that allow for the application of the doctrine (Sections 10–13 of the Private International Law (Miscellaneous Provisions) Act 1995; *Kuwait Airways Corp v Iraqi Airways Co (No 3)* [2002] 3 All ER 209). The second is the doctrine of *lex loci delicti*, which holds that the substantive law that governs international tort claims is the law of the place in which the wrong was inflicted (*lex loci delicti*), while

Consequently, the unique features of warfare do not seem to require a nationality-based distinction for the availability of tort remedies. Nevertheless, when considered within the relevant context, the combatant activities exception appears to discriminate between nationals and non-nationals arbitrarily and without proper justification.

C. No Access to Private Law Remedies

A third issue that arises from the combatant activities exception is that it prevents access to private law remedies. As I argued above, for Dicey, individuals' right to compensation for wrongs inflicted on them by public officials is a key and basic feature of the rule of law, aimed at facilitating accountability and vindicating individuals' rights. Limitations upon, and restrictions of, individuals' ability to seek compensation through private law are a rule of law concern that requires justification, and the elimination of tort claims altogether poses a major challenge to the rule of law. Such limitations and restrictions could be unjust even if they do not discriminate between potential plaintiffs, and there are alternative public law avenues to respond to the wrong.[68] Being able to seek private law remedies is part of what makes individuals into fully formed legal persons.[69] Private law safeguards liberty as independence, dignity, and equality

the procedural law is that of the place of adjudication (*lex fori*). The third doctrine that is applied by many US jurisdictions requires the courts to determine the applicable law according to the jurisdiction which has the most significant relationship to the occurrence of the wrong and the parties. See: Sections 6 and 145 of the American Law Institute, *Restatement of the Law, Second: Conflict of Laws* (American Law Institute 1971).

[68] In HLA Hart's words: 'law might be unjust while treating all alike. The vice of such laws would then not be the maldistribution, but the refusal, to all alike, of compensation for injuries which it was morally wrong to inflict on others. The crudest case of such unjust refusal of redress would be a system in which no one could obtain damages for physical harm wantonly inflicted. It is worth observing that this injustice would still remain even if the criminal law prohibited such assault under penalty.' (Hart, *The Concept of Law* (n 6) 164).

[69] The argument that access to private law remedies is required due to the fact that people are legal persons could be understood in two similar ways. For example, Arthur Ripstein argues that people can only enjoy private rights if there is a mechanism through which disputes could be resolved. See: Arthur Ripstein, 'The Rule of Law and Time's Arrow' in Lisa M Austin and Dennis Klimchuk (eds), *Private Law and the Rule of Law* (OUP 2014) 307. The combatant activities exception disrupts what would otherwise be an available mechanism for dispute resolutions, as it provides states with blanket immunity from liability. The exception does not resolve disputes as much as it withholds remedies from plaintiffs. A similar argument is made by Lisa Austin. She contends that private rights confer legal powers, allowing the individuals who hold them to pursue their ends and secure legal consequences that would not be available otherwise (Lisa M Austin, 'The Power of the Rule of Law' in Lisa M Austin and Dennis Klimchuk (eds), *Private Law and the Rule of Law* (OUP 2014) 269–70). The exception could therefore be said to subvert these powers, as it leaves individuals unable to secure the legal consequences they desire.

by demarcating wrongful from non-wrongful conduct and providing a mechanism through which private law rights can be enforced.[70]

There are instances in which restrictions on access to private law remedies are justified and warranted, as they serve a legitimate public end. For example, if someone stole my car I could, in theory, have an indefinite private right of action against her to return the car to me, as stealing my car does not affect my ownership of it.[71] However, a statute of limitation could narrow down the time during which I can pursue such remedy to several years. The goal of such a restriction could be, for example, to secure fairness[72] and the availability of evidence,[73] or ensuring that disputes are settled so private rights could be utilized.[74]

Hence, an argument could arise that the combatant activities exception is no different than other norms that restrict access to legal remedies, such as statutes of limitation. Indeed, the exception restricts the ability plaintiffs possess to secure remedies for their injuries through private law. Yet, if we accept this restriction as justified or warranted for the purpose of obtaining a legitimate public end, then, according to this argument, the divergence from the rule of law should not raise significant concerns.

But the exception does more than limit private rights of action. It precludes recourse through tort law altogether. A statute of limitation leaves a set time during which individuals can pursue private law remedies. In contrast, the combatant activities exception bars all actions for belligerent losses from the moment they were inflicted, and as it is currently applied it bars actions against the state regardless of whether the loss was wrongful or non-wrongful. In this sense, the exception is not a modest limitation or restriction of individuals' basic rights but a significant divergence from substantive rule of law principles. Put differently, by completely eliminating private rights of action, the combatant activities exception makes the mechanism through which legality is enforced unavailable. Consequently, freedom as independence, dignity, and equality are endangered, and individuals' agency is undermined.

[70] Allan, 'The Rule of Private Law' (n 10) 86, 71; Dyzenhaus, 'Liberty and Legal Form' (n 9) 92–93.

[71] Arthur Ripstein, *Private Wrongs* (Harvard UP 2016) 8.

[72] Paul M Perell and John W Morden, *The Law of Civil Procedure in Ontario* (1st edn, Lexis Nexis 2010) 98.

[73] Thomas Merrill, 'Property Rules, Liability Rules and Adverse Possession' (1984) 79 Northwestern University Law Review 1122, 1128.

[74] Ripstein, 'The Rule of Law and Time's Arrow' (n 69) 324.

D. Unbounded Discretion

The accumulative effect of the exception's ambiguity, discriminatory character, and lack of access to private law remedies is that the discretion of states and combatants is insufficiently bounded by private law. For the substantive rule of law approach, unbounded discretion is a significant concern. The rule of law requires that no public official will hold such a degree of discretion, as unbounded discretion undermines individuals' agency.[75] Every action made by a public official must be authorized by law and reviewable by the courts.[76] Public officials are required to show that they had the power to act in the way they did, especially when they infringed the rights of private individuals. Furthermore, a grant of uniquely public powers does not, of itself, make wrongs into permissible harms. For instance, police officers are allowed to drive over the speed limit in a car chase. Nevertheless, they are not allowed to run down pedestrians in order to stop a car thief. Their discretion and power are, in this sense, bounded.

One way in which public officials' discretion can be kept in check is by allowing individuals to seek remedies for abuse or misuse of public power.[77] Having the ability to impose tort liability on public actors, be they officials or states, is conducive to binding discretion because it assists in demarcating the range of permissible actions. Beyond this range, public power is either wrongly used or it becomes merely the subjection of individuals to private power, under the guise of public power.[78] For example, if a police officer accidently crashes a police car into another vehicle, then it is a wrongful use of public power. However, if the officer intentionally crashes the police car, then it is in fact a wrongful use of private power, as public power can only be used to pursue legitimate public ends.[79] Tort liability is able to respond to both kinds of impermissible actions by public actors, and in doing so, to state clearly how their discretion can and cannot be executed.

In contrast, an immunity to tort liability is detrimental in two ways. First, it frustrates one of the available mechanisms for binding discretion and delineating the range of legitimate actions. Second, the power of public actors increases, since a significant mechanism to bind its use is not available. The

75 Dagan (n 32) 159; Sossin (n 25) 672.

76 Allan, 'The Rule of Private Law' (n 10) 82.

77 Peter H Schuck, *Suing Government: Citizen Remedies for Official Wrongs* (Yale UP 1983) 1.

78 Weinrib (n 5) 53.

79 Allan, *The Sovereignty of Law* (n 9) 91–92; Dyzenhaus, *The Constitution of Law* (n 9) 12–13; Arthur Ripstein, 'Property and Sovereignty: How to Tell the Difference' (2017) 18 Theoretical Inquires in Law 243, 257–60.

more power public actors have, the more possible it is that either public power will be used wrongfully or private power will be used in the guise of public power.[80] Put differently, the availability of tort law remedies provides individuals with the means of resisting arbitrary use of power against them, power that is beyond the authority of public actors.[81] It is through private law that it is possible for individuals to vindicate their rights and ensure that public officials' discretion and power are used legitimately. For individuals to remain independent agents, they must have a way of bringing claims against anyone who inflicts a wrongful loss on them, in order to correct that loss.

Imagine someone taking your car. You would not be free of this person's control unless a court holds that the car is yours, and that it must be returned to you along with any losses you incurred from the wrongful taking. It would not be enough if the court declared only that the car is yours but did not order its restitution, as this result would fail to fully protect individuals' independence from one another. Similarly, if the individual who took the car was a public official, it would not be enough for the court to state that she acted in a way that is unconstitutional or opposed to administrative norms. It would not even suffice if the public official was subject to a disciplinary hearing or held criminally liable. To be free of this individual, you would also have to be able to vindicate your rights through private law.[82]

The combatant activities exception seems to be in opposition to the substantive rule of law requirements that the discretion of public officials should be bounded and that individuals can vindicate their rights through private law. The courts' inability to review administrative action due to the exception results in states holding de facto near-unlimited discretion to act or refrain from acting as they see fit. While they legally have limited authority to act for certain purposes and in certain ways, the lack of judicial oversight means that there is no tort law mechanism for discerning whether an action was a wrongful use of public power or of private power in the guise of public power. Consequently,

[80] In the words of Lord Acton: 'Power tends to corrupt and absolute power corrupts absolutely. Great men are almost always bad men, even when they exercise influence and not authority: still more when you superadd the tendency or the certainty of corruption by authority.' (Lord John Emerich Edward Dalberg-Acton, 'Letter to Archbishop Mandell Creighton' (5 April 1887) paragraph 7 <https://history.hanover.edu/courses/excerpts/165acton.html> accessed 21 November 2019).

[81] Dicey (n 4) 289.

[82] Note, Dyzenhaus' objection to the idea that a private law legal order is a mandatory part of a proper legal system does not pose a difficulty in this context as he contends that if private law was constituted, then it is subject to the principles of the rule of law. See: Dyzenhaus, 'Liberty and Legal Form' (n 9) 102, 109–10. The analysis conducted here is based on the fact that private law was constituted in the relevant common law jurisdictions, and so Dyzenhaus' theoretical critique is inapplicable in this context.

there is also no private law mechanism for redressing states' belligerent wrongs. It is in this sense that states' discretion is not sufficiently bounded.[83]

IV. Failing to Justify Divergence from the Rule of Law

The discussion above illustrates that the combatant activities exception diverges from the rule of law to various degrees, as it places the actions of states beyond the reach of the law by frustrating courts' abilities to review state actions and provide remedies for wrongful losses. The question that must therefore be addressed is, can the combatant activities exception be justified? Indeed, divergences from substantive rule of law principles could be justified if states have acted within their authority to do so *and* the divergence is rationally connected to the achievement of a legitimate and necessary public end.[84] According to the substantive rule of law approach, all of these requirements must be met for a divergence from the rule of law to be properly justified.

Over the years, legislators, courts, and scholars have offered several justifications for the exception, which I classify into four distinct groups. First, due to separation of powers concerns, losses that are inflicted during battle are not justiciable. Second, if states were held liable for belligerent wrongs, they would be over-deterred from engaging in combat. Third, there are procedural difficulties so severe that only by applying the exception can procedural fairness be maintained. Fourth, the exception is required to save judicial and administrative time and resources.

All four justifications seem to comply with the substantive rule of law requirement that the act that constitutes a divergence from the rule of law will be one that a state or a public official has the authority to carry out. Indeed, it is within the authority of legislatures to enact legislation that limits the ability of individuals to pursue private law remedies, and it is within the authority

[83] David Dyzenhaus, 'Recrafting the Rule of Law' in David Dyzenhaus (ed), *Recrafting the Rule of Law: The Limits of Legal Order* (Hart 1999) 10–11; David Dyzenhaus, 'Schmitt v Dicey: Are States of Emergency inside or outside the Legal Order?' (2006) 27 Cardozo Law Review 2005, 2006; Trevor W Morrison, 'Suspension and the Extrajudicial Constitution' (2007) 107 Columbia Law Review 1533, 1539; David L Shapiro, 'Habeas Corpus, Suspension, and Detention: Another View' (2006) 82 Notre Dame Law Review 59, 86–89.

[84] Allan, 'The Rule of Law' (n 9) 218; Allan, 'The Rule of Private Law' (n 10) 72, 82; Allan, *The Sovereignty of Law* (n 9) 108; Dyzenhaus, 'Liberty and Legal Form' (n 9) 107 n63; Dyzenhaus, *The Constitution of Law* (n 9) 12–13, 198. According to Allan, in order for a divergence from the rule of law principles to be justified, the restriction of rights must also be proportionate to the anticipated public benefit: Allan, 'The Rule of Law' (n 9) 215; Allan, *The Sovereignty of Law* (n 9) 108–9. However, as this point is not shared by all substantive rule of law theorists, and because a proportionality analysis requires knowledge of facts that cannot be obtained, I will not take it up in this chapter.

of courts to interpret the law in a fashion that limits individuals' abilities to pursue private law remedies. Statutes of limitation and the principle of estoppel are examples of such abilities.

Additionally, all four justifications appear to meet the requirement that the aim of a divergence from the rule of law will be to pursue a public purpose, as opposed to the private purposes of the relevant public official—such as personal gain or the advancement of personal beliefs. In the context of the combatant activities exception, several such public purposes have been articulated, including saving judicial and administrative time and resources, ensuring procedural fairness, protecting the principle of separation of powers, and frustrating the possibility of over-deterrence.

Accordingly, the discussion below will be limited to examining whether the justifications that have been offered meet the substantive rule of law requirements of rational connection and necessity, which, if met, could justify divergence from the rule of law. I show that the current justifications do not meet these requirements.

A. Separation of Powers

The argument that the combatant activities exception is justified, as it is required by the principle of separation of powers, has been articulated in various cases in Australia, Canada, and the United States. According to this line of reasoning, the decision to wage war and the way in which specific belligerent activities are conducted are issues that should lie entirely with the executive and legislative branches. Courts do not, and should not, examine such operations. Courts lack the knowledge and expertise to assess decisions on whether and how to engage in battle, and if they were to do so through tort law, they would be intervening with matters of policy and foreign relations.[85]

[85] *Aleksic* (n 25) 32, 35, 69; *Shaw Savill* (n 3) 356; *Saleh* (n 51) 26. A related point was raised by Israeli state and district attorneys, who were concerned by the possibility that evidence that was presented to the courts could not be evaluated properly by them. Their main issue in this regard is that judges lack the expertise to make sense of evidence in the context of war. For example, District Attorney Ariel Ararat stated in a Constitution, Law, and Justice Committee meeting regarding Amendment 8, which was aimed at expanding the scope of the combatant activities exception, that: 'Cases of this kind that deal with pure military subject-matters ... require a degree of specialization ... It is difficult for [district and state attorneys] to teach judges in every case the subject-matter de novo ... There are judges who presided over dozens of these cases ... You don't have to teach them the *Zidan* precedence, operation logs, the application of the Military Judiciary Act ... the difficulty of subpoenaing witnesses' ('Protocol 66, Constitution, Law, and Justice Committee, September 14, 2009, 09:00').

It is possible to identify a rational connection between the exception and separation of powers justification if we accept one of two views regarding the inapplicability of the rule of law during warfare. The first view was advanced by Carl Schmitt, who argued that the Sovereign can decide whether a state of emergency exists and that a state of emergency is beyond the reach of law.[86] According this view, combat-related decisions are purely political, and consequently if courts were to review them, then they would be intervening with matters of policy and foreign relations.

The second view is positivist and posits that during emergencies there must be means of acting outside the law, when required to do so, to preserve the legal order.[87] The claim here is not that emergencies are a priori beyond the rule of law. Rather, it is that legislatures have an authority to enact laws that allows the states and its officials to act in ways that would be inconsistent with the rule of law, and hence even emergencies are not completely beyond the law. According to this view, the rational connection between the combatant activities exception and separation of powers also exists, as the exception enables the state and its agents to act beyond the rule of law without accountability.

Nevertheless, both views raise several difficulties. If the rule of law does not exist during warfare, the law of war in its entirety seems pointless; and if the rule of law is maintained by law that excludes its operation, it results in nothing more than a sham.[88] Given these difficulties, the substantive rule of law approach appears to offer a more compelling view. According to this view, times of emergency do not generate a justification or authority to act outside the bound of the rule of law. While the Sovereign can act in ways that are political, its actions are always bounded by what it is legally entitled to do. When states act outside the rule of law, then they are not acting in their capacity as states at all, as they are exercising private rather than public power.[89]

If we accept that the rule of law exists during warfare, and consequently we reject the position that all decisions regarding combat are entirely political or

[86] Carl Schmitt, *Political Theology: Four Chapters on the Concept of Sovereignty (1922)* (University of Chicago Press 2005) 5–13.

[87] John Ferejohn and Pasquale Pasquino, 'The Law of the Exception: A Typology of Emergency Powers' (2004) 2 International Journal of Constitutional Law 210, 210; Cass R Sunstein, 'Minimalism at War' (2004) 2004 Supreme Court Review 47, 108; Richard A Posner, *Not a Suicide Pact: The Constitution in a Time of National Emergency* (OUP 2006) 93; Eric A Posner and Adrian Vermeule, *Terror in the Balance* (OUP 2007) 11–14.

[88] Dyzenhaus, *The Constitution of Law* (n 9) 194–95; David Dyzenhaus, 'The Puzzle of Martial Law' (2009) 59 University of Toronto Law Journal 1, 61, 200.

[89] Hans Kelsen, *Introduction to the Problems of Legal Theory: A Translation of the First Edition of the Reine Rechtslehre or Pure Theory of Law (1934)* (Bonnie Litschewski-Paulson and Stanley L Paulson trs, OUP 1997) 99–106; Dyzenhaus, *The Constitution of Law* (n 9) 194–200; Allan, 'The Rule of Private Law' (n 10) 86.

beyond the law, the rational connection between the combatant activities exception and the separation of powers justification is unclear. Courts routinely pass judgment on states' acts and omissions in tort proceedings, and they might find that an action that was taken was inappropriate and resulted in a wrong. There are no significant differences between courts reviewing the operation of the executive branch for the purpose of determining tort liability in peacetime and in wartime.

The combatant activities exception restricts courts' ability to resolve disputes when their actions are not executive in nature and do not interfere with the executive's policy and foreign relations decision-making. The exception is therefore not conducive to maintaining separation of powers, and in fact seems to undermine separation of powers, as well as the rule of law more generally. When courts cannot review the actions of the executive, there is no mechanism through which it is possible to evaluate whether public officials exercised public power or imposed private power *ultra vires*.[90] Consequently, there is no way of ensuring the conditions necessary to guarantee dignity, equality, and freedom as independence.[91] Indeed, the approach taken by international law and domestic courts is that liability to compensate infliction of wrongful losses during war is a justiciable matter.[92] Put differently, it seems that it is difficult to establish that a rational connection exists between the combatant activities exception and separation of powers.

Even if the rational connection requirement for a deviation from the rule of law could be met, it would nevertheless be challenging to establish the requirement of necessity, that is, that the divergence from the rule of law is minimal and only of the degree required to achieve the relevant public end. Currently, the exception is used to dismiss claims that could otherwise be successful, and

[90] Weinrib (n 5) 53.
[91] ibid 47–54.
[92] For example, Article 3 of The Hague Regulations and Article 91 of Additional Protocol I hold that a state which infringes the law of war and inflicts a loss on another nation is liable to pay compensation for it (Protocol Additional to the Geneva Conventions of 12 August 1949, and relating to the Protection of Victims of International Armed Conflicts 1977; Convention (IV) Respecting the Laws and Customs of War on Land and its annex: Regulations concerning the Laws and Customs of War on Land 1907; Hersch Lauterpacht, 'The Law of Nations and the Punishment of War Crimes' (1944) 21 British Yearbook of International Law 58, 75). Likewise, the US Supreme Court held that federal courts are able to review military decisions, especially when they cause injury to civilians (*The Paquete Habana* 175 US 677 (1900) 686–713; *Scheuer v Rhodes* 416 US 232 (1974) 247–49; *Laird v Tatum* 408 US 1 (1972) 15–16). Additionally, the US Court of Appeals for the Ninth Circuit held that: 'Damage actions are particularly judicially manageable' (*Koohi* (n 34) 1332). Similar views were expressed by Canadian and UK courts. See: *Aleksic* (n 25) 5; *Bici* (n 25) 90; Kenneth Bullock, 'United States Tort Liability for War Crimes Abroad: An Assessment and Recommendation' (1995) 58 Law and Contemporary Problems 139, 147; Andrea Gattini, 'To What Extent Are State Immunity and Non-Justiciability Major Hurdles to Individuals' Claims for War Damages?' (2003) 1 Journal of International Criminal Justice 348, 363.

as such it has the effect of barring courts from reviewing both states' decisions to engage in a belligerent activity and losses that were inflicted during combat.

Yet, it is possible to avoid a violation of the principle of separation of powers in a way that falls short of barring tort litigation for belligerent wrongs entirely, by adopting the tort liability framework I am offering. Accordingly, violations of private law rights are *prima facie* wrongful, but if they are inflicted while complying with international humanitarian law and the rules of engagement, then losses are justified and non-wrongful. My framework allows courts to examine whether the actual conduct of combatant activities was done within the bounds of a state's authority, without venturing into the realm of political questions and policy considerations. Rather, my suggested framework assesses whether acts were done within the bounds of authority. In so doing, my proposed framework does not raise issues of justiciability, while maintaining the ability of individuals to bring claims in tort.

The above suggests that the separation of powers justification does not satisfactorily legitimize divergence from the rule of law based on substantive rule of law principles. This justification is rooted either in a view that the rule of law does not exist during warfare or that the judiciary should defer to the executive on matters relating to security interests. Neither of these views seem accurate or warranted.

B. Over-Deterrence

The existence of the combatant activities exception has also been justified by some courts and scholars on the grounds that it prevents states and combatants from being over-deterred from engaging in warfare by eliminating the potential chilling effects of tort liability.[93] The concern is that were tort liability available, avoiding it would take priority over security interests. For example, states and combatants might refrain from engaging in belligerent activities altogether, hesitate to do all that they could to protect security interests, or would be overly concerned with gathering evidence for possible future litigation.

[93] See, for example: *Koohi* (n 34) 17; *Saleh* (n 51) 18; *Bani Uda* (n 57) 5; *Hardan* (n 34) 14; Thomas Tugendhat and Laura Croft, 'The Fog of Law: An Introduction to the Legal Erosion of British Fighting Power' (Policy Exchange 2013) 33, 54 <https://policyexchange.org.uk/wp-content/uploads/2016/09/the-fog-of-law.pdf> accessed 1 September 2017; Assaf Jacob, 'Immunity under Fire: State Immunity from Harm Caused due to "Combatant Activity"' (2003) 23 The Hebrew University Law Review 107, 129–30.

However, the rational connection between the combatant activities exception and the over-deterrence justification does not seem to exist. As I argued in Chapter 1 and elsewhere, tort liability is likely to under-deter state actors in relation to deciding whether and how to engage in warfare.[94] From a theoretical perspective, the three preconditions for the materialization of deterrence do not seem to exist. Actors either lack the ability to choose whether and how to participate in combat altogether or have very little discretion about such decisions. Actors also generally lack accurate information about the costs and benefits of action versus inaction, as well as an opportunity to analyse rationally the information that is available. Lastly, due to practical and procedural hurdles that disincentivize potential plaintiffs from pursuing claims, and shield defendants from liability, there is little to no internalization of costs by individual state actors that could have resulted in an incentive to act more carefully. Moreover, recent empirical studies suggest that combatants are unlikely to be deterred by an imposition of tort liability on the state and that combatants support various reparation mechanisms for civilians who have been harmed, even during lawful combatant activities.[95]

These theoretical and empirical observations suggest that the concern about states' and combatants' potential over-deterrence by tort liability in relation to engagement in warfare is difficult to support. If indeed tort liability under-deters state actors in relation to their decisions on whether and how to engage in warfare, granting blanket immunity from liability would not assist the avoidance of over-deterrence. Rather, it would hinder any potential deterring effect, even when such deterrence was warranted. The rational connection between the combatant activities exception and the over-deterrence justification does not seem to stand.

Moreover, it is not clear how the over-deterrence justification could meet the necessity requirement. Even if tort liability would have over-deterring effects on individual state actors, an immunity from liability could be extended to them but not to the state. While such an immunity would still be a divergence from the rule of law, as it would frustrate a private law mechanism for holding public officials accountable, it does not go as far as a blanket immunity from liability. A narrower version of the exception that enables liability to be

[94] As I argued in Chapter 1, while instrumental approaches to tort law and theory seem to be less appealing in the context of liability during warfare, the conceptual structure of rights-based approaches is maintained, and for this reason, they are used as the basis for the analysis conducted in this book. For a detailed discussion on why tort liability is under-deterring in the context of warfare, see: Abraham (n 27).

[95] ibid; Jennifer K Robbennolt and Lesley Wexler, 'Service Members' Reactions to Amends for Lawful Civilian Casualties' (2021) 2021 University of Pennsylvania Law Review 399.

imposed on the state maintains tort law as an accountability mechanism and could create reputational incentives to avoid future wrongdoing.

Much like the separation of powers justification, concerns of over-deterrence do not seem to be able to properly justify divergence from the rule of law as required by substantive rule of law principles. For the combatant activities exception to grant states with blanket immunity from liability for all losses that are inflicted during combat, a justification that can withstand scrutiny is warranted.

C. Procedural Fairness

A third justification for the combatant activities exception grounds the need for the exception in unique procedural difficulties that would result in a systematic advantage to potential plaintiffs over the state, forcing it to settle or face a likely finding of liability. According to this justification, as conflicts take place in hostile territories, ascertaining who injured the plaintiff, the extent of the injury, and access to evidence and witnesses more generally are limited and challenging.[96] Moreover, there could be instances in which the state would be forced to settle claims to avoid revealing confidential information even when it would otherwise be able to mount a successful defence.[97] The exception eliminates these procedural biases and was argued to be justified on this basis.

[96] Draft Bill 2645 Handling Lawsuits against the Operations of the Security Forces in Judea and Samaria and Gaza (Amendment 4) (n 56) 4; Michael D Jones, 'Consistency and Equality: A Framework for Analyzing the "Combat Activities Exclusion" of the Foreign Claims Act' (2010) 204 Military Law Review 144, 146; CC (Be'er Sheva) 45043-05-16 *A v Israel* (Nevo, 4 November 2018) 87–89. This issue was particularly concerning for the state and district attorneys as, prior to Amendment 4 of the Civil Wrongs (State Liability) Act in 2002, courts applied rules in the Negligence Ordinance that shifted the burden of proof from the plaintiffs to the state. Section 38 of the Tort Ordinance (1968) shifts the burden of proof to the defendant when she establishes that the loss was caused by a dangerous object which the defendant was the owner of, whereas Section 41 codifies a *res ipsa loquitur* rule. Consequently, at times Israel was left unable to refute the presumption of its wrongdoing due to lack of evidence. See: 'Protocol 493, Constitution, Law, and Justice Committee, June 24, 2002, 11:30' (n 56); 'Protocol 497, Constitution, Law, and Justice Committee, June 26, 2002, 10:30'; 'Protocol 502, Constitution, Law, and Justice Committee, June 15, 2005, 09:00'; 'Protocol 511, Constitution, Law, and Justice Committee, June 23, 2005, 10:00'; 'Protocol 521, Constitution, Law, and Justice Committee, June 30, 2005, 11:00'; Draft Bill 2645 Handling Lawsuits against the Operations of the Security Forces in Judea and Samaria and Gaza (Amendment 4) (n 56).

[97] District Attorney Irit Kalman describes this very dilemma: 'A taxi was driving towards a roadblock with a suicide terrorist who carried a bomb. Intelligence was received regarding the taxi and the immanent terror attack . . . Without the use of targeted killing on the taxi the terror attack would have been executed. The taxi owner filed a claim . . . We came to the courts with affidavits from Brigadier Generals with all the information we could divulge . . . The court wanted to know who we got the information from, maybe it is wrong, maybe we were misled . . . In this case we were not misled but we cannot bring the evidence to court.' ('Protocol 489, Constitution, Law, and Justice Committee, May 31, 2005, 10:20').

Yet, it is difficult to see how the exception meets the rational connection requirements given that it eliminates challenges faced by states at the cost of mounting nearly impenetrable barriers on plaintiffs, shifting any procedural unfairness between parties to litigation. By ensuring that a claim cannot be filed we are not ensuring procedural fairness, but rather that there will be no procedure at all. It is difficult to see how having no recourse to obtain compensation for wrongfully inflicted losses can be described as achieving procedural fairness.

Moreover, to achieve procedural fairness, or at the very least to eliminate systematic disadvantage of the state, it is not necessary to extend an immunity from liability as there are other means of achieving similar results without barring tort remedies. For instance, short limitation periods could assist in ensuring that information is obtainable and that witnesses are available and have a good recollection of the events.[98] Adopting rules that reflect the uniqueness and reality of combat could also be a means of eliminating systematic disadvantages to the state.[99] The concern regarding forced settlement due to the risk of divulging confidential information could also be resolved by means that fall short of an immunity from liability. For example, it could be possible to grant security clearance to special advocates, who could represent plaintiffs in such a context, while deliberations would be held *in camera*.[100]

It seems that the procedural fairness justification of the exception does not meet the rational connection and necessity requirements for divergences from the rule of law. The fact that the exception is a significant factor in creating hurdles for potential plaintiffs could also raise the question of whether the exception furthers a legitimate public end.[101]

[98] For example, in England and Wales, a claim in tort for losses inflicted overseas by the armed forces has a six-year limitation period instead of the ordinary seven-year period (Sections 33(1ZA–1ZC) of the 'Limitation Act'). Israel has a two-year limitation period and requires a notice of intent to be filed within sixty days of the injury (Sections 5A(2)(b) and 5A(3) of the Civil Wrongs (Liability of the State) Act).

[99] For instance, the rule that shifts the burden of proof to the state due to the use of 'dangerous things' could be made inapplicable; and online witness testimony, streamlining the litigation process, and considering operation logs as *prima facie* evidence of correctness could be made available (Sections 483(a) and 488 of the Military Judiciary Act 1955).

[100] For the operation of this mechanism in the context of immigration, see: Dyzenhaus, *The Constitution of Law* (n 9) 163.

[101] In Israel, for instance, the exception, as well as other procedural hurdles such as limitation periods, security bonds, and refusal to grant entry permits to plaintiffs and witnesses, was viewed by some state actors as a means of preventing civilians, who were viewed as the enemy, from being able to access courts. See: Abraham (n 27) 906–13; Bachar (n 61) 849–51, 856–58.

D. Judicial and Administrative Time and Resources

The fourth and final justification raised in support of the combatant activities exception is that it is required to save judicial and administrative time and resources by allowing courts to dismiss claims *in limine*.[102] The concern here is that claims for losses that are inflicted during warfare are likely to be dismissed. Indeed, given the current broad interpretation and application of the combatant activities exception, and the fact that judges often adopt the position of states when it comes to matters of national security,[103] tort claims in this context are, indeed, likely to be dismissed.

Blanket immunity from liability saves the costs and time that would otherwise be required of the courts and the state to litigate such cases. By barring tort remedies for belligerent wrongs, the combatant activities exception saves judicial and administrative time and resources. If there are no civil proceedings, or if they are dismissed *in limine* without the need to provide substantial evidence and cross-examine witnesses, time and resources could be spared. In this sense, the rational connection requirement between the expressed aims of the act that diverges from the rule of law and the effect the act has in practice seems to be met.

Nevertheless, the justification of the combatant activities exception for the sake of saving judicial and administrative time is based on an empirical assertion that most claims are bound to fail. Yet, it is not entirely clear that claims in tort brought against a state in its own courts are *necessarily and inherently* bound to fail more often than not. There is no data in common law jurisdictions to support such a broad assertion.

Furthermore, in Israel—which is the only jurisdiction for which there is data about success rates when the exception is interpreted narrowly—half of all cases were successful.[104] Tort claims for belligerent wrongs are only bound to fail, or highly likely to fail, if there is no way of conceptualizing what would amount to a wrong during warfare or if tort law doctrines could not apply in the

[102] This justification was articulated most clearly by three state and district attorneys in the process of deliberations over Amendment 8 of Israel's combatant activities exception: 'Protocol 66, Constitution, Law, and Justice Committee, September 14, 2009, 09:00' (n 85). Similar arguments were made in response to the possibility of holding states liable in tort for belligerent activities, by Thomas Tudendhat, Lisa Croft, and Yaël Ronen in academic writing (Tugendhat and Croft (n 93) 24, 35; Ronen (n 58) 244).

[103] Dyzenhaus, *The Constitution of Law* (n 9) 218–19.

[104] Between 1959 and 2002, the courts in Israel had an inconsistent approach to the combatant activities exception, some interpreting it narrowly while others implementing a broader approach. However, the broader approach was adopted in 2002. In twenty-eight out of sixty cases in the relevant period of time, a court ruled in favour of the plaintiffs, and in two cases the parties settled. See: Abraham, Bachar, and Ceasefire Centre for Civilian Rights (n 43).

context of warfare. As I demonstrated in Chapter 2, what amounts to a wrong during warfare can indeed be conceptualized, and as I show in Chapters 4–6, tort doctrine can apply even for losses that are inflicted during combat. The resulting liability regime might have narrow applicability, but it is not so limited that all or most cases are likely to fail. Consequently, the rational connection requirement might not be met.

Even if the combatant activities exception could save judicial and administrative time, it is not clear that the necessity requirement is fulfilled. Tort litigation in general has been criticized for its high costs.[105] Yet, tort litigation has not been barred altogether, and there does not appear to be anything unique about litigation relating to losses that were caused during belligerent activities, that *necessarily* results in significantly higher use of judicial and administrative time. Nothing in the arguments that have been made thus far supports differentiating between the judicial and administrative costs that arise from tort proceedings generally, and those that arise in relation to combatant activities particularly. Nor are the number of belligerent tort cases, or their costs, likely to surpass those that arise from tort litigation generally.

Consequently, a blanket immunity from tort liability seems to go beyond the minimal necessary degree for attaining the relevant public end of saving judicial and administrative time. It might save some time, but doing so comes at the significant cost of eliminating a key mechanism for accountability and vindication of private law rights. Other means that fall short of blanket immunity could still offer similar benefits in terms of judicial and administrative time, while having a less severe impact on the rule of law and individuals' rights. Yet, as it stands, the justification of the combatant activities exception as required to save judicial and administrative time and resources seems to fail to meet the necessity requirement and might fail the rational connection requirement as well.

[105] Donald N Dewees, David Duff, and Michael J Trebilcock, *Exploring the Domain of Accident Law: Taking the Facts Seriously* (OUP 1996) 413; John CP Goldberg, 'Twentieth-Century Tort Theory' (2003) 9 Georgetown Law Journal 513, 545; Helene M Goldberg, 'Tort Liability for Federal Government Actions in the United States: An Overview' in Duncan Fairgrieve, Mads Andenas, and John Bell (eds), *Tort Liability of Public Authorities in Comparative Perspective* (The British Institute of International and Comparative Law 2002) 531–32; Harlow (n 21) 95.

V. Conclusions

The ability to impose liability on public officials and bodies for wrongdoing is an essential element of the rule of law.[106] As the discussion above demonstrates, the combatant activities exception diverges from the rule of law by providing broad, and in some jurisdictions complete, immunity from tort liability for any losses that are inflicted during warfare, whether wrongful or not. The justifications that have been articulated for this divergence do not stand up to scrutiny individually or collectively.

As existing justifications for diverging from the rule of law by limiting the right to a remedy through the combatant activities exception are insufficient, and given that there is a corrective justice duty to redress belligerent wrongs, tort liability ought to be available for losses that are inflicted during warfare. The most straightforward way to allow for tort law to apply would be to abolish the exception altogether.

However, if the combatant activities exception was narrow, it might be possible to conceive of some justification that may comply with the substantive rule of law requirements for a divergence from the rule of law. Several limitations seem warranted. First, the exception should extend immunities to combatants only, and it should be possible to impose liability on states, as doing so maintains the availability of an accountability mechanism against a relevant moral agent—the State—even if not against a particular public official. Second, courts should interpret what amounts to a 'combatant activity' and who should be considered a 'combatant' narrowly, limiting the temporal and geographical reach of the exception. For example, applicability should be restricted to losses inflicted while engaging in actual hostilities by the state's forces and should not apply to losses inflicted during auxiliary or policing activities, or to losses inflicted by contractors.

In substantive rule of law terms, allowing tort law to apply is to enable it to fulfil its role in ensuring that the discretion of public officials and bodies is bounded. Public officials and bodies cannot infringe rights with impunity, and their actions are not shielded from the scrutiny of the courts. Rather, public officials and bodies should be subject to liability, and they have to demonstrate how their actions comply with the rule of law. In this sense, through tort law, it is possible to require states to show that they have used public powers for a legitimate public purpose.

[106] See: Dicey (n 4) 126–28; Hart (n 6) 164.

4

Intentional Torts in War

I. Introduction

The analysis undertaken so far has laid the foundations required to support the argument that tort law could and should apply for losses that are inflicted during combatant activities. In Chapter 2, I established that individuals' private law rights remain relevant in warfare, and that losses are justified, and hence non-wrongful, when they are inflicted while international humanitarian law and the rules of engagement are upheld. By articulating wrongdoing in warfare as an unjustified violation of ordinary private law rights, an infliction of such 'belligerent wrongs', as I refer to them, gives rise to ordinary corrective justice duties. Chapter 3 illustrated that a blanket immunity from tort liability is challenging, from a substantive rule of law perspective, and that existing justifications for such immunity cannot be supported. Together, these chapters refute some of the arguments that previously ruled out the applicability of tort law in warfare and argue that tort law should be made available to address belligerent wrongs.

I shall now show that tort law doctrines could apply to belligerent wrongs. In this chapter, I focus on intentional belligerent wrongs, which I argue could be established following direct intentional infringements of states' rules of engagement or international humanitarian law; for example, when combatants directly and intentionally target civilians or engage in a belligerent activity that they know is disproportionate. The account of liability for belligerent wrongs I develop here demonstrates that liability could be imposed on states and combatants using ordinary tort doctrines, while not deeming all losses that are inflicted during warfare as wrongs for which liability could, or should, be imposed.

In this chapter, I articulate the bounds of liability for intentional torts that are inflicted in the course of combatant activities.[1] Some torts, such as false

[1] For a discussion on the ambiguity regarding what is and ought to be considered a combatant activity and who should be considered a combatant, see Chapter 3. My analysis in this chapter shall be based on instances of engagement in actual hostilities, as there is no dispute that this is a form of combatant activity, and the greatest resistance to the availability of tort law is raised in relation to it.

Tort Liability in Warfare. Haim Abraham, Oxford University Press. © Haim Abraham 2024.
DOI: 10.1093/9780191997051.003.0004

imprisonment, battery, conversion, or trespass, could be inflicted in the general context of warfare, but through actions that fall short of engagement in actual hostilities. Inflicted in this way by combatants or military contractors, these torts do not raise the same unique considerations that are typically used to limit liability, nor are they deemed to fall under the combatant activities exception. Ordinary tort law can apply, and indeed courts have imposed tort liability on states in such circumstances.[2] Therefore, I shall not analyse how tort liability operates in response to ordinary wrongs committed in an unusual context.

Instead, I focus only on intentional torts that are inflicted in the process of engaging in actual combat. In doing so, I address the elements shared by all intentional torts—an intentional interference with another person's body or means, without consent or authority.[3] My analysis will demonstrate how international humanitarian law informs the operation of the torts' elements. It will also suggest intentional torts could be available where combatants acted without proper authority and the loss was inflicted in breach of international humanitarian law. Consequently, misfeasance in public office seems to be a particularly relevant cause of action with which to address belligerent wrongs.

II. Intending to Act

When considering under which circumstances intentional torts could be established, the first element that warrants attention is the element of intent, which is often classified into three distinct categories: actual, constructive, or transferred.[4] Actual intent is the plain and intuitive sense in which we understand

[2] See, for example: *Alseran and others v Ministry of Defence* [2017] EWHC 3289 (QB), Leggatt J, paragraphs 9, 13, 17 [finding that imprisonment of individuals contrary to international humanitarian law amounts to false imprisonment and that torture and beating are batteries]; *Bici v Ministry of Defence* [2004] EWHC 786 (QB), Mr Justice Elias, paragraphs 66–72, 101–02 [holding that firing at individuals who created disorder in the street does not fall under the combatant activities exception and amounts to negligence and battery]; CA 623/83 *Levi v Israel* [1986] PD 4(1) 447, 482 [holding that a destruction of property by an auxiliary fuel division is negligent and a trespass to property]; CC (Be'er Sheva) 5709-12-12 *Estate of Iman Elhams v Israel* (Nevo, 05/19/2021), Judge Friedlander, paragraph 21 [holding that looting is not a combatant activity].

[3] Robert Stevens, *Torts and Rights* (OUP 2007) 101; Arthur Ripstein, *Private Wrongs* (Harvard UP 2016) 167–71; Allan Beever, *A Theory of Tort Liability* (Hart Publishing 2016) 55–74.

[4] I will follow this terminology to articulate the bounds of different categories of intent, but it should be noted that this categorization reflects a degree of generalization and abstraction. More specific types of intent that have been identified for various torts could fall under one of the more general categories of actual, constructive, or transferred. For example, in *OBG v Allan*, Lord Hoffmann identified five types of intention, some of which were subsequently treated as species of the same group by Cromwell J in *A.I. v Bram*. See: *OBG v Allan* [2008] 1 AC 1, 30, 35; *AI Enterprises Ltd v Bram Enterprises Ltd* [2014] 1 SCR 177, 221–22.

intent. It is the individual's will to bring about the consequences of her actions.[5] For example, if I run my fingers through your hair, I intend to make contact between us; or if I hit your car's windshield with a baseball bat, I intend to smash it.

In contrast, constructive intent is a situation in which there is substantial certainty that the results of the wrongdoer's conduct would arise, although she may not actually intend to cause such results.[6] Put differently, constructive intent enables courts to deduce that a defendant acted with a sufficient level of intent to bring about certain consequence given the high probability of their materialization. Suppose I place a basketball hoop against the fence that borders my backyard with my neighbour's, behind which she has a large collection of fragile potted plants. While I do not intend for the ball to bounce from the hoop into the neighbour's backyard, it is substantially certain that it will occur, given the nature of the game and the proximity of the hoop to the neighbour's property. It is also substantially certain that when the ball does bounce to my neighbour's backyard, it will damage one or more of her plants. Yet, I play basketball disregarding these risks of which I am well aware. Under these circumstances, it could be said that I have acted with constructive intent to damage her plants.

Lastly, in some jurisdictions, intent could also be transferred to establish an intentional tort. When A has an actual intent to pursue a certain wrongful end against B—say, run her fingers through B's hair without consent. Unexpectedly, B moves from A's path and the person whose hair is touched is C. It could be said that A has an intent to touch B's hair that is transferred to C.[7]

[5] See, for example: Ripstein, *Private Wrongs* (n 3) 46–47; Philip H Osborne, *The Law of Torts* (5th edn, Irwin Law 2015) 264; *Non-Marine Underwriters, Lloyd's of London v Scalera* [2000] 1 SCR 551, 603.

[6] Osborne (n 5) 264–65; *Non-Marine Underwriters, Lloyd's of London v Scalera* (n 5) 603; *Garratt v Dailey* 49 Wn2d 499 (Wash, 29 November 1956) 501; *Wilkinson and Another v Downton* [1895–99] All ER Rep 267, 269; *O v Rhodes* [2016] AC 219, 243. In *O v Rhodes*, Baroness Hale and Lord Toulson critiqued the use of the term 'imputed intent', which sometimes is taken to have the meaning of constructive intent as a means of deducing that the defendant acted with the required level of intent but sometimes is used to assign intention as a matter of law even when none existed, which they argue has no place in modern tort law (ibid 252–53). As my analysis below suggests, the latter understanding of imputed intent will be insufficient to establish liability for belligerent wrongs, and given its controversial character, I will not use it as an analytical tool in this book.

[7] See, for example: *Keel v Hainline* [1958] 331 P2d 397–99; *State v Batson* [1936] 96 SW2d 384, 389; Nancy Moore, 'Intent and Consent in the Tort of Battery: Confusion and Controversy' (2012) 61 American University Law Review 1585, 1597; William Prosser, 'Transferred Intent' (1967) 45 Texas Law Review 650; Vincent R Johnson, 'Transferred Intent in American Tort Law' (2004) 87 Marquetter Law Review 903. It has been suggested that the doctrine of transferred intent should also apply between intentional torts. That is, if an individual intended to shoot another person but instead hit her car, then it would be held that the element of intent was transferred from trespass to person, to trespass to chattels—see: Allen M Linden and Bruce P Feldthusen, *Canadian Tort Law* (9th edn, LexisNexis 2011) 38–42. The use of the transferred intent doctrine in tort law is most prominent in the United States and has also been used or referred to in other jurisdictions such as Canada and England and Wales.

Ordinarily, intent can be established for some intentional torts even when the tortfeasor is unaware that she is using another person's means. For example, trespass to land is an intentional tort even if the person trespassing does not realize she is on someone else's land, as long as she intended to perform the action of walking on that land.[8] The wrong is constituted by the intentional walking, not by the intention to walk on someone else's land coupled with the physical act of walking.

In the context of warfare, the categories of actual, constructive, and transferred intent seem to be analytically helpful. For example, it is possible to suggest that if a combatant intends to shoot an enemy non-combatant, and successfully does so, then this action was done with actual intent. Contrastingly, if a combatant aimlessly shoots towards a crowd of non-combatants with no desire for any of them to actually be shot, and consequently someone is injured, then it could be said that the combatant acted with constructive intent since it is substantially certain that such a result would occur. Lastly, it is also possible to conceive of scenarios in which transferred intent might be applicable—for instance, if a sniper intends to shoot one non-combatant, but misses, and the bullet ricochets and hits another non-combatant instead.

That said, while ordinarily the element of intent could be met when an individual intends her actions (to walk) even if she does not intend to commit a tort (to walk on someone else's land), it seems that a higher threshold is required in the context of warfare. As I have previously argued in Chapter 2, losses brought about by belligerent activities are justified and non-wrongful as long as they adhered to international humanitarian law and the rules of engagement, which states set out in their military manuals.[9] These norms are therefore key to

However, its integration into tort law has been criticized—see, for example: Stevens, *Torts and Rights* (n 3) 102; Ripstein, *Private Wrongs* (n 3) 44–45; Osborne M Reynolds Jr, 'Transferred Intent: Should Its Curious Survival Continue' (1997) 50 Oklahoma Law Review 529, 554–55; Johnson (n 7) 907–10; *Bici* (n 2) 80. For the purpose of this book, there is no need to determine whether indeed the doctrine of transferred intent ought to be a part of tort law, and it is sufficient to establish that it is a part of tort law—though its precise role and scope vary between jurisdictions.

[8] *Superior Oil Co v Harsh* 50 F Supp 358 (D Ill, 8 June 1943) 359–60; *Burns Philp Food, Inc v Cavalea Continental Freight, Inc* 135 F3d 526 (7th Circuit, 1998) 529; Ripstein, *Private Wrongs* (n 3) 44–46; John CP Goldberg, 'The Constitutional Status of Tort Law: Due Process and the Right to a Law for the Redress of Wrongs' (2005) 115 Yale Law Journal 524, 598.

[9] Military manuals might differ between jurisdictions in the ways they concretize international humanitarian law. Some jurisdictions might provide greater or lesser protection to non-combatants, but as these principles are *jus cogens*, no state has the authority to contradict them—see Arthur Ripstein, 'Political Independence, Territorial Integrity and Private Law Analogies' (2019) 24 Kantian Review 573, 595. For a discussion on how military manuals reflect international humanitarian law, see: *Prosecutor v Duško Tadić a/k/a 'Dule'* ICTY IT-94-1-AR72, Decision on the Defence Motion for Interlocutory Appeal on Jurisdiction, 2 October 1995 paragraph 99; HCJ 769/02 *The Public Committee against Torture in Israel v Israel* PD 62(1) 507 (2006) 536–37; James Crawford, *Brownlie's Principles of Public International Law* (9th edn, OUP 2019) 21–22.

demarcating the boundary between what could amount to wrongful and non-wrongful conduct under tort law.

Three international humanitarian law principles are particularly relevant in this context. First, the principle of necessity, which requires that the target of an attack, as well as the attack itself, will have some advantage to the war effort.[10] Second, the principle of distinction, which mandates that all non-combatant individuals and objects sustain losses from combatant activities only as an unintended side effect.[11] Third, the principle of proportionality, which dictates that only actions for which the anticipated military gain is commensurate to the foreseeable harms inflicted by those actions are justified.[12]

The principles of necessity, distinction, and proportionality prohibit certain forms of use of force, but there are still instances where these principles could have been adhered to, even if a belligerent activity injured non-combatants or damaged civilian objects.[13] For example, the principle of distinction is not breached if non-combatants are injured incidentally to attacking a military target. Similarly, the principle of proportionality is maintained so long as the expected incidental losses to non-combatants prior to the attack do not surpass the expected military advantage, even if in hindsight the former was greater than the latter.

The upshot of these principles is that awareness, not ordinarily required, is necessary for establishing an intentional tort in war. As tort liability depends

[10] *Legality of the Threat or Use of Nuclear Weapons* ICJ Advisory Opinion (1996) 245; Michael Newton and Larry May, *Proportionality in International Law* (OUP 2014) 69; Francisco de Vitoria, 'Relectiones: On the Law of War' (1557) 37; Emer de Vattel, *The Law of Nations (1758)* (Béla Kapossy and Richard Whatmore eds, Liberty Fund 2008) 482; Endre Begby, Gregory M Reichberg, and Henrik Syse, 'The Ethics of War. Part II: Contemporary Authors and Issues' (2012) 7 Philosophy Compass 328, 333; Thomas Hurka, 'Proportionality and Necessity' in Larry May and Emily Crookston (eds), *War: Essays in Political Philosophy* (CUP 2008) 130; Jeff McMahan, 'The Morality of War and the Law of War' in David Rodin and Henry Shue (eds), *Just and Unjust Warriors: The Moral and Legal Status of Soldiers* (OUP 2008) 22.

[11] Articles 48, 51(4) of the Protocol Additional to the Geneva Conventions of 12 August 1949, and relating to the Protection of Victims of International Armed Conflicts 1977; *Legality of the Threat or Use of Nuclear Weapons* (n 10) 257; Begby, Reichberg, and Syse (n 10) 337; Michael Walzer, *Just and Unjust Wars: A Moral Argument with Historical Illustrations* (5th edn, Basic Books, a member of the Perseus Books Group 2015) 153–56.

[12] Article 51(5)(b) of Additional Protocol I; *Nicaragua v United States of America* ICJ Reports (1986) 94; Newton and May (n 10) 3; Begby, Reichberg, and Syse (n 10) 333; Emily Crawford and Alison Pert, *International Humanitarian Law* (CUP 2020) 46–47.

[13] The debate about the nature of international humanitarian law as permissive or restrictive goes beyond the scope of this chapter. For an account of this debate, see: Jeff McMahan, *Killing in War* (OUP 2009) 52–53; Jeff McMahan, 'On the Moral Equality of Combatants' (2006) 14 Journal of Political Philosophy 377, 389–90; Thomas Hurka, 'Liability and Just Cause' (2007) 20 Ethics and International Affairs 199, 210; Adil Ahmad Haque, *Law and Morality at War* (OUP 2017) 34; Walzer (n 11); Arthur Ripstein, 'Rules for Wrongdoers' (Berkeley Talks: Tanner Lectures, day 1, 16 May 2019) <https://news.berkeley.edu/2019/05/16/berkeley-talks-transcript-2019-tanner-lectures-01/> accessed 4 November 2019.

on the violation of international humanitarian law and the rules of engagement, being unaware that someone else's means have been used or damaged could not constitute a belligerent wrong. Consider, again, the example of trespass: Ordinarily, if someone walks on another person's land, they are committing trespass even if they thought that the land was unowned. Yet, international humanitarian law would not be violated if combatants were ordered to destroy what appeared to be a wild field, that they suspected enemy combatants were hiding in, even if that field was, in fact, owned and used by non-combatants for agricultural purposes. Losses inflicted under these circumstances would be justified and non-wrongful according to my account of belligerent wrongs. To amount to an intentional belligerent wrong, it seems that combatants and states would have to be aware that the field was a civilian object in order for it to be said they had intended to act in a way that violates the principles of international humanitarian law. It is not that trespass could not be established at all, but rather that it could be established in a narrower set of circumstances than it can be, ordinarily, in peacetime.

Moreover, a belligerent wrong could also result from inflicting a loss while acting in breach of a state's rules of engagement. These rules could be breached negligently or intentionally. For example, the rules of engagement might require soldiers to fire only at a certain angle as a warning to individuals who are perceived to be non-immediate threats. Firing at the wrong angle could be accidental or intentional. When the rules of engagement are breached intentionally, there are strong indications that the breach was meant to inflict an injury. By establishing that the rules of engagement have been infringed intentionally, it seems that the relevant intent for a breach of necessity, distinction, or proportionality could also be established.

That said, there seems to be some ambiguity regarding the concept of intent to establish a breach of the principles of international humanitarian law. Some theorists suggest that intent to perpetrate unlawful conduct must be demonstrated, whereas others propose that foreseeable consequences being virtually or practically certain are sufficient to show acting with intent.[14] As Jens David Ohlin notes, this ambiguity could be attributed to the varying uses and interpretations of the term 'intent' in different bodies of law in common and civil law traditions.[15]

[14] Jens David Ohlin, 'Targeting and the Concept of Intent' (2013) 35 Michigan Journal of International Law 79, 125–28.

[15] ibid 82–95, 129.

For the purposes of my argument, either of these interpretations of intent could plausibly delineate the boundary between wrongful and non-wrongful conduct. Defining intent as acting for the purpose of doing something wrongful results in a narrow liability regime that enables a wider range of belligerent activities, without the risk of incurring the costs of committing a tort. Applying this definition to the example of the destruction of a field, only *actual* intent to destroy what is known to be a non-combatant's field when there is no military gain in so doing could constitute wrongdoing.

In contrast, if the definition of intent encompasses acting with consequences that are foreseeable and virtually or practically certain to materialize, then the tort regime would vindicate non-combatants' rights in a wider range of circumstances. Analysing the field destruction example with this definition in mind, wrongdoing could be established by identifying that a combatant acted with *constructive* intent. If there was substantial certainty that the field was owned by non-combatants and that there are no combatants hiding in it, yet the field was destroyed nevertheless, it could be said that the combatants acted with the relevant intent to breach international humanitarian law.

In my view, the more inclusive approach to intent is more coherent with what is currently required under international humanitarian law. Take Article 51(4)(b) of Additional Protocol I, for example. It prohibits the use of 'a method or means of combat which cannot be directed at a specific military objective'. This prohibition would be violated if a combatant or a state used such prohibited means that do not and cannot distinguish between a military objective and a non-combatant individual or object, even if the combatant or state intended to destroy only the enemy forces' facilities, for instance. Additional Protocol I does not seem to suffice in collateral damage being foreseeable, as it does not prohibit incidental harming of non-combatants merely even when it is foreseeable. Rather, it seems to require at least foreseeable risks that are highly likely to materialize, which is precisely the issue with using methods and means that necessarily cannot distinguish between military and non-combatant targets.

The point I wish to press here is that the foreseeability of risks that are highly likely to materialize is a means of identifying that the intent was essentially to target non-combatants. The International Court of Justice (ICJ) has held that the use of nuclear weapons, arguably one of the least discriminatory types of weapon, is not inherently and necessarily a violation of the principles of distinction and proportionality.[16] If there are circumstances under which the use of nuclear weapons is compliant with international humanitarian law, then

[16] *Legality of the Threat or Use of Nuclear Weapons* (n 10), paragraphs 41–42, 94–95.

the principles of distinction and proportionality are not merely regulating the methods and means of warfare. Rather, they appear to go further and regulate combatants' and states' intent, as well as the implications of engaging in combat. Surely if intentions and military gains had no role to play, nuclear weapons would have been prohibited under all circumstances.

The above analysis demonstrates that the applicability of intentional torts would be narrower in relation to losses inflicted through combatant activities, as opposed to losses inflicted through non-combatant activities. As my account of belligerent wrongs extends tort liability only for losses that infringe international humanitarian law and the rules of engagement, intent is relevant in two ways. First, the ordinary tort categorization of intent to actual, constructive, and transferred are conceptually helpful to the analysis of intentional torts in warfare. Second, combatants and states can only breach the principles of necessity, distinction, and proportionality by acting with a relevant level of intent. The cumulative result of requiring a violation of international humanitarian law and the rules of engagement for losses to be tortious produces a higher bar for liability. While ordinarily it might be enough to intend to walk, touch someone, or take something, to constitute trespass to land, person, or property—in combat, more is required. In addition, combatants and states need to intend to inflict an unnecessary, direct, or disproportionate loss on non-combatants. Consequently, tort remedies will be available in a comparatively narrower range of circumstances.

III. Wrongful Intentional Conduct

Showing that someone intended to act is one element that is required to establish an intentional tort, but what makes an intentional act wrongful is that the act interfered with another person's body or means in a manner that is inconsistent with that person's rights to be in charge of their body or means.[17] For some intentional torts, such as trespass to land, any unilateral interference would be inconsistent with the property owner's rights. Intentionally trampling someone's wheat field is just as much a trespass as walking on concrete road that you thought was a public sidewalk. For other torts, such as assault and battery, not every interference is inconsistent with another's rights. Brushing

[17] Eg Ripstein, *Private Wrongs* (n 3) 47, 167–71; Beever (n 3) 39–40; John CP Goldberg and Benjamin C Zipursky, *Recognizing Wrongs* (Harvard UP 2020) 190; Robert Stevens, 'Private Rights and Public Wrongs' in Matthew Dyson (ed), *Unravelling Tort and Crime* (1st edn, CUP 2014) 115; Stevens, *Torts and Rights* (n 3) 101.

past someone on a packed bus to find a place to stand might mean that you intentionally touch them, yet doing so is not a battery as it is consistent with everyone's rights in a modern society. However, as I have argued in Chapter 2, it seems that all interferences with an individual's rights through belligerent activities are *prima facie* wrongful. What renders them non-wrongful is that states and combatants have a justification to inflict such losses if they act in compliance with international humanitarian law and the rules of engagement.

Ordinarily, there is another key justification that is available for individuals that makes otherwise intentional wrongs into non-wrongful interactions, and that is acting with the other individual's consent. Having consent makes what would otherwise be an inconsistent interaction with another person's body or means into an interaction that is consistent with her rights.[18] In this sense, consent operates as a form of providing the relevant authority for an otherwise impermissible interaction.

For example, you are not allowed to take my car to buy groceries at the supermarket simply because you want to. That would be inconsistent with my rights as the owner of the car, and, generally, other individuals have no authority to use my car. But if you ask to use my car and I consent, then your use of my car is consistent with my rights, and no wrong is established by such use. By providing my consent, I authorize you to use my car for those purposes.

However, in the context of belligerent activities, it is difficult to maintain that non-combatants provide their consent to states and combatants to inflict losses on them during battle. The reason for this difficulty is twofold. First, the laws of war do not operate based on states' consent. Rather, they are *jus cogens* norms that restrict states' authority to act. Second, even if consent were relevant, in order for it to negate a wrongful interference with rights, the relevant individuals would have to voluntarily consent to that particular use.[19] None of these three preconditions (agreement between the relevant individuals, which is given voluntarily, and for a particular use) appear to be met during war.

Non-combatants do not reach an agreement with their potential injurers for the latter to use or damage the former's bodies and means. Even if non-combatants express political support for engaging in belligerent activities, this

[18] *F v West Berkshire Health Authority* [1990] 2 AC 1, 27; Ernest J Weinrib, 'The Monsanto Lectures: Understanding Tort Law' (1989) 23 Valparaiso University Law Review 485, 514–15. Even in the international context, when states exert their authority with the consent of other states, otherwise wrongful conduct could be non-wrongful. See: Article 20 of the Draft Articles on the Responsibility of States for Internationally Wrongful Acts 2001; Kimberley N Trapp, 'Jurisdiction and State Responsibility' in Stephen Allen and others (eds), *The Oxford Handbook of Jurisdiction in International Law* (1st edn, OUP 2019) 361.

[19] Consent that is made under duress is invalid. See, for example: *Norberg v Wynrib* [1992] 2 SCR 226, 304; Osborne (n 5) 294–95.

expression does not amount to consenting to sustaining losses or to a grant of permission to the enemy state or its combatants to inflict losses. There is no agreement between non-combatants and their potential injurers, nor is there such an agreement between non-combatants and their own state.[20]

Seeing this argument through demonstrates another way in which tort liability for intentional torts would be narrower in warfare than it is in peacetime. It appears that the only relevant justification that would deem interferences constituted through combatant activities non-wrongful is acting in compliance with international humanitarian law and the rules of engagement. Consent, which is an available justification for ordinary conduct, is inapplicable in the context of combat.

IV. Belligerent Misfeasance in Public Office

The discussion above demonstrates that in the context of actual engagement in combatant activities, the range of actions that could constitute an intentional tort is narrower than in peacetime. Consequently, some intentional torts might arise in the general context of warfare, rather than through combatant activities—these include, for instance, defamation, privacy, and, more generally, purely economic torts, such as inducing a breach of contract. For such torts, there are usually no special bars to liability, and therefore liability could be imposed in an ordinary fashion.

[20] There is considerable scholarly debate on whether consent exists between combatants of opposing states, and if it can provide the justification for inflicting losses on enemy combatants. It has been argued that if enlistment is made on voluntary basis, then the combatants implicitly or explicitly agreed to being injured in battle—see: Hurka (n 13) 210. This argument concedes that combatants who are under mandatory conscription cannot be said to have freely and voluntarily consented, at least to a certain extent. Voluntarily enlisted combatants seem to be, at most, the only individuals who can offer the relevant consent, and that too is assuming that we accept that they freely give consent to their potential injurers, not their own state. Nevertheless, it is challenging to maintain that voluntarily enlisted combatants' consent to the relevant thing (being injured or killed by enemy forces) and to the relevant individuals (the enemy forces). By agreeing to become a combatant, an individual agrees to take on the status of a combatant that allows enemy forces to lawfully target her, as well as to be deployed at the discretion of their state both in terms of locations and roles. That is true regardless of whether an individual enlisted before or after belligerent activities began. A combatant could be said to be sending a stronger signal about the degree to which she freely and knowingly accepted the risk of being injured in combat if she voluntarily enlisted after warfare began, than a combatant who enlisted before war broke out. Still, it is difficult to maintain that she consented to the enemy killing her on the battlefield. Perhaps, it would be easier to argue that she is willing to give her life or well-being for her state, but that does not amount to giving permission to the enemy to kill or injure her. While there are some differences between voluntary enlisting before or after hostilities take place, in both scenarios, we seem to arrive at the same conclusion that combatants do not consent to the relevant thing or the relevant individuals. They do not give permission to the enemy to kill or injure them.

Other intentional torts seem to lend themselves more readily to actual combatant activities. For example, troops trespassing by walking on someone's land or committing battery by shooting a bystander. Liability for such intentional torts could be available when they were inflicted through actual hostilities, which were intended to, and did, infringe international humanitarian law or the rules of engagement.

This articulation of intentional belligerent torts suggests that their infliction involves an element of misuse or abuse of public power. It is within combatants and states' power to inflict losses on non-combatants, but only as long as doing so complies with the principles of necessity, distinction, and proportionality. Losses that violate these principles could be said to be an instance of abuse of public power, or even *ultra vires*. Given this apparent element of misuse or abuse of public power, one intentional tort seems to lend itself particularly relevant to this context, and that is the tort of misfeasance in public office.

This somewhat controversial tort has an element of intention and an element of misuse or abuse of public power, both of which require further elaboration before I can demonstrate how misfeasance in public office could operate in relation to combatant activities.[21] Intent in misfeasance in public office cases

[21] On the controversial character of misfeasance in public office, see: Kit Barker and Katelyn Lamont, 'Misfeasance in Public Office: Raw Statistics from the Australian Front Line' (2021) 43 Sydney Law Review 315, 316; Ellen Rock, 'Misfeasance in Public Office: A Tort in Tension' (2019) 43 Melbourne University Law Review 337, 363–67; Mark Aronson, 'Misfeasance in Public Office: A Very Peculiar Tort' (2011) 35 Melbourne University Law Review 1, 2–4. John Murphy offers a powerful counter-argument, questioning both the assumption that it is an anomalous tort and the degree to which we should be concerned with a potential clash between misfeasance in public office and any individual theoretical approach to tort law. See: John Murphy, 'Malice as an Ingredient of Tort Liability' (2019) 78 Cambridge Law Journal 355, 356–58.

While Murphy argues that misfeasance in public office fits within tort law, he maintains that it is challenging in the context of rights-based approaches to tort law, due to the lack of a need to establish an infringement of a private law right, the availability of punitive damages, and public law concepts such as *ultra vires*. See: John Murphy, 'Misfeasance in a Public Office: A Tort Law Misfit?' (2012) 32 Oxford Journal of Legal Studies 51, 56, 61. These concerns, as well as the apparent fit of the rationale of misfeasance in public office with that of public law, that is, as a mechanism of accountability and restoring the public's trust in public officials, are the basis for Donal Nolan's argument that misfeasance in public office is a public law tort, not a private law tort at all. See: Donal Nolan, 'Tort and Public Law: Overlapping Categories?' (2019) 135 Law Quarterly Review 272, 282–83; Donal Nolan, 'A Public Law Tort: Understanding Misfeasance in Public Office' in Kit Barker and others (eds), *Private Law and Power* (Hart Publishing 2017) 181–86.

For the purposes of this book, I do not see a reason to be concerned by the issues regarding misfeasance in public office being a tort or the belief that it does not fit with rights-based accounts of tort law and theory. First, misfeasance in public office is currently an available cause of action in tort and as such its applicability to intentional belligerent wrongs could be examined. Second, there are several arguments that suggest that misfeasance in public office is compatible with rights-based accounts of tort law. Although rights-based accounts differ on several points, they all share the notion that liability is imposed for wrongful violations of individuals' private law rights, which must be rectified by holding the wrongdoer liable towards the injured individual for the wrongful loss she inflicted.

For example, Arthur Ripstein argues that misfeasance in public power entails both a public law and a private law wrong. The public law wrong is constituted when public officials use their public powers to pursue any end other than that for which their powers were given. Yet, Ripstein argues, if a public

corresponds, to a degree, to the categories of actual and constructive intent of other intentional torts, though the terminology employed is distinct. One category of intent in misfeasance in public office is 'targeted malice', and it relates to a state of mind in which the public official intends to act unlawfully and injures the plaintiff, or a class of people of which the plaintiff is a member.[22] Targeted malice is similar to 'actual intent' in the sense that both capture mental states whereby an individual desires the consequences of her actions, though targeted malice requires an intent to act unlawfully that the ordinary category of actual intent does not.

The other category of intent in misfeasance in public office is that of 'knowledge and recklessness', which requires that a public official acted with knowledge of, or reckless indifference to, the unlawfulness of the action and its probable outcomes.[23] Put differently, 'knowledge and recklessness' captures situations in which a public official is substantially certain her conduct will result in a wrongful loss, but she is not acting out of targeted malice.

The similarity between 'knowledge and recklessness' and 'constructive intent' seems to vary between jurisdictions, as the courts have adopted different approaches to the required standard of knowledge and recklessness. For example, In Canada, England and Wales, and New Zealand, the requirement is that the public official has subjective knowledge of, or recklessness towards, the unlawfulness of her actions and the probability of the subsequent harm materializing.[24] In contrast, in Australia, the requirement is one of subjective knowledge on the part of the public official to the unlawfulness of her actions, as well as an objective foreseeable risk of harm that will follow from her unlawful conduct. The High Court of Australia held that 'it is sufficient for present purposes to proceed on the basis accepted as sufficient in Bourgoin, namely, that liability requires an act which the public officer knows is beyond power and which involves a foreseeable risk of harm'.[25] Neither approach would result

official acts in a way that is inconsistent with the private law rights of another individual through an inappropriate use of her public powers, then that act establishes a private law wrong—see: Ripstein, *Private Wrongs* (n 3) 182–83. Another articulation is offered by Erika Chamberlain. She argues that when a public official deliberately inflicts a loss on an individual through unlawful or *ultra vires* actions, they are infringing that individual's private law right not to be harmed in this way. See: Erika Chamberlain, *Misfeasance in a Public Office* (Carswell 2016) 55–57.

[22] See, for instance: *Roncarelli v Duplessis* [1959] SCR 121, 42; *Bourgoin SA v MAFF* [1986] QB 716, 776; *Dunlop v Woollahra Municipal Council* [1982] AC 158, 172; *Three Rivers District Council v Bank of England (No 3)* [2003] 2 AC 1, 48.

[23] Chamberlain (n 21) 139–42.

[24] *Three Rivers* (n 22) 7–9; *Garrett v Attorney General* [1997] 2 NZLR 332, 349–50; *Odhavji Estate v Woodhouse* [2003] 3 SCR 263, 22–23.

[25] *Northern Territory of Australia v Mengel* (1995), 185 CLR 307 (HCA) 347. Also see: *Sanders v Snell (no 2)* [2003] FCAFC 150, 38; *State of South Australia v Lampard-Trevorrow* [2010] SASC 56, 264.

in knowledge and recklessness being identical to constructive intent, as the latter is established objectively, though the Australian approach brings the two categories closer together.

That said, the difference between the courts' approaches to knowledge and recklessness might only be theoretical, as it could be established by inference.[26] Inference, to a certain extent, moves away from considering what the official's state of mind was to what it ought to have been, and in this sense, subjective knowledge and recklessness is not too different from objective knowledge and recklessness. Consequently, this account renders subjective knowledge and recklessness as similar to constructive intent, which establishes intent objectively, given the high degree of probability that the risk from a defendant's conduct would materialize.

The second element of misfeasance in public office is misuse or abuse of public power. Courts and academics have noted five types of actions which, if carried out by a public official, could establish misfeasance in public office. These include *ultra vires* actions, actions conducted for an improper purpose (ie for a purpose other than a legitimate public end) in breach of statutory duties, violations of administrative fairness, and omissions.[27] In other words, the act of an official who either assumes a public power not granted to her or abuses a power she possesses can constitute an action in misfeasance in public office.

With the elements of misfeasance in public office clarified, it is now possible to see how they could apply to intentional belligerent wrongs. In relation to the element of intent, both targeted malice and knowledge and recklessness are consistent with my articulation of tortious wrongdoing in warfare. They require that a public official intended to act unlawfully. To act unlawfully in combat means acting in breach of international humanitarian law or the rules of engagement, which would also render inflicting losses on non-combatants wrongful, according to my account.

As for the second element of misfeasance in public office, that is, misuse or abuse of public power, it seems that in the context of engaging in actual

[26] *Three Rivers* (n 22) 48. Also, in *Garrett v Attorney General*, Blanchard J held that 'a person intends to bring about the known consequences of his or her actions or omissions, even if other consequences form the primary motive' [*Garrett* (n 24) 349–50].

[27] See, for example: *Mengel* (n 25); *McGillivray v Kimber* (1915) 52 SCR 146; *Odhavji* (n 24); *Sanders* (n 25); *O'Dwyer V Ontario Racing Commission* [2006] OJ No 4367; *State of South Australia v Lampard-Trevorrow* (n 25); *Three Rivers* (n 22); *Roncarelli* (n 22); Osborne (n 5) 215–16; Ripstein, *Private Wrongs* (n 3) 182–84; Aronson (n 21) 24–26; Andenas Mads and Fairgrieve Duncan, 'Misfeasance in Public Office, Governmental Liability, and European Influences' in Duncan Fairgrieve, Mads Andenas, and John Bell (eds), *Tort Liability of Public Authorities in Comparative Perspective* (The British Institute of International and Comparative Law 2002) 187–91; Chamberlain (n 21) 113–30.

hostilities not all five types of misuse or abuse of public power are applicable. For example, violations of administrative fairness and omissions seem to be irrelevant,[28] as these do not result in the type of losses that would establish a belligerent wrong, either because they would not result in an infringement of international humanitarian law or because they are not of a combatant nature.

Determining whether a combatant activity was a misuse or abuse of power necessitates a consideration of international humanitarian law and the rules of engagement. If a combatant activity infringes the rules of engagement, it is necessarily *ultra vires*.[29] Indeed, combatants and states do not have the authority to act in breach of these rules as they are binding on all states, and no state can unilaterally detract from them. Moreover, once these rules are grounded in legislation or regulations, their infringement can amount to a breach of statutory duty.

In addition, if a combatant were to breach the rules of engagement, she is also engaging in an unlawful act. While a violation of the rules of engagement does not necessarily result in a violation of international humanitarian law,[30] the rules of engagement nevertheless seem to encapsulate the relevant scope of combatants' authority to engage in combat. Alternatively, an intentional infringement of any of the rules of engagement could also result in the conclusion that a combatant activity was pursued for an improper purpose.

[28] Nonetheless, these kinds of actions might be relevant in the context of belligerent occupation. For example, the Supreme Court of the Netherlands found the Netherlands liable for failing to offer male refugees in a compound that was under state control the choice of staying in the compound, resulting in Bosnian Serb forces killing these male refugees. See section 5 of *State of The Netherlands v Mothers of Srebrenica et al* 17/04567 (Eng) (2019). However, my focus in this chapter is on combatant activities that amount to an engagement with enemy forces, and I will not address the issues that arise in relation to administrative fairness and omissions. Furthermore, while there is a way in which omissions could occur in the course of combatant activities, for instance, if an intelligence officer does not pass on information that a certain target is civilian rather than combatant, omissions are nevertheless irrelevant in the context of misfeasance in public office. An omission such as the one described will not infringe international humanitarian law on its own, as it does not cause the loss. Rather, it is the actions of another combatant that might. While the actions of the state as a whole can be considered wrongful, the omission of the individual intelligence officer cannot be a misfeasance in public office. This is another aspect of the narrower application of intentional torts in the context of belligerent activities, as opposed to their application during peace.

[29] An argument could be made here that use of force that is opposed to the rules of engagement is not *ultra vires*, but simply private use of violence. This argument is similar to the discussions that are taking place in the context of vicarious liability as to whether an employee acted within the course of employment or on a frolic of their own. Ultimately, it would be a matter of degree that could only be decided based on the particular circumstances of every case. Still, not every use of force that is a violation of a state's rules of engagement could be said to be only private violence and not acting *ultra vires*.

[30] International humanitarian law grounds the minimal standards that all states must abide by, and every state can add further restrictions and requirements on top of these standards in its rules of engagement. Hence, by adhering to these rules, combatants are also adhering to international humanitarian law but not vice versa. For example, a combatant might be required by the rules of engagement to fire only towards a perceived enemy's legs under certain circumstances. If she fires at the enemy's torso, she is violating the rules of engagement, but is adhering to international humanitarian law.

What follows is that both international humanitarian law and the rules of engagement could be used to determine whether there was misuse or abuse of public power that amounts to unlawful conduct. Nevertheless, determining precisely which category of misuse or abuse of public power most accurately reflects the characteristics of a wrong will ultimately depend on the particularities of each case.

To see how misfeasance in public office might be applicable to combatant activities, consider the following hypothetical situation. A sniper unit is ambushing enemy combatants within enemy territory. The rules of engagement prohibit soldiers from firing unless commanded to do so, or if they are under immediate threat. However, the combatants are bored, and they start to fire blank ammunition for amusement. Eventually, one of the combatants, private Morin, fires a live tracer bullet through a non-combatant's window, which starts a fire and results in the total destruction of the house.

Based on these facts, the elements of misfeasance in public office could be established. Morin shot a live tracer bullet through the window to damage it, while knowing that doing so was both unlawful and in violation of the rules of engagement. Morin fired the shot for her entertainment, directly targeting a civilian object in an action that does not bring about any military gain and is in violation of the rules of engagement. It seems clear that Morin had targeted malice to act unlawfully.

Now consider the following variation. Private Morin identifies an enemy combatant driving a fuel truck. Killing the combatant would delay the fuel's arrival to enemy forces, and so it would achieve a small military gain to Private Morin's state. However, Private Morin knows that since the truck is moving, it is very likely to explode upon collision with nearby civilian buildings, and thus it is very likely to inflict a disproportionate loss on non-combatants. Yet, Private Morin fires at the enemy combatant, causing the risk of explosion and injury to non-combatants to materialize.

Whereas in the first variation of the hypothesis Morin acted with targeted malice, in the second variation of the hypothesis Morin could be described as acting with knowledge and recklessness. In this particular case, prior to shooting the enemy combatant Morin knew, or at the very least was recklessly indifferent to, the very likely disproportionate loss that would be inflicted on non-combatants were she to shoot, which would mean that her actions would violate international humanitarian law. Moreover, she knew, or at the very least was recklessly indifferent to, the fact that she would be violating an order not to open fire without being ordered to and when there is no immediate threat.

As this analysis demonstrates, misfeasance in public office seems to provide a coherent legal structure with which to address the corrective justice duties that arise from intentional belligerent wrongdoing. An infliction of loss through combatant activities that infringe international humanitarian law and the rules of engagement rules out the availability of a justification for the imposition of the loss, leaving it as a wrong that requires redressing. Additionally, inflicting losses in such circumstances could also amount to misuse or abuse of public power, and if done intentionally the wronging could be redressed through misfeasance in public office.

V. Conclusions

The analysis in this chapter demonstrates that tort liability could be imposed for intentional belligerent wrongs using ordinary doctrines, though some appear to be more relevant to actual engagement in hostilities than others. Nevertheless, the articulation of belligerent wrongs as an infliction of a loss that breaches international humanitarian law or the rules of engagement results in intentional torts being available in a narrower set of circumstances than they are for equivalent wrongs inflicted through non-combatant activities. It is not enough for states and combatants to intend to use or damage non-combatants' bodies or means. They must also act with sufficient intent that would deem their combatant activities as breaching international humanitarian law or the rules of engagement. While the resulting liability regime is limited in comparison to peacetime, ordinary tort doctrines could still be used coherently to address wrongs inflicted through combat by properly accounting for the moral and legal features of warfare.

5

Negligent Warfare

I. Introduction

Whereas the discussion in Chapter 4 outlined the operation and applicability of intentional torts for an infliction of intentional belligerent wrongs, in this chapter, I shall demonstrate the applicability of negligence in the context of warfare. Each of the tort of negligence defining elements will be analysed: duty of care, breach of the standard of care, and causation. I demonstrate that policy considerations that have been invoked to rule out the existence of a duty of care during warfare are unconvincing. Instead, states' and combatants' duty of care towards non-combatants while engaging in belligerent activities ought to be understood as the ordinary duty to avoid wrongfully interfering with individuals' rights over their bodies and means. I also argue that the standard of care during warfare could be deduced from international humanitarian law and the rules of engagement independently to questions of whether a justification for belligerent wrongs exists. Doing so suggests that negligence in warfare could mean that individual combatants have breached the rules of engagement or that states' overall conduct amounts to a direct infringement of the international humanitarian law. Lastly, I show that ordinary rules of causation and treatment of causal uncertainty could be used to establish that combatants and states have inflicted a belligerent wrong. As the form of belligerent wrongs both informs and constrains the applicability of negligence in the context of combatant activities, the upshot of this chapter is, once more, that liability could only arise in a narrow set of circumstances compared to the context of non-combatant activities.

II. States and Combatants' Duty of Care

In negligence, duty of care is the requirement that every individual will use their body and means only in a way that is consistent with the rights of others.[1]

[1] See, for example: Arthur Ripstein, *Private Wrongs* (Harvard UP 2016) 83; Ernest J Weinrib, *The Idea of Private Law* (OUP 2012) 164–65; Robert Stevens, *Torts and Rights* (OUP 2007) 2; John CP

Tort Liability in Warfare. Haim Abraham, Oxford University Press.
DOI: 10.1093/9780191997051.003.0005

This duty is based on the principle that all people are free and equal agents who are not subject to the arbitrary choices of others.[2] In order to comply with this principle, individuals must act in ways that are consistent with the rights of others. This duty is constrained, however, by a qualification that is referred to by courts as 'remoteness' or 'proximate cause'.[3] Only those kinds of interferences that are foreseeable and real, rather than those that are unforeseeable and far-fetched, would be considered wrongful interference with the rights of others.[4]

As I have established in Chapter 2, even during warfare individuals' private law rights remain relevant. The right to life, bodily integrity, and property are not extinguished or over-ridden, and as such everyone has a duty of care to avoid wrongfully infringing these rights. States' and combatants' authority to engage in hostilities does not negate their duty of care, but rather provides a justification for losses that are inflicted while acting in compliance with international humanitarian law or the rules of engagement, making such losses non-wrongful.[5]

Goldberg and Benjamin C Zipursky, *Recognizing Wrongs* (2020) 154, 352; John Gardner, 'What Is Tort Law For? Part 1: The Place of Corrective Justice' (2011) 30 Law and Philosophy 1, 9–11, 22–23. Note, I will not address the economic approach to negligence, as it is often in conflict with the rights-based analysis that informs my discussion throughout the book.

[2] Arthur Ripstein, *Force and Freedom: Kant's Legal and Political Philosophy* (Harvard UP 2009) 55.

[3] See, for example: *Palsgraf v Long Island R Co* 248 NY 339 (NY 1 January 1928) 346; *Overseas Tankship (UK) Ltd v The Miller Steamship Co Pty Ltd [The Wagon Mound (No 2)]* [1966] 2 All ER 709, 719; *AIB Group (UK) plc v Mark Redler & Co Solicitors* [2015] 1 All ER 747, 767; *Saadati v Moorhead* [2017] 4 LRC 458, 473–74; Ripstein, *Private Wrongs* (n 1) 91; Weinrib, *The Idea of Private Law* (n 1) 158–70.

[4] See, for example: *Bolton and Others v Stone* [1951] 1 All ER 1078, 1085; *McCarthy v Wellington City* [1966] NZLR 481 (CA) 521; *MacPherson v Buick Motor Co* 217 NY 382 (NY, 14 March 1916) 389–90; *Palsgraf* (n 3) 344; *Donoghue v Stevenson* [1932] All ER Rep 1, 11; *Home Office v Dorset Yacht Co Ltd* [1970] 2 All ER 294, 297–98; *Anns and others v London Borough of Merton* [1977] 2 All ER 492, 498; *Caparo Industries Plc v Dickman* [1990] 1 All ER 568, 573–74; *Cooper v Hobart* [2001] 3 SCR 537, 548–51, 555; Ripstein, *Private Wrongs* (n 1) 89; Weinrib, *The Idea of Private Law* (n 1) 164.

It should be noted that the identification of the existence of duty of care is usually not restricted to questions of foreseeability and proximity, but there is also an element of justice or policy that courts rely on. I address some aspects of this element in the discussion below, but the arguments I have made in Chapters 2 and 3 are helpful in this context as well. The duty to refrain from wrongfully injuring others and their property is an ordinary duty that exists even during warfare. Compliance with international humanitarian law does not rule out the existence of the duty, but rather provides a justification for the infliction of losses that would otherwise be wrongful. Any limitation of the duty requires further justification, and those currently advanced—the risk of over-deterrence, unjust compensation, crippling claims, and judicial encroachment over the government's discretion—all appear unconvincing when properly examined.

[5] In an interview, Colonel Dr Gabi Siboni, a former fighter and commander in the Golani Brigade, explained that the source of the duty of care during battle directly stems from international humanitarian law: '[When engaging in warfare], the duty of care is always there . . . Of course there is a duty of care. What are the principles of warfare if not constantly operating the system of checks and balances and making sure you are acting appropriately?' ('Interview with Colonel Gabi Siboni' (February, 2019)). This argument is slightly different from my own, as I locate the existence of a duty of care in the fact that individuals' rights remain relevant during war, which means that there is a general duty to

Yet, it has been argued by some courts that in the course of conducting belligerent activities, combatants and states do not owe a duty of care to civilians and other combatants at all, and it is helpful to differentiate between two versions of the combatant activities exception. In some jurisdictions, such as Canada, Israel, and the United States, the combatant activities exception operates as a legislative immunity from liability. It bars the recourse to tort law altogether, rather than declaring that the state does not have a duty of care.

In other jurisdictions, such as Australia and England and Wales, the combatant activities exception is a doctrine that negates the existence of a duty of care during armed conflicts due to policy considerations. Two main reasons were offered. First, that a duty of care would limit the ability of the military to achieve its objectives. Second, that such a duty cannot exist as it is impossible to articulate and enforce a standard of care.

For example, in the *Shaw Savill* case, the Australian High Court held that there is no duty of care during combat, to avoid limiting the military's ability to act. In this case, a commercial merchant ship called *Coptic* collided with an Australian Commonwealth ship called *Adelaide* on the night of 3 September 1940.[6] The naval authorities had given the *Coptic* its course.[7] The *Adelaide* was taking the same route between Brisbane and Sydney, although in the opposite direction, uninformed by the naval authorities about the *Coptic's* route.[8] Both ships were advancing without lights, and the *Adelaide* was proceeding without a proper lookout and at a higher speed than normal when they collided.[9] The majority ruling of the Australian High Court, as given by Dixon J, held that no liability in negligence was to be imposed.[10] Dixon J stated that in times of actual engagement with enemy forces, broadly construed, the Commonwealth and its combatants owe no duty of care towards others who may be injured by their actions:

> It cannot be enough to say that the conflict or pursuit is a circumstance affecting the reasonableness of the officer's conduct as a discharge of the duty of care, though the duty itself persists. To adopt such a view would mean

avoid an imposition of a wrongful loss. International humanitarian law does not generate a duty of care according to my view, but instead it provides a justification that renders a wrongful loss non-wrongful. Consequently, a duty of care to avoid inflicting wrongful belligerent losses remains in force, while there is no duty of care to avoid an infliction of non-wrongful losses.

6 *Shaw Savill & Albion Co v Commonwealth* (1940) 66 CLR 344, 364.
7 ibid 358.
8 ibid.
9 ibid.
10 ibid 363.

> that whether the combat be by sea, land or air our men go into action accompanied by the law of civil negligence, warning them to be mindful of the person and property of civilians . . . To concede that any civil liability can rest upon a member of the armed forces for supposedly negligent acts or omissions in the course of an actual engagement with the enemy is opposed alike to reason and to policy.[11]

Dixon J held that augmenting the standard of care to meet the reality of the battlefield, while maintaining that combatants have a duty of care to others while engaging in belligerent activities, would not do enough to eliminate tort law's deterring effect on combatants. Deterrence might, in turn, hinder combatants' ability to achieve their military goals. To avoid this hindrance, Dixon J holds that combatants must be deemed to lack any duty of care when conducting 'active operations' against enemy forces.[12]

The UK Supreme Court's decision in the *Smith* case recognizes Dixon J's ruling but offers a different articulation as to why the combatant activities exception rules out a duty of care towards civilians and fellow combatants during combat. Here, relatives of British army combatants, who died while serving in Iraq, brought a suit against the Crown. The plaintiffs claimed that the military acted negligently and in breach of Article 2 of the European Convention for the Protection of Human Rights and Fundamental Freedoms when it deployed its combatants with insufficient protective gear.[13] Lord Hope DP delivered the majority decision:

> While in the course of actually operating against the enemy, the armed forces are under no duty of care to avoid causing loss or damage to those who may be affected by what they do. But, as Dixon J also said (at 362), there is a real distinction between actual operations against the enemy and other activities of the combatant services in time of war . . . At the stage when men are being trained, whether pre-deployment or in theatre, or decisions are being made about the fitting of equipment to tanks or other fighting vehicles, there is time to think things through, to plan and to exercise judgment. These activities are sufficiently far removed from the pressures and risks of active operations against the enemy for it to not to be unreasonable to expect a duty of care to

[11] ibid 361–62.
[12] ibid.
[13] *Smith v Ministry of Defence* [2013] 4 All ER 794, 805–7. The combatants were deployed using Snatch Land Rovers with light armour that offered insufficient protection against improvised explosive devices, which were a known threat at the time.

> be exercised, so long as the standard of care that is imposed has regard to the nature of these activities and to their circumstances.[14]

The upshot of the *Smith* case seems to be that when there is a possibility of exercising care, there would also be a duty of care to do so. Yet, under circumstances where there is no possibility of exercising care, there would be no duty of care. Duty of care exists, according to Lord Hope DP, when the pressures of battle are distant, and individuals are able to consider the possible consequences of their actions. However, during actual engagement with the enemy, Lord Hope DP seems to hold that the intensity of belligerent activities makes it either impossible or extremely difficult for combatants to assess the consequences of their actions and act with due care. As neither care nor foresight are reasonable expectations during battle, an imposition of a duty of care would be unwarranted as complying with it would be impossible.

The *Shaw Savill* case and the *Smith* case identified policy considerations for non-recognition of a duty of care for acts and omissions done while engaging in actual combatant activities. And indeed, to date, courts in Australia and England and Wales have not held that states and combatants owe such a duty. Yet, both cases support the conclusion that a duty of care could and should be recognized in the context of warfare for acts and omissions that fall short of actual combatant activities. Moreover, it remains conceptually possible to establish the argument that a duty of care should be recognized for actual combatant activities as well, were the policy considerations that guided the courts shown to be inaccurate or irrelevant.

As I have argued in previous chapters, there is a way to articulate a duty of care during warfare and there are policy considerations to support its existence in this context. I argue that the ordinary principle of duty of care—that every person is always presumptively under a duty to avoid acting in a way that is inconsistent with the rights of others—exists even during war. Consequently, injuring or killing another person in combat, as well as damaging her property, are *prima facie* breaches of one's duty of care towards another person. However, inflicting a loss while acting in accordance with international humanitarian law or the rules of engagement is within the scope of states and combatants' authority to wage war, thus the loss is justified and non-wrongful. Action that is justified in these ways is akin to acting in a way that is *careful enough.*

[14] ibid 830–31.

Moreover, as the duty of care during warfare is ordinary, and a breach of it creates a corrective justice duty to redress belligerent wrongs, the onus of proof ought to be on those who wish to exclude the existence of a duty of care during warfare—not those who wish to establish that there is one. This analytical starting point is also warranted from a substantive rule of law perspective, according to which the availability of tort remedies is an essential element of the rule of law that holds public bodies and officials accountable.

The policy considerations in the *Shaw Savill* case and the *Smith* case do not seem to meet this requirement. In *Shaw Savill*, Dixon J's main concern was about over-deterrence. However, empirical and theoretical studies suggest that combatants are unlikely to be deterred by an imposition of tort liability on the state and that combatants support various reparation mechanisms for civilians who were harmed, even during lawful combatant activities.[15] These findings undermine deterrence as a relevant policy consideration towards excluding the existence of a duty of care in the context of warfare. Legally recognizing and enforcing an ordinary duty of care in instances where a loss was inflicted while acting in breach of international humanitarian law or the rules of engagement does not generate an additional restriction on the military's ability to pursue its goals. Rather, it is an expression of restrictions that states are already subject to.

Furthermore, Lord Hope DP's view that during engagement in active hostilities combatants have no time to exercise judgment, but simply act, overlooks the requirements set out by international humanitarian law and the rules of engagement. Combatants and states are required to consider whether an activity is necessary, if it properly discriminates between combatants and non-combatants, and whether the expected military gains are proportionate to the anticipated losses. Each of these principles obligates combatants to actively reflect upon the implications of their actions on the civilian population, whom they are putting at risk.[16] Even under attack, combatants are not allowed to aimlessly fire in all directions.

[15] *Shaw Savill* (n 6) 361–62; Jennifer K Robbennolt and Lesley Wexler, 'Service Members' Reactions to Amends for Lawful Civilian Casualties' (2021) University of Pennsylvania Law Review 399; Haim Abraham, 'Tort Liability, Combatant Activities, and the Question of Over-Deterrence' (2022) 47 Law & Social Inquiry 885.

[16] Article 57(1) of Protocol Additional to the Geneva Conventions of 12 August 1949, and relating to the Protection of Victims of International Armed Conflicts 1977. This Article clearly states that a duty of care exists even in the context of belligerent activities: 'In the conduct of military operations, constant care shall be taken to spare the civilian population, civilians and civilian objects'. A similar statement is found in Article 13(1) of the Protocol Additional to the Geneva Conventions of 12 August 1949, and relating to the Protection of Victims of International Armed Conflicts 1977. According to this Article, 'the civilian population and individual civilians shall enjoy general protection against the dangers arising from military operations'. The duty of care that is owed to non-combatants is also expressed in military manuals, states' practice, and officials' statements. See: International Committee of the Red Cross,

While states and combatants cannot be expected to exercise judgment in the same way individuals can in ordinary activities during peace, holding that combatants are excused from any exercise of judgement raises difficulties. It would mean, for instance, that international humanitarian law is nothing more than what David Dyzenhaus refers to as a 'grey hole'.[17] It would stand as a façade of a legal order without any real substance. Yet, if we accept that, for the purposes of international humanitarian law, there is and can be a possibility of preventing the realization of foreseeable and wrongful risks, then it is very difficult to justify the claim that no duty of care should exist on grounds of reason or policy.

Since the policy considerations that negate the existence of a duty of care are apparently unconvincing, it would seem it is indeed possible to articulate states and combatants' duty of care towards non-combatants while engaging in belligerent activities. It is the ordinary duty to avoid wrongfully interfering with individuals' rights over their bodies and means. Nevertheless, such interferences during combat are justified and non-wrongful, as long as they comply with international humanitarian law and the rules of engagement.

III. Being Negligent in Battle

Being negligent means that an individual created an unreasonable risk towards another, to whom she owes a duty of care, which ultimately materialized in a loss.[18] Ascertaining which risks are reasonable, and which are not, is done in reference to the standard of care. This standard can be understood, in general terms, as acting in a way that creates ordinary and inevitable risks that people impose on each other while using their bodies and means carefully.[19] Being able to use your own body and means necessitates an ability to impose such risks on others that are either minor or are unlikely to materialize.[20]

'Customary IHL: Rule 15. Precautions in Attack' <https://ihl-databases.icrc.org/customary-ihl/eng/docs/v1_rul_rule15#Fn_C9F91DAD_00004> accessed 19 October 2018.

[17] David Dyzenhaus, *The Constitution of Law: Legality in a Time of Emergency* (CUP 2006) 50.

[18] John Gardner, *From Personal Life to Private Law* (OUP 2016) 49–51; Weinrib, *The Idea of Private Law* (n 1) 147; Stevens (n 1) 2, 107–8; Jules Coleman, *Risks and Wrongs* (OUP 2002) 331–32; George P Fletcher, 'Fairness and Utility in Tort Theory' (1972) 85 Harvard Law Review 537, 548.

[19] Goldberg and Zipursky (n 1) 107, 189; Ripstein, *Private Wrongs* (n 1) 103; Fletcher (n 18) 543, 556; Gregory C Keating, 'Reasonableness and Rationality in Negligence Theory' (1996) 48 Stanford Law Review 311, 324–25; Stephen Perry, 'The Moral Foundations of Tort Law' (1992) 77 Iowa Law Review 449, 497–98.

[20] Ripstein, *Private Wrongs* (n 1) 103.

However, this standard can also be understood in particular contexts, in which case the question is not about how ordinarily careful people act, but how ordinarily careful people of a certain affiliation act.[21] Reasonable conduct of professionals, for example, can be determined by the courts as that which conforms to the norms of practice of that particular community, even though conforming with such norms is not necessarily synonymous with acting with the appropriate standard of care.[22]

The particular standard according to which the conduct of professionals is evaluated can stem either from social practices or legal norms. For example, if physicians have a common practice to which they are not obligated to adhere to by law, but it is the acceptable standard of the profession, then courts might choose to adopt this common practice as the legally required standard.[23] In contrast, some professionals are obligated by law to act in accordance with a certain standard. In this scenario, even if there is a common practice that is deviating from the legal standard, the conduct should nevertheless be evaluated in relation to its compatibility with the latter, rather than the former. In this sense, common practice can provide context on how the legal standard is applied in practice, but it has no ability to override the legal standard simply by being the acceptable social rule.

The standard of care while engaging in belligerent activities should be understood in this way, identifying what a reasonable combatant or state ought to do in the heat of battle, not what a reasonable, ordinary person ought to do.[24] When the man on the Clapham Omnibus is deployed in the field of battle,[25] his actions should not be judged as if he is still riding that hypothetical Clapham

[21] For example, a reasonable physician, a reasonable lawyer, a reasonable police officer, and so on. For a discussion on the specialized standard of care of professionals and experts, see: John G Fleming, *The Law of Torts* (9th edn, LBC Information Services 1998) 121–24.

[22] For instance, in one case, the Supreme Court of Canada deferred to the practice among anaesthetists, in relation to the question of whether placing a can of ether on the operating table, which subsequently exploded, was a form of reasonable conduct: *Sylvester v Crits* [1956] SCR 991, 1–3. In another case, the High Court of Australia determined that an architect who failed to properly oversee the construction of a swimming pool, and so did not meet the professional practice of the time, was negligent due to this deviation from the professional practice: *Florida Hotels Pty Ltd v Mayo* (1965) 113 CLR 588, 593, 601. In England, the standard of care to determine medical negligence tracks the practice that is accepted as proper according to a responsible body of medical opinion, unless it is incapable of withstanding logical analysis: *Bolam v Friern Hospital Management Committee* [1957] 1 WLR 582, 587; *Bolitho v City and Hackney Health Authority* [1998] AC 232, 243.

[23] For instance: CA 542/82 *Credit and Savings Mutual Benefit Society Inc v Awad* PD 44(1) 422 (1990) 436; CA 3521/11 *Adv Daniel Wagner v Mazal Abadi* (Nevo, 22 June 2014) 58.

[24] *Smith* (n 13) 831; *Bici v Ministry of Defence* [2004] EWHC 786 (QB) 46; *Attorney General for Northern Ireland's Reference (No 1 of 1975)* [1977] AC 105, 138; CA 3889/00 *Lerner v Israel* PD 56(4) 304 (2002) 312–16.

[25] Collins MR attributed the phrase 'Man on the Clapham Omnibus' to Lord Bowen in *McQuire v Western Morning News Co* [1900-03] All ER Rep 673, 675.

Omnibus. Rather, they should be judged by the norms that are expected from a combatant in his position.

Reasonableness in warfare could be deduced from the legal norms that regulate and dictate the appropriate conduct of hostilities as enshrined in international humanitarian law and the rules of engagement. As I have noted in previous chapters, every state's rules of engagement must comply with international humanitarian law, and although further restrictions could be added, unilateral deviations from international humanitarian law are prohibited. Consequently, while the standard of care in warfare could, at its core, be identical across states, reliance on the rules of engagement could result in some variations of the standard between states. However, similar variations are common to all tort law doctrines, and as such do not raise particular concerns.

To illustrate what the standard of care during warfare could be for combatants and states, consider the following example. State A's rules of engagement permit shooting at individuals if they pose a clear and immediate threat, but if the threat they pose is unclear or non-immediate, combatants are required to take escalating steps to get individuals to stop and identify themselves. These steps include such actions as calling out to suspects to stop, firing in the air, aiming at the suspect's legs, and only aiming at the torso as a last resort. The rationale of these steps is to minimize harm to non-combatants.

One of State A's combatant identifies an individual at a distance, whom she mistakenly identifies as an enemy combatant. The combatant shoots at the individual as he was walking away from her, injuring his knee. In doing so, the combatant has infringed State A's rules of engagement, as the individual did not pose a clear and immediate threat and she was authorized to use force only by following the required escalating steps. Drawing on the rules of engagement to determine the standard of care in warfare, it is possible to argue that in the example above a reasonable combatant would have followed the required escalating steps. In inflicting the injury, the combatant's ordinary duty of care not to cause bodily harm to others was infringed and she acted in a manner that breached the required standard of care in the context of warfare. As the wrong was inflicted while acting in breach of the rules of engagement, the combatant's actions cannot be justified and remain wrongful.

As this example illustrates, states' rules of engagement could be infringed unintentionally. However, as I have argued in Chapter 4, in order to infringe international humanitarian law, combatants or states must act with intent to violate its norms. For instance, targeting individuals who were believed to be combatants but were in fact non-combatants is not a breach of the principle of distinction, whereas knowingly targeting non-combatants is. This conclusion holds true even if the belief that individuals are combatants is erroneous, for example if intelligence mistakenly identified the wrong building as one where enemy forces were located.

Nevertheless, the fact that international humanitarian law can only be infringed intentionally does not mean that courts cannot rely on it to deduce the relevant standard of care that is expected from states and combatants during warfare. In doing so, civil courts could differentiate between the element of intent and the principles of necessity, distinction, and proportionality. The resulting regime could mean that a combatant activity that inflicted a loss on non-combatants is unreasonable for tort law purposes, even if international humanitarian law is not infringed.

Consider the following. An intelligence unit accidentally classifies a building as hosting enemy forces, spots the error, but fails to update its records despite having ample time and opportunity to do so. As a result, an attack force targets the building, which results in massive injuries to non-combatants. Considered separately, neither unit has infringed the principles of discrimination or proportionality, nor has any individual combatant violated the rules of engagement. Since the intelligence unit did not carry out the attack, they cannot have infringed international humanitarian law. Likewise, because the attacking force acts based on the information they had *ex ante*, they, too, have not violated international humanitarian law and the rules of engagement.

However, by understanding that states' military forces are not composed of entirely self-sustaining units, but rather on collaborative units with a deep division of labour, it is possible to see how a state can inflict a loss while acting in a manner that breaches the standard of care. On the whole, the state had knowledge of the non-combatant character of the building. By failing to pass on this information to the strike force, the state did not comply with its obligation to minimize harm to non-combatants and distinguish between legitimate military targets and non-combatants.[26] Given this information, a reasonable state would have taken active steps to ensure that an attack was not launched, as the target is illegitimate and the collateral damage would be disproportionate. Put differently, courts could evaluate *ex post* whether a state's acts and omissions overall resulted in a loss that does not comply with the principles of necessity, distinction, and proportionality unintentionally.

Two possible conclusions could follow based on my account of belligerent wrongs. The first is that, based on the facts of this hypothetical example, if both

[26] A state's obligation to do all it can to verify it is targeting legitimate individuals or structures could be found in Article 57(2)(a)(i) of Additional Protocol I.

international humanitarian law and the rules of engagement are adhered to by individual combatants, the losses are justified. While it is conceptually possible to hold that the state's overall conduct is incompatible with its duty of care and standard of care, liability could not be imposed because the losses are justified. The resulting tort liability regime would be consistent with international humanitarian law and states' responsibility under international law to a high degree.[27] Consequently, some accidental collateral damage to non-combatants would not be addressable.

An alternative possibility would be to limit the scope of the justification of acting in compliance with international humanitarian law and the rules of engagement due to policy considerations. For example, it could be argued that failing to provide a remedy for losses brought about due to gross negligence and incompetence is unjust, or that the lack of tort remedies might result in insufficient incentives for states to develop efficient intelligence exchange networks. Addressing these policy concerns could be achieved, for example, by limiting the justification of combatant activities, requiring more than compliance with international humanitarian law and the rules of engagement for the justification to apply.

For the purpose of this book, there is no need to elaborate further on which of these possibilities ought to be advanced. It is sufficient to note that either could result in a coherent regime, and neither rule out the ability to articulate a standard of reasonable care during warfare. The standard of care, much like the duty of care, could draw on international humanitarian law and the rules of engagement independently from questions of whether a justification for belligerent wrongs exists.

IV. Causing Wrongful Belligerent Losses

So far, the discussion has surveyed several key elements of liability for negligent warfare. I argued above that states and combatants are under an ordinary duty of care to avoid wrongfully interfering with other individuals' bodies and means. Furthermore, I maintained that the standard of care could be derived from the norms governing combatant activities and thus would require states and combatants to act in compliance with international humanitarian law and

[27] On the interplay between international law of state responsibility in warfare and tort law, see: Haim Abraham, 'Frameworks for Accountability: How Domestic Tort Law Can Inform the Development of International Law of State Responsibility in Armed Conflicts' (2023) 64 Virginia Journal of International Law Online 1.

the rules of engagement. I now analyse how the element of causation could operate in relation to belligerent wrongs.

Causation is the materialization of an unreasonable risk through an interference with the plaintiff's rights that constitutes a wrong.[28] For example, texting while driving creates an unreasonable risk that another road user will sustain an injury, but in the absence of such an injury, private individuals do not have a claim in tort against the negligent driver, nor would a corrective justice duty arise. It is only when a wrongdoer's tortious conduct can be shown to have caused the injured individual's loss that a claim could succeed, and a corrective justice duty is triggered.

A causal analysis has a factual and a legal dimension to it. Factual causation is ordinarily determined by using a hypothetical counterfactual: would the plaintiff's injuries have materialized if the defendant's actions were not negligent?[29] If the answer is positive, then the defendant is not the factual cause of plaintiff's injury. Legal causation (or proximate cause in the United States) determines which losses factually caused by the defendant could be recoverable by the plaintiff's tort claim. To meet the requirement of legal causation, losses must not be deemed too remote, that is, that they are a consequence of a kind which is not reasonably foreseeable.[30] Even if losses are not too remote, were they to materialize due to the acts or omissions of an intervening cause, such as another person or acts of nature, legal causation would not be established.[31]

In some instances, establishing factual and legal causation for belligerent wrongs may be straightforward. Consider the example of the combatant who negligently fires at a suspicious individual, who was not posing an immediate risk, in breach of her state's rules of engagement. As the identity of the combatant and the chain of events are known, a factual causation analysis is simple. The individual would not have sustained that loss were the combatant to have followed the rules of engagement. Similarly, legal causation is also relatively clear. It is reasonably foreseeable that negligently using firearms could lead to injuries to life, body, and property—and, as such, these types of losses that are not too remote. Furthermore, under the factual scenario of this example, there

[28] *Palsgraf* (n 3) 344–46; Goldberg and Zipursky (n 1) 286; Ripstein, *Private Wrongs* (n 1) 116; Weinrib, *The Idea of Private Law* (n 1) 157; Stevens (n 1) 129–36; Coleman (n 18) 276–77.

[29] See, for instance: *Barnett v Chelsea and Kensington Hospital Management Committee* [1969] 1 QB 428, 433–34; Stevens (n 1) 129–33. On the difficulties of causal underdetermination when the contrasting forms of conduct indicate that the injury would both occur and would not occur, see: Maytal Gilboa, 'Multiple Reasonable Behaviors Cases: The Problem of Causal Underdetermination in Tort Law' (2019) 25 Legal Theory 77.

[30] *Overseas Tankship (UK) Ltd v Morts Dock & Engineering Co Ltd* [1961] AC 388, 418–26; Goldberg and Zipursky (n 1) 218–19.

[31] *Home Office v Dorset Yacht Co Ltd* (n 4).

are no other factors that might break the chain of causation. Both dimensions of causation could, therefore, be established.

Factual and legal causation could also be established when a state's actions overall are negligent. Think again of the state whose intelligence unit failed to inform an attacking force that a building was housing only non-combatants, resulting in their misidentification and injury. As it is known that the loss was inflicted by the acts and omissions of the forces of a single state, concluding that but for the state's overall negligent conduct, the loss would not have materialized is straightforward. Additionally, and much like the example of the negligent combatant, the type of losses that are inflicted do not appear to be too remote and there are no intervening factors that might break the chain of causation. When the circumstances are clear and simple, no particular issues relating to the establishment of factual and legal causation appear to arise.

This is not to say that every infliction of a loss on non-combatants through combatant activities will be clear and simple. As past and recent examples of warfare demonstrate, causal uncertainty can arise in a variety of ways. It might not be possible to identify the combatant who caused the loss, even if the identity of her state is known. Also, it might be impossible to attribute the loss to one state if several different forces are operating simultaneously in a particular area. Furthermore, it might be challenging to establish whether a loss was inflicted in accordance with international humanitarian law and the rules of engagement, or in breach of them.

Such challenges are not unique to the battlefield and stem from the conceptual limitations of a counterfactual analysis. The hunter who was shot by a single bullet, that could have been fired by any of his fellow hunters who fired simultaneously using the same ammunition, could never establish who caused his injuries using a counterfactual analysis.[32] The children who developed cancer due to generic prescription medication their mothers took while pregnant, that was manufactured by several different corporations, face a similar problem.[33] In both cases, while it is clear that one defendant caused the injury, a counterfactual analysis results in no defendants being the factual cause of the injury, since the injury cannot be traced to a single defendant.

The above examples are of instances in which the negligence of the defendants is not questioned, just their contribution to the materialization of the actual loss. However, the counterfactual analysis also results in an inability to

[32] *Cook v Lewis* [1951] SCR 830; *Summers v Tice* 33 Cal 2d 80 (Cal, 1948); *Oliver v Miles* 144 Miss 852 (Miss, 1926).

[33] For instance: *Sindell v Abbott Laboratories* 26 Cal 3d 588 (Cal, 1980) 612–13; *Brown v Superior Court* 44 Cal 3d 1049 (Cal, 1988) 1070–75; *Hymowitz v Eli Lilly & Co* 73 NY2d 487 (NY, 1989).

hold any potential defendant liable in other circumstances. For example, when wrongful or non-wrongful conduct created the risk of a loss and it is impossible to identify which of the two forms of conduct caused it to materialize,[34] and when a third party created the risk that could have materialized regardless of the negligence of the defendant.[35] An opposite difficulty arises when a counterfactual analysis results in all of the potential defendants being the cause of the loss, while the conduct of any one of them was sufficient to have caused it.[36]

Several possible solutions have been suggested and implemented in response to these causal uncertainties, and there is nothing to suggest that they could not apply in the context of warfare as well. For example, one way of bypassing the difficulty of establishing who committed the wrong is offered by the doctrine of joint and several liability. According to this doctrine, liability can be imposed jointly and severally for the wrongful losses caused, even though it is not entirely clear which parts of the wrong was caused by which of the tortfeasors.[37] Another solution lies in the market share liability doctrine, which determines the scope of liability according to the proportion of the defendants' activity in the particular 'market', even though the loss cannot be attributed with certainty to the conduct of any defendant in particular.[38] An additional

[34] In the McGhee case, for instance, an employee argued that he contracted dermatitis due to his employer's admitted negligent failure to provide shower facilities. Yet, the employee could not establish that he would not have contracted dermatitis even if he had showered, due to the lack of scientific evidence. See: *McGhee v National Coal Board* [1972] 3 All ER 1008.

[35] For instance, when, due to medical malpractice, a patient loses the chance of recovery from a condition, for which it is doubtful that she would have recovered regardless of the quality of treatment she could have received. Under these circumstances, in all instances in which chances of recovery are low, it will not be possible to establish on the balance of probabilities that a loss would not have occurred if the doctor acted non-negligently. Consequently, any patient who lost over 50% chance of recovery could obtain a remedy in tort, while all patients who lost less than 50% chances of recovery cannot. See: *Laferrière v Lawson* [1991] 1 SCR 541; *Gregg v Scott* [2005] UKHL 2; FH 4693/05 *Carmel-Haifa Hospital v Malul* PD 64(1) 533 (2010).

[36] The case of *Fitzgerald v Lane* demonstrates this point. Here, the plaintiff was crossing the road when he was struck by the first negligent driver, tossed in the air to the other side of the road, and hit by the second negligent driver. As a result, the plaintiff became tetraplegic. The Court of Appeal held both defendants liable, even though, on the balance of probabilities, it was impossible to identify which defendant's negligence caused the injury, as both were sufficient individually. See: *Fitzgerald v Lane and another* [1987] 2 All ER 455.

[37] See: *Cook v Lewis* (n 32); *Summers v Tice* (n 32); *Fitzgerald v Lane and another* (n 36); Nancy Lee Firak, 'Alternative Forms of Liability: Developing Policy Aspects of the Cause-in-Fact Requirement of Tort Law' (1988) 20 Arizona State Law Journal 1041, 1052–54; Ariel Porat and Alex Stein, *Tort Liability under Uncertainty* (OUP 2001) 59–60; Joachim Dietrich and Pauline Ridge, *Accessories in Private Law* (CUP 2015) 93–98.

[38] See, for instance: *Sindell v Abbott Laboratories* (n 33) 612–13; *Brown v Superior Court* (n 33) 1070–75; Firak (n 37) 1060–64; Susan Rose-Ackerman, 'Market-Share Allocations in Tort Law: Strengths and Weaknesses' (1990) 19 Journal of Legal Studies 739; Mark A Geistfeld, 'The Doctrinal Unity of Alternative Liability and Market-Share Liability' (2006) 155 University of Pennsylvania Law Review 447, 477–85; Alessandro Romano, 'God's Dice: The Law in a Probabilistic World' (2016) 41 University of Dayton Law Review 57, 82–83. Variations of this doctrine suggest that liability should be imposed based on the proportion of the increased risk the defendant's behaviour has caused. See, for example: Glen O Robinson, 'Probabilistic Causation and Compensation for Tortious Risk' (1985)

solution turns the focus from the violation of a substantive right to the frustration of a remedial right. By shifting the focus in this way, the evidential damage doctrine allows for the imposition of liability for the spoliation of evidence that is needed to establish a causal link.[39]

Given belligerent activities do not give rise to unique causal uncertainties, it is possible to see how such issues could be resolved. When uncertainty is in reference to the identity of the particular combatant who inflicted the loss, while the identity of the state whose agents inflicted the loss is known, causation could be established by directly or vicariously attributing the wrong to the state. In contrast, if several states acted negligently, but the loss could only have materialized due to the acts of one of them and it is impossible to determine whose, the doctrine of joint tortfeasors could be used. The defendant states violate different aspects of the same right—one inflicted the physical injury, the other or others frustrated the ability to establish a claim in tort.[40] Because all states created wrongful risks that have materialized, uncertainty regarding which state inflicted which loss should not frustrate liability. Consequently, if, for example, two states negligently and simultaneously fired at non-combatants in violation of international humanitarian law or the rules of engagement, both states could be held liable for the wrong they committed.

Additionally, when a loss could have materialized due to either the wrongful or non-wrongful conduct of a state and its combatants, and it is unclear due to which of these it arose, it might be possible to shift the burden of proof to the state since it created the risk that materialized. On this account, causation of the loss is attributed based on the activity as a whole, while acknowledging that states create a risk by engaging in combatant activities, and so they have a responsibility to minimize the potential for the materialization of these risks.[41] For instance, intelligence about potential targets should be as accurate and

14 Journal of Legal Studies 779, 790; Lee Firak (n 37) 1064–67; Ariel Porat, 'Offsetting Risks' (2007) 106 Michigan Law Review 243, 246–47; Ariel Porat and Eric A Posner, 'Offsetting Benefits' (2014) 100 Virginia Law Review 1165, 3. However, Ernest Weinrib argues that the market share liability doctrine is incompatible with tort law's structure, as it is based on distributive justice rather than corrective justice. See: Ernest J Weinrib, 'Causal Uncertainty' (2016) 36 Oxford Journal of Legal Studies 135, 152.

[39] Porat and Stein (n 37) 160–70. This doctrine has been adopted in some jurisdictions to the extent that causing a loss of evidence results in shifting the burden of proof to the defendant, as, due to the absence of the records, the plaintiff's ability to establish a *prima facie* case is hindered. See: CA 361/00 *Azam D'aher v Captain Yoav* PD 59(4) 310 (2005) 327; *Public Health Trust v Valcin* 507 So 2d 596 (Fla, 1987) 599; *Welsh v United States* 844 F2d 1239 (6th Cir Ky, 1988) 1246–47; *Cook v Lewis* (n 32) Rand J, paragraphs 13–15.

[40] Weinrib, 'Causal Uncertainty' (n 38) 145–47.

[41] ibid 153–55. The responsibility to minimize the risks battle imposes on non-combatants is grounded in international humanitarian law as well as Article 57 of Additional Protocol I.

up-to-date as possible, and failures to gather this intelligence, or to relay it to a strike force, could establish the necessary causal link.[42]

It is important to note that the solution that has been used to resolve causal uncertainty that arises in instances where the plaintiff might have sustained an injury by a third party, regardless of the defendant conduct, seems relevant in a narrow set of cases in the context of warfare. In these situations, causation could be attributed when the plaintiff and the defendant have a special relationship that creates reliance and an *in personam* right for the plaintiff towards the defendant for the fulfilment of a particular goal.[43] Such relationships appear to exist between states and their own combatants. By sending troops into battle, combatants rely on their state to provide them with the means that are required for their safety, such as food, clothing, and armour. If their state fails to provide them with these means, then they can establish a causal link between their injuries and the state's conduct, even though they might have sustained these injuries in battle, as the state did not properly fulfil its part.

It might also be possible to imagine a limited set of circumstances in which a state could have the necessary relationship towards non-combatants. In the context of belligerent occupations, the occupying force could create mechanisms with non-combatants to ensure that they are not subject to attack. For example, some individuals in the Occupied Palestinian Territories can call a dedicated phone line when operations are being conducted in proximity to their homes to identify as non-combatants.[44] In other instances, peacekeeping forces might invite non-combatants to rely on them to ensure that they will not be injured by other states, and non-combatants might come to indeed rely on this invitation.[45] However, it is difficult to envision instances where this kind of a special relationship could be established between states and non-combatants more generally.

The upshot of this analysis is that although the exact mechanism for addressing various cases of causal uncertainty might vary, belligerent activities do not give rise to unique issues of causal uncertainty, and these issues could be addressed using ordinary solutions. Even though the possibility of causal uncertainty might be greater during warfare than in peacetime, it is possible

[42] In one recent case, an Israeli bombing of an outdated target from a 'target bank' that had not been updated for months resulted in the deaths of eight non-combatants. See: Yaniv Kubovich and Jack Khoury, 'Outdated Intelligence, Social Media Rumors: Behind Israel's Killing of Gaza Family' *Haaretz.com* (15 November 2019) <https://www.haaretz.com/israel-news/.premium-outdated-intelligence-social-media-rumors-behind-israel-s-killing-of-gaza-family-1.8131101> accessed 4 December 2019.

[43] Weinrib, 'Causal Uncertainty' (n 38) 161–63.

[44] CA 220/19 *The Estate of Abuelaish v Ministry of Defense* (Nevo, 24 November 2021) (Isr).

[45] *State of The Netherlands v Mothers of Srebrenica et al* 17/04567 (Eng) (2019).

to follow the same rules to establish causation both in combat and in ordinary activities.

V. Conclusions

In this chapter, I demonstrated that combatants and states can be held liable in negligence for unintentional losses they inflict during warfare. While engaging in belligerent activities, combatants and states owe an ordinary duty of care to avoid wrongfully interfering with individuals' rights. Concerns that a duty of care in tort would result in over-deterrence are not supported by theoretical and empirical studies of the impact of liability on state actors. Furthermore, arguments that a duty of care in tort would be unjust due to an inability exercise judgment during armed conflicts are outweighed by rule of law considerations. There are, therefore, sufficient reasons to recognize a legal duty of care in belligerent activities. I also argued that it is possible to deduce the relevant standard of care by examining what international humanitarian law and the rules of engagement require of combatants and states. Lastly, I showed that while warfare can raise complex causal issues, these issues could be addressed through ordinary doctrines, such as joint and several liability, and shifting the burden of proof.

That said, the account of liability I advance both in this and the previous chapter focuses mainly on direct liability, and thus far I have only briefly discussed the possibility of imposing vicarious liability on states. In Chapter 6, I turn to address in greater detail the particular considerations that vicarious liability raises in the context of belligerent activities.

6

Unpacking States' Vicarious and Direct Liabilities

I. Introduction

As the arguments in previous chapters demonstrate, tort liability could and should be available against states and combatants when a wrongful loss is inflicted on civilians during actual hostilities. I articulated both the infliction of the wrongful loss and the imposition of liability as direct in form—the infliction of a loss through an act that breaches international humanitarian law or the rules of engagement is an unjustified wrong for which a state or a combatant could be liable. In doing so, I treated the acts and omissions of a state's combatants as the acts and omissions of an entity that is operating through its actors. After all, states are artificial persons and as such they can only act through real people. In this chapter, I expand the analysis to assess the viability of vicarious and direct impositions of liability on states for wrongful losses inflicted by their combatants, contractors, and citizens.

I begin by demarcating the scope of states' vicarious liability for belligerent wrongs. I show that the relevant relationship between the state and the wrongdoer, usually described as one of employment or agency, clearly exists towards its combatants but not necessarily towards its contractors or civilians. Only in some jurisdictions have statutes extended the scope of the state's vicarious liability to wrongs of its independent contractors, and consequently it could be available for belligerent wrongs as well. Furthermore, and generally, the doctrine's second limb of acting 'in the course of employment' could be met when a belligerent wrong was inflicted negligently. Yet, the applicability of vicarious liability to intentional torts across jurisdictions is not sufficiently unified and consistent to be able to make a similar general claim in relation to intentional belligerent torts. It could only be established in this context on a case-by-case basis.

I then discuss three additional instances in which states could be held directly liable under circumstances that preclude the availability of vicarious liability, namely that the wrong was inflicted by a third party. First, that states'

Tort Liability in Warfare. Haim Abraham, Oxford University Press. © Haim Abraham 2024.
DOI: 10.1093/9780191997051.003.0006

own failures result in the creation and materialization of the wrongful loss. For example, by failing to properly train, supervise, or select its combatants and contractors, the state could be held directly liable. However, I show that this form of liability is unlikely to be available in relation to wrongs that a state's civilian population inflicts on enemy non-combatants. Second, I argue that states have non-delegable duties to ensure the health and safety of prisoners of war and occupied populations. Furthermore, I show that a non-delegable private law duty to ensure that civilians do not sustain belligerent wrongs might be established. Third, I demonstrate that in some jurisdictions direct liability could be imposed on states through the doctrine of ratification when states explicitly or implicitly adopt the wrongful conduct of their combatants or contractors as their own.

II. Vicarious Liability

The doctrine of vicarious liability enables courts to impose tortious liability on an individual or an entity for losses that were inflicted by a third party on the plaintiff. Generally, there are two cumulative elements that must be met for vicarious liability to be imposed.[1] First, that the third-party tortfeasor is in a relationship of sufficient agency with the individual or entity for which vicarious liability is sought, often referred to as a relation of employment or one that is akin to employment. Second, that the wrong was inflicted in connection with the performance of duties that stem from the relationship of sufficient agency.

Consider the following example. Alice, a wealthy homeowner, employs Bob to do the daily cleaning and gardening work throughout her estate. One day, while Bob is mowing the lawn, he tosses a small rock out of his way, which unintentionally goes over the hedges and damages a neighbour's window. In doing so, Bob has committed a wrong for which he could be held liable in tort. Alice, on the other hand, did not directly cause the damage, yet she could be held liable through the doctrine of vicarious liability. Bob committed the tort while working as Alice's employee, and the incident occurred while he was performing his duties.

[1] American Law Institute, *Restatement (Third) of Agency* (2006) §7.03, §7.07; Section 13 of the Tort Ordinance 1968; *BXB v Trustees of the Barry Congregation of Jehovah's Witnesses* [2023] 2 WLR 953, 957; *Bazley v Curry* [1999] 2 SCR 534, 559–60; *Prince Alfred College Inc v ADC* [2016] HCA 37, paragraphs 39–40; Paula Giliker, *Vicarious Liability in Tort: A Comparative Perspective* (CUP 2010) 1–6, 13–18; Jason W Neyers and Jerred Kiss, 'Vicarious Liability: The Revolution in Canada' in Paula Giliker (ed), *Vicarious Liability in the Common Law World* (Hart 2022) 21.

Given that vicarious liability can be imposed on an individual who has not committed a wrong but was merely in a relationship of sufficient agency with the wrongdoer, liability could be viewed as strict in the sense that fault has no role in its imposition.[2] Going back to the gardening example, Alice could be held liable simply because she was Bob's boss and he broke the neighbour's window while doing his job for Alice. Liability is not imposed because Alice did something wrong that causally contributed to the window being broken. Furthermore, if liability was imposed because of Alice's own wrongdoing, for instance if she hired Bob despite his reputation for damaging neighbours' property, she would be held directly liable.

Theoretical analyses of the doctrine of vicarious liability have characterized it either as a means of merely allocating liability or as a means of imputing wrongdoing.[3] As a means of allocating liability, the wrongful act is not considered to have been done by the defendant who is vicariously liable. Instead, liability is imposed for reasons that are not necessarily related to any possible fault on the defendant's side but are more properly aligned with instrumental approaches to tort law and distributive justice. For instance, notions such as the ability to pay, deter, or spread the costs associated with losses have been argued to be the conceptual basis of the doctrine and its strict liability character.[4] An alternative justification, according to which the individual or enterprise that creates the risk and enjoys the benefits of the risk-creating activity should bear the costs of the risk materializing, also tracks this line of thought.[5]

[2] *Bernard v A-G of Jamaica* [2005] 2 LRC 561 569; *Bazley* (n 1) 539; *Majrowski v Guy's and St Thomas's NHS Trust* [2006] 4 All ER 395, 400; Arthur Ripstein, 'Reasonable Persons in Private Law' in Giorgio Bongiovanni, Giovanni Sartor, and Chiara Valentini (eds), *Reasonableness and Law* (Springer 2009) 125–26; Luke McCarthy, 'Vicarious Liability in the Agency Context' (2004) 4 Queensland University Technology, Law, and Justice Journal 1, 1; Philip Morgan, 'Recasting Vicarious Liability' (2012) 71 Cambridge Law Journal 615, 617.

[3] For a detailed review of the development of the doctrine of vicarious liability in Australia, Canada, England and Wales, and the United States, see: Anthony Gray, *Vicarious Liability: Critique and Reform* (Hart Publishing 2018) 5–95; Christine Beuermann, 'Vicarious Liability in Australia' in Paula Giliker (ed), *Vicarious Liability in the Common Law World* (Hart 2022); Paula Giliker, 'Vicarious Liability in England and Wales' in Paula Giliker (ed), *Vicarious Liability in the Common Law World* (Hart Publishing 2022); Neyers and Kiss (n 1).

[4] *Armes v Nottinghamshire County Council* [2018] 1 All ER 1, 18; *Lister and others v Hesley Hall Ltd* [2001] 2 All ER 769, 793–94; *Bazley* (n 1) 559; Patrick S Atiyah, *Vicarious Liability in the Law of Torts* (Butterworths 1967) 27; Bryant Smith, 'Cumulative Reasons and Legal Method' (1948) 27 Texas Law Review 454, 458–59; John G Fleming, *The Law of Torts* (9th edn, LBC Information Services 1998) 410.

[5] *Armes* (n 4) 18; *Bazley* (n 1) 560; *JGE v Trustees of the Portsmouth Roman Catholic Diocesan* [2012] 4 All ER 1152, 1177; Gregory C Keating, 'The Idea of Fairness in the Law of Enterprise Liability' (1997) 95 Michigan Law Review 1266, 1360; Jane Stapleton, *Product Liability* (Butterworths 1994) 186; Jennifer H Arlen and W Bentley MacLeod, 'Beyond Master–Servant: A Critique of Vicarious Liability' in M Stuart Madden (ed), *Exploring Tort Law* (CUP 2005) 121; Robert Stevens, *Torts and Rights* (OUP 2007) 258; Morgan (n 2) 618; Douglas Brodie, 'Enterprise Liability: Justifying Vicarious Liability' (2007) 27 Oxford Journal of Legal Studies 493, 495–96; Neyers and Kiss (n 1) 41–44.

In contrast, viewing vicarious liability as imputing wrongdoing goes further, and some accounts result in a conceptualization of vicarious liability that is consistent with a rights-based approach to tort law, while others would still consider vicarious liability as external to a rights-based approach.[6] According to this view, vicarious liability is the idea that a person should be liable for wrongful losses that ought to be considered as if she has caused them. Thus, the vicariously liable person is considered to also have caused the loss alongside their employee or agent. For example, one justification places emphasis on agency and holds that vicarious liability is justified as the direct tortfeasor acts as an agent of another.[7] In order to impose liability on one person or entity for the actions of another, there needs to be a high degree of closeness between the two to the extent that it is possible to hold that one person acted through another.[8] It is this quality of 'acting through' that makes this type of liability both vicarious and direct, simultaneously. Liability is vicarious as it is imposed for acting through another person. Nevertheless, liability is also direct, as the wrongful acts of another are also the wrongful acts of the defendant.

Applying these articulations of vicarious liability to the context of belligerent activities raises two questions. First, which individuals' actions could be considered as the state acting through its agents? For instance, can the actions of combatants who are public officials result in vicarious liability? Can the actions of combatants who are part of private military companies have the same effect? Second, and assuming that states can be held vicariously liable for either or both types of combatants, what types of losses inflicted by a state's agent would still be within the ambit of the state acting through its agents? As I have argued above, in the context of warfare, belligerent wrongs could be imposed negligently and intentionally.[9] The question is whether either or both forms

[6] Allan Beever, *Rediscovering the Law of Negligence* (Hart Publishing 2007) 35–36.

[7] *Launchbury v Morgans* [1973] AC 127 135; *Armes* (n 4) 18; *Bazley* (n 1) 559; *Scott and others v Davis* (2000) 175 ALR 217 277–78; Arlen and MacLeod (n 5); Morgan (n 2) 625–28; Giliker (n 1) 110–16; Arthur Ripstein, *Force and Freedom: Kant's Legal and Political Philosophy* (Harvard UP 2009) 125; Gray (n 3) 270–71.

[8] Ernest Weinrib discusses this aspect in relation to the *respondeat superior* doctrine, holding that it fits with corrective justice principles to the extent the actions of an employee can be imputed to the employer. See: Ernest J Weinrib, *The Idea of Private Law* (OUP 2012) 186–87. Robert Stevens similarly situates his view of vicarious liability in the *respondeat superior* doctrine, holding that vicarious liability incorporates rules of attribution, making the acts and omissions of the employee those of the employer: Stevens, *Torts and Rights* (n 5) 260–69.

[9] I do not address potential torts that arise in the general context of warfare but from activities that fall short of engagement in actual hostilities, such as injuries caused by combatants' intoxicated driving, acts of vandalism, or false imprisonment. These torts can be, and in some jurisdictions are, resolved through ordinary tort law and are not included in most states' combatant activities exception. Vicarious liability could apply to these ordinary torts in an ordinary fashion, and as such I will not analyse such instances in this chapter. For a further discussion on which activities should be considered as 'combatant activities', see Chapter 3.

of wrongdoing could result in states' vicarious liability. Ultimately, these questions can only be answered in the particular context in which they arise. Still, some general theoretical observations can be made.

A. Agents of the State

The contemporary theatre of war has many actors in it, including combatants, contractors, civilians, animals, and even robots. But for which actors could a state be held vicariously liable? Ordinarily, this question is answered by examining whether the relationship between the wrongdoer and the defendant is one of sufficient agency. The clearest example is of an employer and an employee, but other examples include partners in a partnership towards one another and owners of vehicles and individuals who drive them.[10]

In some instances, the existence of such relationships is established based on various factors, such as control over conduct, resources, and explicit or implicit acknowledgement by the parties of the character of their relationship.[11] At times, policy considerations are taken into account as well, including the ability to pay compensation, incentivizing safer conduct, or loss-spreading.[12] There are also instances in which a relationship of sufficient agency is deemed to exist through legislation.[13]

With these clarifications in place, it is possible to examine whether a state could be held to have a relationship of sufficient agency with its combatants, contractors, and civilians when they engage in combat. From these three groups, the statuses of the relationships between states and their combatants, and between states and their civilians, seem the most straightforward to determine. Whether subject to mandatory or voluntary conscription, combatants are public officials. Even if they are not employees in a traditional sense, combatants are clearly in a relationship that is akin to employment with their state. The state selects, trains, and directs its combatants' activities, as well as paying their salaries and providing them with the means of performing their roles. The relevant relationship of sufficient agency exists between states and

[10] See, for example: Sections 9–10 of the Partnership Act 1890; *Launchbury v Morgans* (n 7) 149–51; *Scott and others v Davis* (n 7), paragraphs 250–58; GHL Fridman, 'The Doctrine of the "Family Car": A Study in Contrasts' (1976) 8 Texas Tech Law Review 323.

[11] Giliker (n 1) 55–59, 69–77.

[12] *Armes* (n 4) 18; *Lister and others v Hesley Hall Ltd* (n 4) 793–94; *Bazley* (n 1) 559; Atiyah (n 4) 27; Smith (n 4) 458–59; Fleming (n 4) 410.

[13] For example, in New Zealand and England and Wales, independent contractors are treated as the Crown's agents for the purpose of tort liability. See: Sections 2(1)(a) and 38(2) of the Crown Proceedings Act 1947 [UK]; Sections 2 and 6(1)(i) of the Crown Proceedings Act 1950 [New Zealand].

their combatants for vicarious liability to apply. Indeed, an examination of key cases from Australia, Canada, England, Israel, and the United States indicates that the state is the defendant that is sued for torts inflicted by its combatants, although liability is imposed directly and vicariously almost interchangeably. The upshot is that from both theoretical and doctrinal perspectives, a relationship of sufficient agency exists between states and their combatants to establish the first limb of vicarious liability.

The status of the relationship between a state and its civilians is a mirror image of the relationship between a state and its combatants. There is no doubt that combatants who engage in warfare are the state's agents. It is similarly clear that if civilians decided to take up arms, without the state conscripting them or encouraging this conduct, then they cannot be considered to have a relationship of sufficient agency with the state. Rather, they ought to be treated as third parties for whose wrongs generally vicarious liability cannot be imposed. Under these circumstances, civilians are not in a relationship of employment with their state, nor are there sufficient indications that would suggest that they are in a relationship that is akin to employment with their state. The state does not control, direct, benefit, or provide means to its civilians, and its civilians are not integrated into its military operations.

However, if civilians are engaging in warfare under certain conditions, such as being under the control and direction of a state, it could be argued that a relationship of sufficient agency exists to attribute the conduct of the civilians to the state. This is the approach that seems to have been taken by Article 8 of the Draft Articles on the Responsibility of States for Internationally Wrongful Acts 2001. Put differently, the fact that wrongs are inflicted by civilians does not necessarily suggest that their state could not be held vicariously liable. Nevertheless, there appears to be a rebuttable presumption that vicarious liability could not be imposed on a state for wrongs its civilians inflict in the context of warfare.

Things are somewhat more complicated when considering independent contractors. In relationships that do not involve the state, parties cannot be held vicariously liable for the actions of independent contractors who provide a service that they were hired to do.[14] Once more, there seems to be a presumption, in this context, that the degree of closeness required for an imposition of

[14] See, for instance: *Lister and others v Hesley Hall Ltd* (n 4) 784–88; *D & F Estates Ltd v Church Commissioners* [1989] AC 177, 208; *Lane v Shire Roofing Co (Oxford) Ltd* [1995] IRLR 493, 495; *671122 Ontario Ltd v Sagaz Industries Canada Inc* [2001] 2 SCR 998–1003; *Northern Sandblasting Pty Ltd v Harris* (1997) 146 ALR 572, 608–9; Ewan McKendrick, 'Vicarious Liability and Independent Contractors: A Re-Examination' (1990) 53 Modern Law Review 770, 702; McCarthy (n 2) 3; Morgan (n 2) 622; Brodie (n 5) 503. For the purpose of this book, there is no need to detail a test to determine who might be considered an independent contractor beyond the discussion that follows footnotes 16–19. Different jurisdictions can approach this issue in a variety of ways. For the argument that I am

vicarious liability does not exist.[15] Similarly, vicarious liability cannot be imposed on defendants for the actions that third parties undertook of their own accord, even if these actions benefited the defendants. However, in relationships that involve states, it is possible to identify a divergence in approaches between jurisdictions.

For example, in Canada, Israel, and the United States, the state cannot be held liable in tort for wrongs inflicted by independent contractors and third parties. In Canada, the Crown Liability and Proceedings Act limits liability to torts committed by 'a servant of the Crown' including its agents but excluding independent contractors.[16] In Israel and the United States, the liability the of the state seems to be more restricted, allowing an imposition of vicarious liability only for acts of the state's employees.[17] In contrast, in New Zealand and England and Wales, the state can be held vicariously liable for the acts of its servants and agents, and legislation assigns a specific definition to the term 'agent' that is inclusive of independent contractors who are employed by the Crown.[18]

The potential imposing of vicarious liability on states for losses inflicted during combat by private military contractors could follow these approaches.[19] Private military contractors are independent contractors, and their employees

advancing here, it is sufficient to state that there is a conceptual category of 'independent contractor' that impacts the applicability of the rules relating to the availability of vicarious liability.

[15] In Australia, Canada, England and Wales, and the United States, evaluating the degree of closeness for imposing vicarious liability for the actions of an independent contractor is based on the defendant's control over the contractor; the degree to which the contractor was integrated into the defendant's operations; or how much discretion the contractor had. See: Gray (n 3) 204; Richard Kinder, 'Vicarious Liability: For Whom Should the "Employer" Be Liable?' (1995) 15 Legal Studies 47, 63–64; Morgan (n 2) 641–43.

[16] Sections 2 and 3(b) of the Crown Liability and Proceedings Act (RSC, 1985, c C-50) 1985.

[17] Section 2 of the Civil Wrongs (Liability of the State) Act 1952 [Israel]; Section 13 of the Tort Ordinance [Israel]; 28 USC §1346, 1948 (b)(1); 28 USCS §2671, 1948.

[18] Sections 2(1)(a) and 38(2) of the Crown Proceedings Act 1947 [UK]; Sections 2 and 6(1)(i) of the Crown Proceedings Act [New Zealand]. Such treatment seems consistent with both instrumental and rights-based theoretical accounts of vicarious liability. For instance, a state is more likely to be able to pay an award of compensation, and spread the costs associated with liability. Furthermore, as it created the risk of injury by relying on independent contractors instead of its employees, it could be argued that the state should shoulder the costs. That said, a state seems less likely to be deterred by tort liability, particularly in the context of warfare (see: Haim Abraham, 'Tort Liability, Combatant Activities, and the Question of Over-Deterrence' (2022) 47 Law & Social Inquiry 885). Moreover, for a state to be acting through its independent contractors, in the sense used by rights-based scholars, a high degree of closeness between them must be established, which could limit the scope of vicarious liability considerably.

[19] There is no uniform definition of private military companies in scholarly writing. See, for example: Christopher Kinsey, *Corporate Soldiers and International Security: The Rise of Private Military Companies* (Routledge 2006) 9–11; Emanuela-Chiara Gillard, 'Business Goes to War: Private Military/Security Companies and International Humanitarian Law' (2006) 88 International Review of the Red Cross 525, 529–30; Peter Warren Singer, *Corporate Warriors: The Rise of the Privatized Military Industry* (Cornell UP 2008) 89–100. For the purpose of this book, I will refer to private military companies as those corporations who provide combat or combat-related services to states, as they can commit belligerent wrongs.

are not public officials even when they perform what appear to be public functions. Depending on the approach adopted by different jurisdictions, belligerent wrongs committed by private military contractors could meet the first requirement—a relationship of sufficient agency—for an imposition of vicarious liability on the state.

B. In the Course of Combat

The second requirement that must be met for vicarious liability to be imposed is that the wrong was inflicted in a way that is sufficiently connected to the wrongdoer's 'employment'.[20] Emphasis is placed not only on whether the employment created an opportunity for wrongful conduct but also on whether the employment increased the risk of a wrong being inflicted.[21] In some jurisdictions, additional policy considerations such as deterrence, loss spreading, and ability to compensate have been considered by courts to determine whether a loss was inflicted in the course of employment.[22] Consequently, there is some lack of clarity regarding which actions would give rise to an imposition of vicarious liability.[23]

While it is possible to identify variations between jurisdictions in their approaches to determining whether a sufficient connection exists, some common features are identifiable.[24] First, courts can consider a variety of factors to

[20] *Restatement (Third) of Agency* (n 1) §7.03, §7.07; *WM Morrison Supermarkets plc v Various Claimants* [2020] UKSC 12, paragraphs 25–26, 31; *Bazley* (n 1) 545–51, 559–60; *Lister and others v Hesley Hall Ltd* (n 4) 776; *State of New South Wales v Lepore and Another* (2003) 195 ALR 412 446–47; Giliker (n 1) 185–86.

[21] *Bazley* (n 1); *Lister and others v Hesley Hall Ltd* (n 4); *State of New South Wales v Lepore and Another* (n 20); *Ryan v Fildes* [1938] 3 All ER 517; *Lloyd v Grace, Smith, & Co* [1912] AC 716; *Mattis v Pollock* [2003] EWCA 887; Giliker (n 1) 162. An extreme version would be the employer's failure in hiring, supervising, or retaining the employee, in which case liability could be directly imposed rather than vicariously (Catherine M Sharkey, 'Institutional Liability for Employees' Intentional Torts: Vicarious Liability as a Quasi-Substitute for Punitive Damages' (2018) 53 Valparaiso University Law Review 1, 17–18). It should be noted that in *Mattis v Pollock* the court found that the employer encouraged the employee to act aggressively as a factor that was relevant for the imposition of vicarious liability (*Mattis v Pollock* 2168–69). This conclusion is not surprising given that ordinarily acting aggressively towards other people entails creating a risk that a wrong will be inflicted. However, the same cannot be said in the context of warfare, which is mostly conducted in violent means. The wartime parallel of *Mattis v Pollock* would not be an instance in which a state encourages its combatants to act aggressively while engaging in belligerent activities. Rather, the relevant parallel would be if the state encourages its combatants to execute their orders in disregard of the international humanitarian law or the rules of engagement, as in doing so the state is increasing the risk that a wrong will be inflicted.

[22] For example: *Restatement (Third) of Agency* (n 1) §2.04 comment b, §7.07 comment b; *BXB v Trustees of the Barry Congregation of Jehovah's Witnesses* (n 1) 971–72.

[23] Giliker (n 1) 171.

[24] For example, in Australia, whether a wrong was inflicted 'in the course or scope of employment' requires judges to consider what the employee was employed to do and whether the employment provided a mere opportunity to inflict the wrong of the occasion for it (*CCIG Investments Pty Ltd v*

assess whether there is a close connection between the wrongdoing and employment. This assessment is not limited to a closed list of factors, and depends on the circumstances of each case. Second, temporal and geographical proximity could be relevant, but they are not sufficient or necessary to establish a close connection with employment. Third, and in contrast, if an employee intended to harm their employer through the wrongful conduct, even if that required directly wronging a third party and causing an indirect harm to the employer, this factor would be given considerable weight. Fourth, policy considerations shape the analysis, either by defining the doctrine or informing its application and interpretation of the various factors accounted for. All of these factors aim to assess whether the wrongful conduct was sufficiently connected with the acts that the tortfeasor was authorized to do, in order that the tort could be regarded as having been inflicted in the course of employment.

Moreover, there appears to be a difference between negligent and intentional torts in relation to the possibility that vicarious liability could be imposed. Losses that are inflicted negligently while engaging in authorized acts, even if the mode of operation was unauthorized, are generally seen as inflicted while acting within the scope of employment.[25] In contrast, intentional wrongdoing is generally faced with greater scrutiny and scepticism, and will not easily be held to have been inflicted while acting within the scope of employment.

The applicability of vicarious liability to belligerent wrongs could follow this distinction between negligent and intentional wrongdoing. Negligent belligerent torts, such as those losses that combatants inflict while breaching the rules of engagement unintentionally, appear to be sufficiently closely

Schokman [2023] HCA 21, paragraphs 14, 34, 95; *State of New South Wales v Lepore and Another* (n 20) 471–72). Similarly, in the United States, courts also need to establish what employees were employed to do, but there is an additional element of assessing whether the employee conducted assigned work that the employer controls (*Restatement (Third) of Agency* (n 1) §7.07(2)). If the employee's actions are not connected to assigned work, are outside of the employer's control, or solely benefit themselves or third parties, they are not in the course of employment (*Restatement (Third) of Agency* (n1) §7.07, comment b). The approach in England and Wales is fairly similar, though the assessment of the close connection of the wrongful conduct to the employment requires assessing considerations of policy and justice slightly more directly. A wrong will be considered closely connected when 'it can fairly and properly be regarded as done [as part of] . . . the tortfeasor's authorised activities' (*BXB v Trustees of the Barry Congregation of Jehovah's Witnesses* (n 1) 971–72). Here too, it was held that 'a causal connection (i.e., that the "but for" causation test is satisfied) is not sufficient in itself to satisfy the test', and that policy considerations should be considered in difficult cases as a cross-check on the determination of whether an imposition of vicarious liability would be just (*BXB v Trustees of the Barry Congregation of Jehovah's Witnesses* (n 1) 972). By comparison, policy considerations have an active role in Canada, particularly if a precedent for an imposition of vicarious liability does not exist in the circumstance. In such cases, a wrong is closely connected to employment if employment increased the risk of, and created the opportunity for, the infliction of the wrong beyond incidental temporal and geographical elements (*Bazley* (n 1) 545, 560, 567).

[25] Giliker (n 1) 157–60.

connected with combatants' 'course of employment' (or 'quasi-employment'). Using force is part of what combatants are authorized to do. If combatants use force while failing to comply with the rules of engagement, not for pursuing an independent purpose or furthering their own benefit, this should be deemed as a wrongful and unauthorized mode of engaging in an authorized act.

The analysis would be different if the rules of engagement or international humanitarian law were breached intentionally and constituted an intentional belligerent tort. In this context, it is much more difficult to identify clear categories of cases in which it will or will not be possible to determine that an actor was acting within the course or scope of their employment. Consequently, a range of factors would have to be considered on a case-by-case basis. Still, there is nothing unique in the intentional infliction of a loss through combatant activities that suggests that vicarious liability should be altogether inapplicable in the context of warfare. Such a stance does not seem to be required by doctrine or theory.

The discussion above shows that vicarious liability could be imposed on states when belligerent wrongs are inflicted as a matter of doctrine and theory. However, the scope of states' vicarious liability would vary greatly between jurisdictions. For example, in Australia, Canada, New Zealand, and England and Wales, it is possible for the state to be held liable for intentional torts.[26] In contrast, the US Federal Tort Claims Act does not revoke the federal government's sovereign immunity for several, though not all, intentional torts committed by its officials, while Israel's approach excludes the state's liability in tort for all intentional wrongs.[27] In all of these jurisdictions, it seems that states could be held vicariously liable for wrongs that were inflicted negligently during combatant activities, but the same cannot be said of intentional belligerent torts.

While variations in doctrine and plurality of theoretical approaches to vicarious liability create a challenge to theorists who wish to articulate a single clear explanation and justification of it, for the purposes of this book they are an asset. These variations demonstrate that the doctrine could, both in fact and in theory, be implemented in the context of belligerent activities. There is nothing in the doctrine of vicarious liability that inherently rules out its applicability in this context.

[26] Sections 56 and 64 of the Judiciary Act 1903 [Australia]; Sections 3 and 10 of the Crown Liability and Proceedings Act [Canada]; Section 6 of the Crown Proceedings Act [New Zealand]; Section 2(1) of the Crown Proceedings Act 1947 [UK].

[27] 28 USC §2680(h), 1948; Sections 2–3 of the Civil Wrongs (Liability of the State) Act [Israel].

III. Direct Liability for Wrongs Inflicted by Non-Combatants

Thus far, I have sketched the contours of states' vicarious liability for wrongful losses that were inflicted in the heat of battle by individuals with whom states have a relationship of sufficient agency. I now turn to discuss the possibility that states could be held directly liable for belligerent wrongs. In Chapter 5, I analysed one such possibility that could be relevant in instances that a belligerent could be said to have been inflicted by the state itself, when its overall conduct through its actors amounts to a wrong. The analysis below is focused on a different issue, namely to examine under what circumstances could states be held directly liable for belligerent wrongs that are inflicted by individuals who are not their actors.

A. The State's Own Failures

One context in which states could be held directly liable for wrongs inflicted by third parties is instances in which there is an identifiable form of wrongdoing by the state that could be said to have been a relevant factor in the causation and materialization of the wrong. For example, outside of the battlefield, direct liability has been imposed on individuals who were negligent in selecting, instructing, or supervising hired independent contractors.[28] It is possible to imagine a similar scenario in the context of warfare, such as a state that hired the private military contractors and negligently failed to properly select or instruct them, or supervise their operations.[29] Were a belligerent wrong to be inflicted as a result of this failure, it could be viewed as a breach of the state's own duty of care, as I have defined it in Chapters 2 and 5. Only those injuries that comply with international humanitarian law and the rules of engagement

[28] For example: *Ferguson v Welsh* [1987] 1 WLR 1553, 1560; *CA 1051/14 Eden Health Teva Market Ltd v National Insurance* (Nevo, 30 August 2015), Justice Zilbertal, paragraphs 28–29. Similar failures by a state in relation to the selection, training, and supervision of its own combatants could establish direct liability as well as vicarious liability on the state as the relevant relationship of sufficient agency exists, assuming that the second requirement of 'in the course of employment' is met.

[29] Examples include the US' employment of Blackwater during the Iraq War, and Russia's use of the Wagner group in its war with Ukraine (Rod Nordland, 'Blackwater Is Soaked' *Newsweek* (9 October 2007) <https://www.newsweek.com/blackwater-soaked-103437> accessed 19 August 2023; 'European Parliament Resolution of 25 November 2021 on the Human Rights Violations by Private Military and Security Companies, Particularly the Wagner Group' (2021) <https://www.europarl.europa.eu/doceo/document/TA-9-2021-0482_EN.html> accessed 19 August 2023). Similar issues could arise in the context of activities that are auxiliary to combat. See, for instance: *Badilla v Midwest Air Traffic Control Service, Inc* 8 F4th 105 (2021): negligence in providing air traffic control to a civilian airport in the context of the war in Afghanistan; *Saleh v Titan Corp* 580 F3d 1 (CADC, 2009): companies that were hired to provide interpretation and interrogation services during the war in Iraq were accused of torture.

can be said to be justified and non-wrongful, for they fall within the scope of a state's authority to inflict these kinds of belligerent losses. Failing to impose direct liability under such circumstances is not only inconsistent with existing doctrine, but it also assists the use of private military contractors as a shield from liability.

This form of direct liability does not seem to be applicable to instances in which wrongs are inflicted by civilians during warfare when they are not under the control and direction of the state. After all, civilians are generally free to pursue any non-prohibited ends using any means at their disposal, and states are not under a private law obligation to prevent their civilians from inflicting wrongful losses.

Even in the context of belligerent military occupation, finding that states could be held directly liable for belligerent wrongs committed by their civilian populations upon enemy non-combatants seems unlikely. Indeed, states have positive duties in international law towards the occupied population, which could include protection against infringement of international humanitarian law even by third parties, including its own civilians.[30] Yet, this international humanitarian law duty does not easily translate into a private law duty, particularly as the wrongful conduct on part of states in this context is an omission to act in a way that would prevent a wrong from being inflicted by a third party.

Generally, liability for omissions could be imposed if the defendant assumed responsibility towards the plaintiff; a previous positive act created the risk that materialized by failing to take further actions; the defendant had control over the tortious third part; or if there is a special relationship between the defendant and the plaintiff.[31] I will discuss the last category of cases in the next section on non-delegable duties. As for the remaining categories, it is difficult to see how any of them might be applicable to the context of warfare. An assumption of responsibility is usually in relation to a particular activity and risk, whereas if we were to find an implicit assumption of responsibility towards the occupied civilian population it would be in relation to all activities and risks that might arise from governance. Such a conclusion seems to create a liability that is far more extensive than that which exists ordinarily. Moreover, states do not usually create the risk that their civilians would inflict belligerent wrongs on occupied civilian populations, making this category potentially relevant only in unique cases. Lastly, the form of control that is ordinarily required to

[30] *Armed Activities on the Territory of the Congo (Democratic Republic of the Congo v Uganda)* Reparations Judgment, 9 February 2022, ICJ Reports 2022, paragraph 70.

[31] Sandy Steel, 'Rationalising Omissions Liability in Negligence' (2019) 135 Law Quarterly Review 484, 495–505.

impose liability for omitting to prevent an infliction of a wrong by a third party is not one that is likely to be found between a state and its citizens in warfare. Were such a degree of control to exist, it may very well be that the relevant status of the state's citizens would be that of combatants, not civilians.

B. Non-Delegable Duties

States might also be held directly liable for belligerent wrongs inflicted by independent contractors if it could be established that they have non-delegable duties, the breach of which materialized in the loss. Non-delegable duties are held to exist despite the delegation of certain tasks or responsibilities from one person to another, usually when the former is responsible for the safety of a third party who exhibits 'special dependence or vulnerability' or when an activity is especially dangerous.[32] This means that a duty of care cannot be transferred or avoided by delegating it to another person. Examples of non-delegable duties include employers' duty to ensure a safe workplace; schools' duty to ensure a safe environment for their students; and medical institutions' duty to ensure that proper care and safety protocols are followed.[33]

Beyond this general framing, it is difficult to assert that there is a unified theory of the form and substance of non-delegable duties.[34] For example, in Australia two different conceptualizations of the doctrine have been identified: a form of direct liability for failing to ensure that proper care is taken, or as an exception to the general rule that vicarious liability cannot apply for independent contractors.[35] Similarly, in the United States, case law also developed two different theories of non-delegable duties, one deeming it a form of vicarious liability and the other a form of direct liability for a breach of one's own

[32] See, for example: American Law Institute, *Restatement (Second) of Torts* (1977) §416, §427–427A, §519–524A; *McMillan v US* 12 F 3d 1040 (1997) 1045–47; *State of New South Wales v Lepore and Another* (n 20) 438–39; *Burnie Port Authority v General Jones Pty Ltd* (1994) 179 CLR 520, 551; *Woodland v Swimming Teachers Association* [2013] UKSC 66, Lord Sumption JSC, paragraphs 6–7; John Murphy, 'Juridical Foundations of Common Law Non-Delegable Duties' in Jason W Neyers, Erika Chamberlain, and Stephen GA Pitel (eds), *Emerging Issues in Tort Law* (Hart Publishing 2007) 369–92.

[33] Robert Stevens, 'Non-Delegable Duties and Vicarious Liability' in Jason W Neyers, Erika Chamberlain, and Stephen GA Pitel (eds), *Emerging Issues in Tort Law* (Hart Publishing 2007) 352–65.

[34] McLachlin CJC remarked that a single comprehensive definition of non-delegable duties might not exist in the common law, and instead we should simply identify all of the instances in which non-delegable duties have been recognized: *B (KL) v British Columbia*, paragraph 31. See also: John Murphy, 'The Liability Bases of Common Law Non-Delegable Duties: A Reply to Christian Witting' (2007) 30 University of New South Wales Law Journal 86, 87–88; Stevens, 'Non-Delegable Duties' (n 33) 368.

[35] *Leichhardt Municipal Council v Montgomery* 230 CLR 22 [2007], Gleeson CJ, paragraphs 23–24, 27; Kirby J, paragraph 73; Hayne J, paragraph 155.

duties.[36] However, in Canada and England and Wales, there appears to be only one theory of non-delegable duties, according to which liability is direct, not vicarious, and is imposed for failing to ensure that care is taken.[37]

Despite the variety of approaches to the doctrine, an imposition of liability on a state for belligerent wrongs using the doctrine of non-delegable duties seems possible, but requires identifying that the state has such a duty and that its breach materialized in the wrongful loss.[38] The question that needs addressing at this stage is whether a non-delegable duty could and should be recognized in the context of warfare.

Private military contractors have been employed by states to fulfil various functions in conflict zones.[39] Some of these functions have a more ordinary character, such as building structures and providing air traffic control. Others have an auxiliary-to-combat character, including guarding suspects and prisoners, operating checkpoints, and gathering intelligence, to name a few. However, private military contractors have also been employed to engage in active combat. It is possible to argue that states should have non-delegable duties in each of these scenarios.

For instance, when an ordinary non-combatant activity, for which a non-delegable duty has already been recognized, is conducted and warfare is merely a background condition, it seems reasonable for courts to continue to apply the doctrine of non-delegable duties. One such example arises in the context of employment as employers have a non-delegable duty to provide a safe work environment for their employees. There is nothing to suggest that the mere fact that belligerent activities take place should change the obligations owed between parties, even if the 'employer' is a state and the 'employees' are its combatants. Outside of the theatre of battle, should the state be able to discharge its duty of care to its combatants by having a private military contractor construct sleeping quarters that expose the combatants to asbestos? Or by building shoddy recreational facilities that expose soldiers to a high risk

[36] *McGarry v US* 370 F Supp 525 (1973) 564.

[37] *Lewis v British Columbia* [1997] SCC 1145, McLachlin J, paragraph 50; *Woodland v Swimming Teachers Association* (n 32), Lord Sumption JSC, paragraphs 3–7.

[38] For instance, in the United States, the federal government waived its immunity from liability for wrongful losses that are inflicted by its employees [28 USC §1346 (b)(1); 28 USCS §2671]. Consequently, if a wrong was inflicted by an independent contractor, the federal government could not be held under the first theory of non-delegable duties in the United States, that views it as a form of vicarious liability, but only under the second theory of non-delegable duties as directly breaching its own duties (*McGarry v US* (n 36) 564).

[39] Kinsey (n 19); Gillard (n 19) 529–30; Singer (n 19).

of serious injury? Nothing in the unique moral and legal feature of warfare suggests that the state should enjoy this lower standard just because combat is taking place.[40]

There also appears to be reason to identify states' non-delegable duties in relation to functions that are auxiliary to combat. In part, these functions could be ordinary, such as driving fuel trucks, or providing training or compound security. When non-delegable duties have been recognized in relation to such ordinary functions, the fact that they are provided for a state during warfare does not seem to offer a reason to treat them differently.

Moreover, international humanitarian law seems to support a recognition of non-delegable duties in relation to functions that are auxiliary to combat in two particular circumstances. The first is in relation to prisoners of war. Under the Third Geneva Convention, states are obliged to ensure the prisoners' health and safety throughout their detention, including in instances in which they perform work or are being transported.[41] In particular, Article 12 of the Convention indicates that these duties are owed by the capturing state to the prisoners, as well as to other states, regardless of who detains the prisoners—as long as the prisoners have not been transferred to another state.[42] These are *jus cogens* norms that bind all states, from which no state can unilaterally deviate, and clearly ground states' positive obligation to ensure the safety of prisoners of war.

Given these characteristics of state duties, as well as the particular vulnerability of prisoners of war,[43] it seems that an argument that states should have private law non-delegable duties in this context could be sustained. I argue that compliance with international humanitarian law provides states with a justification during warfare, turning *prima facia* wrongs to non-wrongful losses. Accordingly, if a state infringes its obligations towards prisoners of war and

[40] As was held in the *Smith v Ministry of Defence* case, a state has a duty of care to provide its combatants with these means that cannot ensure their safety but do provide them with some safety measures (*Smith v Ministry of Defence* [2013] 4 All ER 794, paragraph 95). The fact that the theatre of battle is an extremely dangerous place in which injuries are likely to occur does not seem to justify sending forces with an even higher degree of risk. Nor does the ultrahazardous character of conflict zones seem to suggest that employers' non-delegable duties towards their employees should be delegable and absolve employers from liability. These decisions take place outside of the battlefield and should be treated accordingly as ordinary decisions the employer takes in relation to the working conditions and the risks they expose their employees to.

[41] Articles 12–14, 20, 29, 46, 51 of the Geneva Convention (III) relative to the Treatment of Prisoners of War 1949.

[42] Commentary of 2020 on Article 12 of the Geneva Convention (III) relative to the Treatment of Prisoners of War 1949. Yet, a residual obligation to protect the prisoners remains if the receiving state fails in respecting the obligations under the Convention.

[43] 'Prisoners of War: What You Need to Know' (19 May 2022) <https://www.icrc.org/en/document/prisoners-war-what-you-need-know> accessed 3 August 2023.

consequently the prisoners sustain a loss, no justification will be available to that state for its actions, making them wrongful. The non-delegable character of these obligations simply indicates a relevant cause of action that ought to be available in tort.

The second instance is in relation to belligerent occupation. Occupying states are required to protect the occupied population from acts of violence and ensure its health and safety, food and medical supplies, and public order as far as possible.[44] These obligations place a significant burden on the occupying state, requiring it to utilize all available means to achieve these ends. Importantly, these duties are owed to the occupied population and to other states, are not transferable, and remain with the occupying state even if they are carried out by its agents.[45] In this context too, an argument in support of private law non-delegable duties to an occupied population seems plausible. The duty is to ensure health and safety, is owed to a defined class of vulnerable individuals, and is not transferable. Infringing this duty would leave a state without a justification that would make a loss non-wrongful.

The discussion thus far demonstrated that there are valid reasons to recognize states' non-delegable duties during warfare in relation to functions for which a non-delegable duty has already been established during peacetime and in relation to certain functions regarding the treatment of prisoners of war and occupied populations. There are also reasons to hold that states should have non-delegable duties in relation to active engagement in combat. However, these duties are not to ensure individuals' safety. Rather states' non-delegable duty in this context should be much narrower to ensure that warfare is conducted in accordance with international humanitarian law, which is akin to acting in a way that is careful enough.

Under customary international law and international treaties, states are obligated to minimize the harms that civilians are exposed to during warfare.[46]

[44] Article 43 of the Geneva Convention (IV) respecting the Laws and Customs of War on Land and its annex: Regulations concerning the Laws and Customs of War on Land 1907. Refugees, women, and children are considered particularly vulnerable (Yoram Dinstein, *The International Law of Belligerent Occupation* (2nd edn, CUP 2019) 194).

[45] Article 29 of the Geneva Convention (IV) relative to the Protection of Civilian Persons in Time of War 1949; *Application of the Convention on the Prevention and Punishment of the Crime of Genocide (Bosnia and Herzegovina v Serbia and Montenegro)* Judgment of 26 February 2007, ICJ Reports 2007, paragraph 430; Marco Longobardo, *The Use of Armed Force in Occupied Territory* (1st edn, CUP 2018) 172–73. Additionally, occupying states have a duty to ensure adherence to international humanitarian law and international human rights law within the occupied territory, even non-state actors (*Armed Activities,* Reparations Judgment (n 30), paragraph 70).

[46] The principles of *jus in bello* require states to take adequate care towards civilians, ensuring that they will only sustain those losses that are proportionate and necessary to obtain a military gain while refraining from targeting them directly. As these are *jus cogens* norms, states are not able to do away with this duty by relegating elements of their belligerent activities to independent contractors. See: Geneva Convention (IV); Protocol Additional to the Geneva Conventions of 12 August 1949, and relating to

As I argued in Chapters 2 and 5, the duty of care that states have towards non-combatants is ordinary, and losses are non-wrongful only when they are inflicted while complying with international humanitarian law and the rules of engagement. Accordingly, states do not have a duty to ensure that proper care is taken to see that non-combatants will not be injured during warfare. Indeed, states can intentionally inflict losses on non-combatants without these losses being wrongful. Nevertheless, states still owe a duty that the law of armed conflict will be adhered to.

This obligation, to wage war in accordance with the law of war, is one that states owe under customary international law to other states, and they cannot discharge this obligation by employing third parties, including private military contractors, to engage in belligerent activities on their behalf. If a state fails to do all that it should have done to see that international humanitarian law is adhered to, it is in breach of its own duty.[47]

Given that states' non-delegable duty to conduct hostilities in accordance with the law of war is owed under customary international law to other states, as opposed to private individuals, two possible conclusions could follow. First, that this non-delegable duty is under international law, and therefore it could not be a basis for an imposition of tort liability on states for losses inflicted by third parties. This non-delegable duty is different from states' ordinary duty to refrain from wrongfully inflicting a loss on civilians during warfare. The ordinary obligation stems from the fact that rights remain relevant during warfare, which means that everyone, including states, have a private law duty to refrain from wrongfully injuring others. This private law duty is owed to all individuals. States can only inflict losses on civilians if doing so is justified and therefore non-wrongful. Compliance with international humanitarian law and the rules of engagement outlines the limits of states' authority to engage in combat. Only those losses that are inflicted while complying with these norms could be justified and non-wrongful. Accordingly, while a breach of states' non-delegable duties could give rise to liability under international law, it could not bring about a similar result under tort law.

the Protection of Victims of International Armed Conflicts 1977; Protocol Additional to the Geneva Conventions of 12 August 1949, and relating to the Protection of Victims of Non-International Armed Conflicts 1977; Rebecca Crootof, 'War Torts' (2022) 97 New York University Law Review 1063, 1101–2.

[47] Compare with the Draft Articles on Responsibility of States for Internationally Wrongful Acts: states are held responsible for acts and omissions that are committed by their organs, individuals, and groups who are under the state's control, and for conduct a state has adopted as its own (Articles 4–11 of the Draft Articles on the Responsibility of States for Internationally Wrongful Acts 2001). The Draft Articles use a model of imputation of the wrongful act to the state, which fits some theories of non-delegable duties but not all.

Alternatively, it is possible to conclude that despite the non-delegable duty's international law character, there are sufficient reasons to conclude that tort liability should nevertheless be available through the doctrine of non-delegable duties. Such reasons could be instrumental. For example, if tort liability were not available, states might have an incentive to conduct hostilities through independent contractors while refraining from control and oversight to avoid liability. It is doubtful that this form of engaging in battle would maintain international humanitarian law to a high standard or would see to it that civilian harm is minimized. Moreover, as private military contractors have less means compared to states, and could be uninsured or under-insured, plaintiffs' ability to successfully obtain compensation would be far more limited.

Such reasons could also be rights-based. For instance, states' non-delegable duties under international law could be understood as a form of statutory duty, thus moving beyond the ordinary negative duty states owe to refrain from wrongfully injuring civilians. Rather, states could be said to have an additional positive duty to ensure that hostilities that are conducted on their behalf, or in territories that they are responsible for, comply with the law of war. Under this view, if a private military contractor were to inflict a belligerent wrong, the state's own duty towards civilians would be breached as well.

Both conclusions seem plausible, and for the purposes of this book, there is no need to determine which of the two ought to be adopted. This determination has to be made by considering the implication of rejecting or adopting the availability of the doctrine of non-delegable duties to belligerent wrongs vis-à-vis the doctrinal and institutional realities in a particular jurisdiction.

C. Ratification and the Domestic Act of State Doctrine

Another possible source for holding states directly liable for belligerent wrongs inflicted by their combatants or contractors is offered through the doctrine of ratification. If an individual does something for another person without authority, that person can later express their agreement with it, explicitly or implicitly, and in doing so, the law treats the act as if it was their own and a relationship of agency existed.[48] For example, it has been held that by accepting

[48] *Restatement (Third) of Agency* (n 1) §4.01, §4.03; *Halsbury's Laws of England*, vol 1 (5th edn, 2022) 58, 61, 66, 70; Anthony W Kraus, 'Ratification of Torts: An Overview and Critique of the Traditional Doctrine and Its Recent Extension to Claims of Workplace Harassment' (1997) 32 Tort & Insurance Law Journal 807, 809–11; Deborah A Demott, 'Ratification: Useful but Uneven' (2009) 17 European Review of Private Law 987, 987–88.

profits from a sale of goods a company ratified the actions of a non-employee, who delivered the goods on their behalf and in doing so negligently broke a window.[49] Yet, for the ratification to result in an imputation of liability, the ratifier needs to either know the relevant facts or have expressed their assessment while being aware that they do not know all of the facts.[50]

Though in use, ratification is a somewhat controversial doctrine that varies in scope between jurisdictions and does not have a single theoretical approach that justifies its existence.[51] Much like vicarious liability, it is an exception to the general structure of tort law, according to which individuals are held liable for the wrongs they have inflicted, not those done by others.[52] However, ratification goes further, as it retroactively establishes, by means of a legal fiction, a relationship of agency that pre-existed the infliction of the wrong. In doing so, there is no need for the ratifier to have been a causal factor in the creation of the risk of the wrong, or in its materialization.

In the context of warfare, the ability to impose liability on states due to ratification could be narrow due to exceptions to the state's own tort liability that preclude classes of individuals, wrongs, or locations. Classes of individuals are precluded in the United States and Israel, for example, as the state could only be held liable for wrongs inflicted by its employees, excluding its agents and independent contractors.[53] Classes of wrongs are excluded in some jurisdictions, namely intentional torts, for which a state could not be held liable.[54] Lastly, in some jurisdictions extraterritorial torts are excluded from the scope of torts for which the state could be held liable.[55]

[49] *Dempsey v Chambers* 154 Mass 330 (1891) 331, 334.

[50] *Restatement (Third) of Agency* (n 1) §4.01, comment b; *Halsbury's Laws of England* (n 48) 60, 70; Kraus (n 48) 812–13.

[51] Kraus (n 48) 818–25; Demott (n 48) 988, 999 fn 39.

[52] *CA 2362/19 Plonim v The Palestinian Authority* (Nevo, 10 April 2022), Amit J, paragraph 29; Oliver W Holmes, 'Agency' (1891) 5 Harvard Law Review 1, 14.

[53] Section 2 of the Civil Wrongs (Liability of the State) Act [Israel]; Section 13 of the Tort Ordinance [Israel]; 28 USC §1346 (b)(1); 28 USCS §2671. Note the leading precedent on ratification in Israel in a Supreme Court of Israel decision, in which it held the Palestinian Authority liable, *inter alia*, under the doctrine of ratification, for payments the Palestinian Authority made to the families of Palestinian prisoners detained by Israel for security offences, even though the prisoners have no organizational affiliation with the Palestinian Authority (CA 2362/19 *Plonim v The Palestinian Authority* (n 52), Amit J, paragraphs 35, 44). The approach taken by the Supreme Court of Israel towards the Palestinian Authority is, therefore, more extensive than that accorded to the State of Israel.

[54] For example: 28 USC §2680(h); Sections 2–3 of the Civil Wrongs (Liability of the State) Act [Israel].

[55] For example, in England and Wales, the Crown Act of State doctrine acts as a bar to courts' ability to impose tort liability on the state and its officials, for some wrongs its officials commit abroad. To apply, the state must ratify the conduct of the official's actions, which are sovereign acts in character, that is, conducting high policy in the context of foreign relations, and the acts are closely connected with execution of policy. That said, the doctrine only applies to acts that are lawful under domestic and international law. It does not apply to claims under the Human Rights Act, to the torture and maltreatment of prisoners (as these are not conceived of as sovereign acts), or generally to the expropriation or

More generally, the scope of applicability of the doctrine of ratification would be limited in the context of warfare, in line with the definition I provided for a belligerent wrong as an infliction of a loss that is done in breach of international humanitarian law or the rules of engagement. As a result of this definition of belligerent wrongs, the availability of both negligence and intentional torts in the context of warfare seems to be more restricted than during peacetime.

Nevertheless, in those jurisdictions where ratification could be available for extraterritorial losses, state liability could arise in a wide range of scenarios. Consider the following example: A state uses a private military contractor during an armed conflict for logistical and security support. The contractor's security guards repeatedly open fire at anyone walking towards the military base, in violation of the state's rules of engagement. Ratification could be explicit, such as a proclamation by the government or legislature that adopts the contractor's wrongdoing as its own; or implicit, such as defending the contractor's actions,[56] or ignoring the repeated violations of the rules of engagement.

The range of possible ways in which a state can ratify the unauthorized acts of its combatants and military contractors seems to be as wide and variable as the doctrine itself. It is beyond the scope of this chapter to attempt to address

destruction of property. That said, the Supreme Court held that the doctrine could apply if property was destroyed during combat: *Rahmatullah v Ministry of Defence* [2017] AC 649, 799; Uglješa Grušić, 'Civil Claims against the Crown in the Wake of the Iraq War: Crown Act of State, Limitation under Foreign Law and Litigation Funding: *Alseran v Ministry of Defence*' (2018) 37 Civil Justice Quarterly 428, 432–33.

It is unclear whether a similar Domestic Act of State doctrine exists in other jurisdictions. For instance, in Israel, the applicability of the Act of State doctrine was mentioned in obiter only (HCJ 8276/05 *Adallah v Minister of Defense* PD 62(1) 1 (2006) 44–45; HCJ 1730/96 *Sabikh v General Biran* PD50(1) 353 (1996) 367). In Australia and Canada, case law mentions the Foreign Act of State doctrine, according to which domestic courts will not review the lawfulness of the sovereign acts of a foreign state, but there is no mention of a doctrine similar to the England and Wales Crown Act of State that would apply to the acts of the domestic state's public officials' actions abroad (*Nevsun Resources Ltd v Araya* [2020] SCJ No 5, paragraphs 28–29, 44–45; *Habib v Commonwealth of Australia* (2010) 113 ALD 469, paragraphs 91–120, 134–35).

In contrast, the Federal Tort Claims Act extends a far wider immunity from liability to the United States for wrongs it inflicts abroad. All tort claims that could arise under the Act but have been inflicted by US employees in a foreign country are excluded (28 USC §2680(k), 1948). This immunity has been interpreted to apply widely, extending even to torts inflicted in the sovereignless territory of Antarctica (*Smith v US* 113 SCt 1178, 1181–83). While it is possible that a claim in tort under a different cause of action could be sustained, the Supreme Court's general approach seems to be to limit the federal government's liability abroad. The Court held that by enacting 28 USC §2680(k) Congress intended to limit the possibility of foreign countries holding the United States liable in tort, and maintained that there is a general approach against interpreting the applicability of US domestic tort law extraterritorially: *Hernandez v Mesa* 140 S Ct 735 (US, 25 February 2020) 747, 759.

[56] *Persons v Valley City* 144 NW 675 (1913) 680.

the doctrine's general lack of clarity, as well as its theoretical incoherence with the basic structure of tort law. What I have been able to show is that given that ratification is currently an available mode of imputing liability in those instances where vicarious liability cannot be established, it could also be available in relation to states' liability during warfare.

IV. Conclusions

In this chapter, I offer an illustration of the scope of states' vicarious and direct liability in tort during warfare. Vicarious liability could be imposed on a state, most notably when that state's own combatants have acted negligently; but under certain circumstances, it could also be held vicariously liable for intentional belligerent torts and torts inflicted by its independent contractors or its civilian population. In contrast, direct liability could be imposed for wrongful losses that were inflicted by third parties when a state's own failures created the risk that materialized, when the state had a non-delegable duty, or when it ratified the wrongful conduct.

My analysis in Chapters 2, 4, and 5 suggests that even though tort liability could be imposed for belligerent wrongs, the applicability of negligence and intentional torts would be narrow. This narrow application of tort law is consistent with the narrow definition I have offered of belligerent wrongs, as the infliction of a loss that is done in breach of international humanitarian law or the rules of engagement.

The liability regime I advance is consistent with, and has the potential to further, international humanitarian law's requirement to minimize potential harm to the civilian population from combatant activities. Still, arguments could be made against the relevance or merit of relying on tort law to remedy belligerent wrongs, as I suggest it ought to be, due to its narrow application.[57] In Chapter 7, I address this critique by assessing the advantages and disadvantages of tort law vis-à-vis its two main alternatives that are used in this context: *ex gratia* payments and state-operated insurance schemes.

[57] For example, Rebecca Crootof, Emanuela-Chiara Gillard, and W. Michael Reisman argue that broad models of compensation should be adopted, which include not only what I argue are belligerent wrongs but also non-wrongful belligerent losses more generally. See: Crootof (n 46) 1109–13; Emanuela-Chiara Gillard, 'Reparation for Violations of International Humanitarian Law' (2003) 85 International Review of the Red Cross 529, 551; W Michael Reisman, 'Compensating Collateral Damage in Elective International Conflict' (2013) 8 Intercultural Human Rights Law Review 1, 10.

7
The Comparative Merits of Tort Liability and Its Alternatives

I. Introduction

The tort liability regime I offer to redress belligerent wrongs is narrow, given the narrow definition of belligerent wrongs I advance—that is, the infliction of a loss that is carried out in breach of the principles of international humanitarian law and the rules of engagement. As private law rights remain relevant in armed conflict, losses are *prima facie* wrongs that could only be non-wrongful if they were inflicted while adhering to international humanitarian law and the rules of engagement. Otherwise, losses would be unjustified belligerent wrongs, for which there is a moral corrective justice duty to redress the wrongs. Yet, establishing that a belligerent has been inflicted would require plaintiffs more than similar losses that are inflicted through ordinary non-combatant activities.

Consequently, arguments could be made against the relevance or merit of relying on tort law to remedy belligerent wrongs. For example, both Emanuela-Chiara Gillard and W Michael Reisman argue that justice can be guaranteed only by adopting broad models of compensation, which include not only what I argue are belligerent wrongs but also non-wrongful losses more generally.[1]

The purposes of this chapter are twofold. First, I analyse whether tort law is, in fact, an appropriate avenue through which belligerent wrongs should be addressed. Second, I compare the merits of tort liability to its two main

[1] Gillard's argument is based on notions of substantive equality, according to which two individuals who have sustained a loss during war should equally be entitled to compensation regardless of whether the *in bello* principles were violated or not (Emanuela-Chiara Gillard, 'Reparation for Violations of International Humanitarian Law' (2003) 85 International Review of the Red Cross 529, 551). In contrast, Reisman bases his argument on distributive justice notions, claiming that as the losses are sustained for the benefit of the injuring state, the injured individuals should not be left to shoulder the costs alone (W Michael Reisman, 'Compensating Collateral Damage in Elective International Conflict' (2013) 8 Intercultural Human Rights Law Review 1, 10). Rebecca Crootof advances a somewhat more nuanced argument, holding that the ideal liability regime would be one that offers a remedy for all losses inflicted in warfare on civilians regardless of whether international humanitarian law was infringed or not, but she does not go so far as to suggest that other regimes will necessarily be unjust. See: Rebecca Crootof, 'War Torts' (2022) 97 New York University Law Review 1063, 1109.

Tort Liability in Warfare. Haim Abraham, Oxford University Press. © Haim Abraham 2024.
DOI: 10.1093/9780191997051.003.0007

alternatives that are currently used to redress losses that are inflicted during combat in various jurisdictions: *ex gratia* payments and insurance schemes.[2] My comparative analysis is based on the assumption that the alternatives to tort liability exist as a source of payment when injured individuals do not have the additional option of pursuing compensation in tort. This is, in fact, the current legal reality, due to the combatant activities exception.

I show that in some respects—such as the consistency and transparency of payment decisions, the question of whether the payment reflects the actual costs of the injuries, the identity of the administrating body, and the ability to correct wrongs—tort liability surpasses its alternatives. However, in other respects—for example the duration, cost, and location of the redress mechanism—the merits of *ex gratia* payments and state-operated insurance schemes appear to indicate that they are superior to tort liability. In doing so, I also demonstrate that the tort liability regime I offer cannot be completely ruled out, despite its limited scope and the concerns it may raise. Furthermore, I establish that the current *ex gratia* and state-operated insurance schemes produce unsatisfactory results, while tort law has significant advantages despite its shortcomings. In particular, I argue that given tort law's ability to achieve corrective justice, as well as its expressive value, it seems to be a preferable means of redressing belligerent wrongs when compared with its current alternatives.

The structure of this chapter is as follows. I begin by offering a gloss of what *ex gratia* and state-operated insurance payment schemes are, and how they operate in the context of belligerent activities. I then turn to compare the merits of these schemes to those of tort liability. In this context, I distinguish between two groups of factors. First, I analyse contingent empirical factors, which are subject to variations based on the circumstances in each jurisdiction, but which nevertheless provide important insights into the operation of the redress mechanisms. Second, I assess a formal factor, namely the three mechanisms'

[2] It is also possible to argue that an additional alternative to tort liability is settling claims through peace or ceasefire treaties at the end of belligerencies, or state-to-state settlement agreement, in which parties to the conflict agree to waive private law claims in exchange for an agreed payment (see, for example: The Islamic Republic of Iran and the United States of America, 'Settlement Agreement on the Case Concerning the Aerial Incident of 3 July 1988 before the International Court of Justice' <https://www.icj-cij.org/files/case-related/79/11131.pdf> accessed 31 March 2020). However, my focus is on the relationship between individuals and the state and its agents, while the relationship in peace and ceasefire treaties is between two states. As such, I will not be analysing this latter alternative to tort liability, as the relationship within it is not of the kind that is at the heart of this project. I will also not analyse jurisdiction-specific alternatives to tort liability that are grounded in public law, such as the UK's Human Rights Act 1998, Section 8 of which provides courts with the authority to offer remedies they deem just and appropriate in response to an unlawful act of a public authority that is incompatible with individuals' rights under the European Convention of Human Rights. Instead, I focus on alternatives that are commonly used by states in the context of armed conflicts.

ability to correct wrongs and consequently to restore the normative relationship between the parties and vindicate the rights and social standing of injured individuals. I conclude by arguing that my analysis indicates that the liability framework I offer is in fact relevant and that the deficiencies of its alternatives necessitate re-examining the mechanism of redress for losses that are inflicted during battle.

II. *Ex Gratia* Payments

The basic definition of *ex gratia* payments is that they are voluntary payments made by public bodies that do not arise from a legal obligation of the public body to award them.[3] These payments have been made in the service of various purposes. For example, Australia made *ex gratia* payments to persons affected by the Bali bombing in October 2002;[4] India offered *ex gratia* payments to the next of kin of those who died in a dust storm that hit north India in 2018;[5] and New Zealand provided *ex gratia* payments to veterans of the Vietnam War.[6] In this sense, *ex gratia* payments are not only a way to address losses that the law does not resolve, but they could also be a way in which public authorities may advance various goals, such as soothing public outrage, promoting equity, or gaining the public's favour.[7]

In addition, *ex gratia* payments have also been used as a means of reducing the number of cases brought before the courts. These payments are entirely discretionary, and there might not be any right to appeal decisions regarding whether to award payments, or what their value will be, to courts. Moreover, payees are often required to sign a liability waiver that acts as a bar to civil proceedings based on the same grounds for which an *ex gratia* payment was

[3] Duncan Fairgrieve, *State Liability in Tort: A Comparative Law Study* (OUP 2003) 244.

[4] Guy Barnett, *Review of Government Compensation Payments* (Commonwealth of Australia 2010) 40 <https://www.aph.gov.au/Parliamentary_Business/Committees/Senate/Legal_and_Constitutional_Affairs/Completed_inquiries/2010-13/govtcomp/report/~/media/wopapub/senate/committee/legcon_ctte/completed_inquiries/2010-13/govt_comp/report/report.ashx> accessed 6 March 2024.

[5] 'PM Narendra Modi Announces Compensation for Storm Victims' (*NDTV.com*, 5 May 2018) <https://www.ndtv.com/india-news/pm-narendra-modi-announces-compensation-for-storm-victims-1847475> accessed 6 March 2024.

[6] Cabinet Social Wellbeing Committee, 'Memorandum of Understanding (2006) between the Crown and Representatives of New Zealand's Vietnam Veterans' 1 <https://www.nzdf.mil.nz/assets/Uploads/DocumentLibrary/Mou-2006-between-the-Crown-and-Representatives-of-NZs-Vietnam-Veterans.pdf> accessed 6 March 2024.

[7] See, for example: 'The Mutual Security Act of 1956' 9–10; HC Deb 16 April 2012, vol 543, col 13WS <https://hansard.parliament.uk/commons/2012-04-16/debates/1204169000019/ExGratiaPaymentsToVictimsOfOverseasTerrorism> accessed 6 March 2024.

made. As such, courts play little to no role in processing these claims, as the decision on the amount of, and eligibility for, payment is not determined by them. By diverting claims from the court system to alternative public bodies, the *ex gratia* payment scheme assists in reducing the workload of the courts.[8]

Ex gratia payments are used by many countries that have inflicted losses on civilians due to the operation of their armed forces, and each country has its own guidelines and policies in regard to the amounts paid, procedures of request of payment, and awarding circumstances. For some countries, such as Australia, Germany, Italy, and Norway, very little information is publicly available about the guidelines, policies, and procedures relating to *ex gratia* payments for losses to life, bodily integrity, and property damage in warfare.[9] In the United Kingdom, records do not distinguish *ex gratia* payments from what are referred to as 'public liability payments', which are awarded when liability to compensation could be established under the law of England and Wales in the circumstances of an injury or damage by UK forces.[10] Still, the partial data that is available is helpful to identify some common features. In the following subsections, I analyse the *ex gratia* payment scheme of three jurisdictions, for which data is comparatively more readily available, to draw some general conclusions about the character and scope of *ex gratia* payments.

A. Canada

In Canada, the authority to make *ex gratia* payments is currently grounded in the Ex Gratia Payments Order, 1991. According to the order, the Treasury Board of Canada may authorize the award of these payments and delegate authority to approve such payments to officials in different ministerial departments.[11] Managers with delegated authority can approve payments of

[8] Fairgrieve (n 3) 239.

[9] See: Yaël Ronen, 'Avoid or Compensate? Liability for Incidental Injury to Civilians Inflicted during Armed Conflict' (2009) 42 Vanderbilt Journal of Transnational Law 181, 214–15; Center for Civilians in Conflict, 'Addressing Civilian Harm in Afghanistan: Policies & Practices of International Forces' 9–13 <https://civiliansinconflict.org/wp-content/uploads/2017/10/Addressing_civilian_harm_white_paper_2010.pdf> accessed 7 March 2024; Michael Friscolanti, 'Canadian Military Payments for Death and Destruction in Afghanistan', *The Canadian Encyclopedia* (15 December 2013) <http://www.thecanadianencyclopedia.ca/en/article/canadian-military-payments-for-death-and-destruction-in-afghanistan/> accessed 6 March 2024.

[10] Roseanne Burke and Mark Lattimer, 'Reparations for Civilian Harm from Military Operations: Towards a UK Policy' 29–32 <https://www.ceasefire.org/wp-content/uploads/2021/12/CFR_Reparations_Nov21_Final.pdf> accessed 7 March 2024.

[11] Sections 2–4 of the Ex Gratia Payments Order [(PC 1991-8/1695)] 1991.

up to 2,000 CAD, and payments over this amount require the approval of a department's deputy head.[12]

Several resources reveal the way in which the scheme operates.[13] When losses are inflicted in the context of belligerent activities, JAG lawyers can approve *ex gratia* payments of up to 2,000 CAD, whereas higher amounts require the approval of the Deputy Minister of Defence. *Ex gratia* payments are offered for civilian property loss, injury, or death in instances where applicants can prove that the harm was caused to them by Canadian forces.[14] Generally, civilians need to file a claim for payment in a military base, and patrols sometimes provide civilians with information on filing claims and evidence to assist in the process. Once a claim is submitted, JAGs can deny, approve, or escalate them to the Deputy Minister of Defence, and there is no clear process of appeal over these decisions.

Both the amounts paid and the duration of processing claims vary greatly. For example, between 2006 and 2010, Canada made *ex gratia* payments for incidental injury caused to civilians in Afghanistan, in amounts as low as 185 CAD to as high as 21,420 CAD, without a consistent approach to valuation. While decisions aim to take into account the local value of the harm, the payments do not—and are not meant to—fully cover the actual costs sustained by the claimants. Additionally, claim approval time could be hours—if the claim is made for amounts under 2,000 CAD and is supported by sufficient evidence—or months, if approval from the Deputy Minister of Defence is required.

B. Israel

Israel offers an interesting point of comparison, as it has three *ex gratia* payment schemes for non-citizens and non-residents who suffer injuries during combat activities. The first *ex gratia* scheme Israel operates is aimed at addressing losses inflicted by Israel's administrative authorities and officials in the West Bank. In 1968, following Israel's belligerent occupation of the West Bank, Decree 271 was issued by Brigadier-General Rafael Vardi. This decree established the legal authority for designated officers of the Israel Defense Forces

[12] Government of Canada, 'Directive on Payments' subsections A.2.2.1.2 and A.2.2.3.1 of Appendix A <https://www.tbs-sct.canada.ca/pol/doc-eng.aspx?id = 32504> accessed 7 March 2024.

[13] Friscolanti (n 9); Ronen (n 9), 214 fn 152; Center for Civilians in Conflict, 'Addressing Civilian Harm in Afghanistan: Policies & Practices of International Forces' (n 9) 11.

[14] For example, in claims relating to property, claimants need to prove both ownership over the property and that the property was damaged or destroyed by Canadian forces.

('IDF') to award *ex gratia* payments to residents of the West Bank who have been injured by the IDF or the Civil Administration that operates the civilian aspects of the belligerent occupation.[15] Yet, the right to submit and obtain payments is qualified, as losses that are inflicted during a military activity pursued for a military purpose are excluded.[16] In addition, claims of individuals who are subjects of enemy states, members of illegal organizations, or their agents, as well as claims for insured losses, are also excluded.[17]

Individuals must submit notice about the injurious act within sixty days of its occurrence, and the claim must be submitted no later than two years from that time.[18] The designated officers have full discretion to decide whether to accept or reject claims and to determine the payable amounts,[19] and their decisions can be appealed via a special Claims Appeals Committee, within thirty days.[20] However, in an interview I conducted with Advocate Ahaz Ben Ari, who served as the chief legal advisor to the Ministry of Defense, he stated that despite the wide discretion granted by law, these claims are processed in accordance with the tort law standard.[21]

The second *ex gratia* payment scheme Israel operates provides payments for Palestinians who have suffered property damage due to illegal actions taken by Israeli citizens. According to Ben Ari, the legal basis for this scheme is a directive of the chief legal advisor to the Ministry of Defense.[22] Claims for payments are received and processed by a committee that is composed of representatives from different ministries, and they are deducted from the general

[15] Section 2(a) of Decree No 271 Regarding Claims 1968.

[16] Section 2(c) of Decree No 271 Regarding Claims 1968. This exclusion did not exist in the original wording of the decree. However, in 1970, the decree was amended to exclude losses that were inflicted in an area that was deemed a theatre of battle, and in 1984, this exclusion was amended again to include all military operations done in pursuit of a military objective.

[17] Sections 2B and 5 of Decree No 271 Regarding Claims 1968.

[18] Sections 2A(2) and 4 of Decree No 271 Regarding Claims 1968.

[19] Section 7(a) of Decree No 271 Regarding Claims 1968.

[20] Sections 8 and 9(a) of Decree No 271 Regarding Claims 1968. Note, according to an empirical study that was conducted by Gilat Bachar, this mechanism is rarely used: Gilat Bachar, 'Access Denied—Using Procedure to Restrict Tort Litigation: The Israeli-Palestinian Experience' (2017) 92 Chicago-Kent Law Review 841, 845.

[21] Interview with Advocate Ahaz Ben Ari (February 2019). Ben Ari also served as Assistant Military Advocate General on International Law, and the Legal Advisor to the Gaza Strip and West Bank. Ben Ari added that the decisions that are reached in this process do not establish *res judicata*, and that Palestinian plaintiffs often file subsequent claims in tort in ordinary civil Israeli courts and use the military decision as the starting point for settlement negotiations. That said, a decision by the Claims Appeals Committee pointed out that even when ordinary tort law standards and norms are applied by the designated officers, their interpretation and application could be done in a way that discriminates Israeli nationals from other applicants: Hagar Shezaf, 'Israel to Compensate Five Palestinians for Property Destroyed in Second Intifada' *Haaretz* (Tel Aviv, 13 January 2020) <https://www.haaretz.com/israel-news/.premium-israel-to-compensate-five-palestinians-for-property-destroyed-in-second-intifada-1.8384303> accessed 7 March 2024.

[22] Interview with Advocate Ben Ari (n 21).

budget of the Ministry of Finance. 'What motivated the establishment of this payment scheme is the feeling of general responsibility of Israel and the IDF towards the Palestinians, and the fact that there is no symmetrical legal mechanism for Palestinians in cases of hostile actions against them', Ben Ari explained.

Lastly, the third *ex gratia* scheme was established in 2000, when a special committee in the Ministry of Defense called Vaadat Lam'ed (literally translated as 'the *ex gratia* committee') began accepting applications for *ex gratia* payments from civilians who have been injured by the Israeli forces, and are not citizens or residents of Israel.[23] The committee is composed of three representatives: two legal advisors from the Ministry of Defense and one member of the Ministry's finance department.[24]

The committee's work is not grounded in any legislation or decree. Rather, it is acting in accordance with guidelines set by the Ministry of Defense and the Attorney General.[25] As a general rule, the committee will only consider cases with extraordinary circumstances, and it distinguishes between Palestinians from Gaza and the West Bank, and all other potential applicants. For Palestinian applicants, the committee will only discuss possible payment for injuries to life and body, and only if these injuries have led to an extreme medical or financial distress that amounts to an urgent humanitarian need.[26] Property damage will not be considered, unless it has caused significant financial distress and there are political or security considerations that justify a consideration of payment.[27] For non-Palestinians, payments will be considered if there are political or security considerations, with the following reservation: individuals can only apply for injury to life and body, whereas states and other entities can apply for property damage.[28]

The committee's discretion is unlimited, and it can take into account any consideration it sees as relevant, from the applicant's medical and financial records to the Ministry's own budgetary considerations.[29] Payment to the

[23] Dina Poliak, 'Request of Information in Accordance with the Freedom of Information Act 1998' (30 May 2016) 2; The State Comptroller, '55A Yearly Report' (2004) 55A 5.

[24] Section 8 of the Ministry of Defense, 'Work Guidelines and Details of the Criteria Guiding the Ministry of Defense's Committee Regarding *Ex Gratia* Payments'.

[25] Poliak (n 23) 1.

[26] Section 2(a)(1) of the 'Work Guidelines and Details of the Criteria Guiding the Ministry of Defense's Committee Regarding *Ex Gratia* Payments' (n 24).

[27] Section 2(b) of the 'Work Guidelines and Details of the Criteria Guiding the Ministry of Defense's Committee Regarding *Ex Gratia* Payments' (n 24).

[28] Section 2(c) of the 'Work Guidelines and Details of the Criteria Guiding the Ministry of Defense's Committee Regarding *Ex Gratia* Payments' (n 24).

[29] Section 7(b) of the 'Work Guidelines and Details of the Criteria Guiding the Ministry of Defense's Committee Regarding *Ex Gratia* Payments' (n 24).

applicant will only be made if she signs a waiver of any liability she might have against the Ministry in regard to her injuries.[30] All of the committee's decisions are final, and there is no option of appeal.[31]

Other information on the committee's work is rather vague, and some details have been obtained through a Freedom of Information Request.[32] The Ministry has no detailed account of the number of applications submitted every year, but they estimate that two to four applications are made.[33] Furthermore, and unlike the United States, there are no clear caps dependent on types of injury. However, there are also no payments for minor injuries, only for severe losses that either amount to an urgent humanitarian need or present clear political or security justifications for payment. Between 2006 and 2014, the Ministry of Defense accepted fifty-eight applications. Apart from one application, in which over 5 million ILS were paid, and payment still continues, in most cases the average sum of payment is a mere 33,000 ILS.

C. The United States

Since the Korean war, the United States has offered three distinct kinds of *ex gratia* payments for losses that are inflicted during battle: solatia, condolence, and battle damage.[34] Successful applications for payments by injured individuals or their relatives are made through funds that are provided by Congress and the units' operations and maintenance budgets.[35] All three payment types

[30] Section 12 of the 'Work Guidelines and Details of the Criteria Guiding the Ministry of Defense's Committee Regarding *Ex Gratia* Payments' (n 24).

[31] Poliak (n 23) 2.

[32] ibid 1.

[33] One possible explanation for the apparent difference between the United States and Israel in number of applications for *ex gratia* payments could be the availability of courts. For Afghan and Iraqi individuals, US courts are inaccessible due to their physical distance, the foreign language they use, and the high costs they entail. However, for Palestinians, Israeli courts are relatively accessible, as they are close, and language is often not a barrier for proceedings. Still, procedural costs may deter potential applicants.

[34] Center for Civilians in Conflict, 'United States Military Compensation to Civilians in Armed Conflict' (2010) 3–4 <https://civiliansinconflict.org/wp-content/uploads/2017/09/CENTER_Condolence_White_Paper_2010.pdf> accessed 28 March 2024; Headquarters Department of the Army, 'The Commanders' Emergency Response Program (CERP)' (2013) 3–27 <armypubs.army.mil/doctrine/DR_pubs/dr_a/pdf/atp1 + 062x2.pdf>; Amsterdam International Law Clinic, 'Monetary Payments for Civilian Harm in International and National Practice' (Center for Civilians in Conflict 2013) 13 <https://civiliansinconflict.org/wp-content/uploads/2020/12/2013_civic_report_on_monetary_payments.pdf> accessed 18 March 2016.

[35] US Government Accountability Office, 'Military Operations: The Department of Defense's Use of Solatia and Condolence Payments in Iraq and Afghanistan' (2007) 1–2 <www.gao.gov/products/GAO-07-699> accessed 28 March 2024.

are referred to as symbolic gestures without admission of fault on the part of US forces and are not viewed as means of compensation.[36]

Solatia payments, for example, are an expression of sympathy towards a victim or her family, for injuries that are not directly tied to a combatant activity.[37] An injuring act will not be considered directly tied to combatant activities if it was not done by US forces during active combat. In other words, solatia payments are awarded not because the United States caused an injury to local civilians, but because the presence of the US forces attracted fire and led to subsequent injuries to adjacent civilians. For example, if a bomb targeted at US forces exploded and injured civilians, solatia payments might be in order, even though the US forces did not create the risk directly. Furthermore, these payments are made in keeping with local custom—that is, when the local population have a custom of providing aid to injured individuals or their relatives, if they suffered losses under such circumstances, then the US forces may follow the custom and provide solatia payments.

In contrast, condolence payments are paid to individuals in cases of death or injury caused by US, coalition, or supporting military operations, to express sympathy and to provide urgent humanitarian relief that is not otherwise compensable under the Foreign Claims Act ('FCA').[38] These payments could be

[36] The definitions of these forms of payments are mostly based on the information provided by: Center for Civilians in Conflict, 'CIVIC, 2010' (n 34) 3; Headquarters Department of the Army, 'The Commanders' Emergency Response Program (CERP)' (n 34) 1–12. These payments are symbolic in two ways. First, they are not meant to be compensation, but a token of good faith. Second, their total amount can be relatively low. For instance, for the destruction of 200 grape vines, 30 mulberry trees, and a well, the United States paid a total of 1,316 USD, while for allegedly incidentally killing a man, the US forces paid 1,494 USD (Cora Currier, Josh Begley, and Margot Williams, 'Our Condolences, Afghanistan' (*The Intercept*) <theintercept.co/condolences> accessed 7 March 2024).

[37] It is important to note in this context that there are sources which describe 'a loss caused by US or coalition forces during combat' as grounds for payment for both solatia and condolence payments (US Government Accountability Office (n 35) 13, 24; Amsterdam International Law Clinic (n 34) 14). This is just another indication of the confusion about the different types of payments, on which I elaborate further below. However, from a methodological perspective, it is important to have a clear understanding of the payments. I find the definition used by the Army Headquarters the most reliable account of the differences between solatia, condolence, and battle damage. This is due to several reasons. First, it comes directly from the organization which awards the payments. Second, the language used is explicit: 'CERP condolence payments are not Solatia payments and will not be referred to as such. Solatia payments must not be tied directly to a combat action and are given because it is local custom to do so. Solatia payments are paid with Operations and Maintenance, Army' (1–12). Third, it is the latest out of the different accounts of solatia and condolence which I have found, and hence it might represent their most current understanding.

[38] Headquarters Department of the Army, 'The Commanders' Emergency Response Program (CERP)' (n 34), 1–12; US Government Accountability Office (n 35), 19. US Congress passed the first iteration of the FCA scheme in 1918, in order to allow for administrative claims for payments to be made to allied European civilians who were harmed during World War I. At the time, it was titled 'An Act to Give Indemnity for Damages Caused by American Forces Abroad', 18 April 1918, ch 57, 40 Stat 532 (1918) (John Fabian Witt, 'Form and Substance in the Law of Counterinsurgency Damages' (2008) 41 Loyola of Los Angeles Law Review 1455, 1458; Emily Gilbert, 'The Gift of War: Cash, Counterinsurgency, and "Collateral Damage"' (2015) 46 Security Dialogue 403, 405). The standard of review adopted the local military liability standard, meaning that if the local military would pay a

made in response to injuries that were inflicted on civilians as a side effect of the US forces' engagement in either non-combatant or active combat activities. For instance, if a US soldier shoots at an enemy combatant and a bullet unintentionally ricochets and hits a civilian, condolence payments might be appropriate.

Lastly, battle damage payments are awarded when property is damaged by US, coalition, or supporting military operations, and the damage is not compensable under the FCA.[39] These payments are only available when the losses were inflicted on the civilian population during combat. Considering the last example, if a civilian's car, rather than the civilian herself, is hit by a ricocheting bullet, then battle damage payment might be in order.

Table 7.1 illustrates the capped payable amounts for each type of *ex gratia* payment according to the severity of the harm caused.[40] Payments are usually capped at 2,500 USD for the most severe harms. It is possible, however, for payments to be made over this cap and up to the amount of 10,000 USD with a special approval from a general. Yet, such approvals are rare and require extraordinary circumstances. For example, between the years 2003 and

civilian for that kind of a loss in those circumstances so would the United States (Witt 1458). The Act was amended in 1942 and renamed the Foreign Claims Act, making it applicable to all foreign civilians, and it became a permanent statute in 1956 (10 USC 2734, 1956; Headquarters Department of the Army, 'Claims Procedures, Department of the Army Pamphlet 27–162' 135 <https://armypubs.army.mil/epubs/DR_pubs/DR_a/pdf/web/p27_162.pdf> accessed 10 June 2019; Witt 1461). However, the FCA excludes payments for losses that are related to combat operations (Foreign Claims Act §2734(b)(3)). This exception in the FCA has been criticized for impeding the efforts of the military to gain support from local foreign populations who might be harmed by the military's operations (Center for Civilians in Conflict, 'CIVIC, 2010' (n 34), 2). The FCA allows for administrative payments to be made to civilians based on local standards of liability (32 CFR §536.139(a); Headquarters Department of the Army, 'Claims, Army Regulation 27–20' <http://35zsuoz9rs33qykh78u0h6ul.wpengine.netdna-cdn.com/wp-content/uploads/2014/01/r27_20.pdf> accessed 10 June 2019, paragraph 10-5(a)). Nonetheless, it is an *ex gratia* form of payment for several reasons. First, the FCA does not waive US sovereign immunity, and federal courts have no authority to review appeals on claim decisions (*Broadnax v United States Army* 710 F2d 865 (DC Cir, 24 June 1983) 867; *Saltany v Reagan* 702 F Supp 319 (DDC, 23 December 1988), n 4; Witt 1463). Second, the FCA does not define the payment process as akin to litigation, but rather as a settlement process (FCA §2734(a) defines the goal of the FCA as 'settlement of meritorious claims'). Third, the claims are processed by a single- or three-person panel of the Foreign Claims Committee, which is appointed by the US Army Claims Service or a senior Judge Advocate (Headquarters Department of the Army, 'Claims Procedures, Department of the Army Pamphlet 27–162' 137). Normally, members of this committee will have a legal education or be lawyers, and they have wide discretion to decide on the amount granted (Headquarters Department of the Army, 'Claims, Army Regulation 27–20', paragraphs 10-6(f), 10-8).

[39] Headquarters Department of the Army, 'The Commanders' Emergency Response Program (CERP)' (n 34) 1–9; US Government Accountability Office (n 35) 19.

[40] Based on data from: Center for Civilians in Conflict, 'CIVIC, 2010' (n 34) 4; US Government Accountability Office (n 35) 13, 20, 24–25, 42, 44, 50, 52. For a graphic illustration of some condolence and battle damage payments that were made in Afghanistan, see: Currier, Begley, and Williams (n 36). As this illustration shows, payments could be made when US forces engage in either non-combatant or combatant activities, as well as when they cause either intentional or unintentional harm to civilians.

Table 7.1 Payable amounts in the US *ex gratia* schemes

	Solatia	*Condolence*	*Battle damage*
Death	*2,000 USD*	*2,500 USD*	*n/a*
Severe injuries	*500 USD*	*1,600 USD*	*1,600 USD*
Minor injuries	*200 USD*	*600 USD*	*600 USD*
Severe property damage	*n/a*	*n/a*	*2,500 USD*
Minor property damage	*200 USD*	*n/a*	*200 USD*

2006, the United States paid about 31 million USD in solatia and condolence payments for an undisclosed number of claims, and about 26 million USD for 21,450 successful claims filed under the FCA, for harms caused in Iraq and Afghanistan. There is no data on dismissed claims.

D. Common Features

While the reasons and procedures for operating *ex gratia* payment schemes vary across jurisdictions, they all seem to share a few common features. First, payments are generally low and offer partial redress without admission of guilt or legal liability. Second, procedures for obtaining *ex gratia* payments are not extensively transparent to the injured individuals and the general population, and often require civilians to approach military bases in person.[41] Third, evidentiary requirements for proof of harm by the state from which payment is sought are not necessarily lower than would have been required in an ordinary tort proceeding. Fourth, discretion for awarding payments and rejecting applications for them is wide, resulting in inconsistent application.[42]

[41] For example, in my interview with Advocate Ben Ari, he stated that he believed many of the lawyers who often represent Palestinian plaintiffs are unaware of the various *ex gratia* payment schemes, as well as the military and district attorneys (Interview with Advocate Ben Ari (n 21)). Furthermore, none of these schemes or the required forms and procedures are published online in the Ministry of Defense, Military Advocate General, or the Coordinator of Government Activities in the Territories' websites.

[42] The US *ex gratia* payment scheme has been criticized for failing to achieve its goal of winning the hearts and minds of the civilian population. Due to the payments' low value and inconsistent application, the local population is left bitter and frustrated with the United States. As Jonathan Tracey puts it: 'The sum of these problems creates a program where hearts and minds are not won and victims are not offered redress. With firsthand experience meeting over 1,000 Iraqis, this author knows well that the current system is not meeting its goals.' (Jonathan Tracey, 'Responsibility to Pay: Compensating Civilian Casualties of War' (2007) 15 Human Rights Brief 16, 18).

Lastly, generally, there is no opportunity to appeal decisions to a higher or independent authority.

III. Insurance Schemes

Another alternative to tort liability is a state-operated insurance scheme, such as social insurance or statutory entitlements.[43] According to these schemes, claims are not processed through the ordinary tort system. Rather, they are diverted to specialized designated bodies that administer payments in accordance with predetermined eligibility criteria. The exact structure of these bodies, scope of eligibility for payments, and amounts vary widely, and my aim here is to identify general features and themes, not to provide a complete taxonomy.

For example, in 1972, New Zealand introduced a no-fault state-operated insurance payment scheme that eventually replaced tort liability for some losses that stem from personal injury and its consequences.[44] Claims for compensation for this type of loss cannot be pursued through the civilian courts and tort law. Instead, they are processed by the Accident Compensation Corporation, which is a government agency. Payments are made on a no-fault basis, provided that the eligibility criteria are met.

State-operated insurance schemes have also been used to respond to losses that were inflicted as a result of armed conflict. For instance, Israel provides payments to its citizens and residents, who sustained body or property losses during war or terror activities, through national insurance and a statutory entitlement scheme.[45] Claims are submitted either to the National Insurance, in

[43] Note, I will not discuss the aspects of private insurance schemes that are aimed at providing coverage for public authorities against liability. Such schemes exist, for example, in the United States, where municipalities buy insurance against liability for wrongs inflicted by its police force (see: John Rappaport, 'How Private Insurers Regulate Public Police' (2017) 130 Harvard Law Review 1539, 1552–53). Private insurance also exists for private individuals who wish to insure themselves against losses that are inflicted by warfare or terrorist activities (see, for instance: Carter Andress, *Contractor Combatants: Tales of an Imbedded Capitalist* (Thomas Nelson 2007) 39; Richard Ericson and Aaron Doyle, 'Catastrophe Risk, Insurance and Terrorism' (2004) 33 Economy and Society 135, 141–42). Nevertheless, the possibility of states insuring themselves through private corporations against wrongs they might inflict during combat seems remote, as states are risk-neutral due to their ability to spread the costs of risks through a broad base of taxpayers. Thus, I will not address this topic as it is both theoretically unlikely and practically non-existent.

[44] Section 5 of the Accident Compensation Act 1972; Sections 3 and 317 of the Accident Compensation Act 2001; Accident Compensation Corporation, 'Our History' <https://www.acc.co.nz/about-us/who-we-are/our-history/> accessed 7 March 2024; Peter H Schuck, 'Tort Reform, Kiwi-Style' (2008) 27 Yale Law and Policy Review 187, 189–90.

[45] Property Tax for Compensating War Losses Act 1951, 3; Property Tax and Compensation Fund Act 1961, 35–36; Compensation for Victims of Hostile Activities Act 1970, 4. The total amount paid by the National Insurance between 2000 and 2006 was 2,048,927,000 ILS, which

cases of bodily injuries,[46] or the Tax Authority in cases of property damage. However, there is no prohibition on pursuing compensation through tort law against the state.

As the examples from New Zealand and Israel demonstrate, state-operated insurance schemes can divert all cases from the civil courts system to other designated bodies, but they do not necessarily do so. The US Victims of State Sponsored Terrorism Fund is an example of a hybrid model, in which payments are awarded by relying on the work of both the civil courts system and another designated public body. This fund provides payments for individuals who hold a final judgment from a US court that awarded them compensatory damages for losses inflicted through acts of international terrorism.[47]

There appear to be two main strands of thought to the possible rationale behind the state-operated insurance schemes. The first suggests the schemes provide individuals with a quick and efficient payment system to redress their injuries when the tort system is deemed inadequate.[48] This inadequacy can stem from a variety of issues, such as the costs associated with tort-based liability and delays in providing payments,[49] to apprehensiveness towards imputing wrongdoing.[50] State-operated insurance schemes avoid these

includes both payments and services provided by it: Shuli Baer, 'Recipients of Hostile Action Benefits' 8–10 <https://www.btl.gov.il/Publications/survey/Documents/seker_212.pdf> accessed 7 March 2024, 30–31. As for payments made by the tax authority, data from a Freedom of Information letter shows that following the Israel–Gaza War in 2014, 25,706 individuals and businesses submitted claims for payments, and 1,521,024,159 ILS was paid (Israel Tax Authority, 'Request of Information in Accordance with The Freedom of Information Act 1998' (23 October 2018) 2 <https://foi.gov.il/sites/default/files/%D7%AA%D7%A9%D7%95%D7%91%D7%94%20%D7%91%D7%A0%D7%95%D7%A9%D7%90%20%D7%A4%D7%99%D7%A6%D7%95%D7%99%D7%99%D7%9D%20%D7%9C%D7%90%D7%96%D7%A8%D7%97%D7%99%D7%9D%20%D7%91%D7%A2%D7%95%D7%98%D7%A3%20%D7%A2%D7%96%D7%94_0.pdf> accessed 7 March 2024).

[46] However, in terrorist activities or violent conflicts in which there are mass casualties, the National Insurance is proactive and seeks out individuals who could be benefactors of this beneficial scheme: Baer (n 45) 3.

[47] 34 USC §20144(c)(1–2) 2015.

[48] Draft Bill 860 Compensation for Victims of Hostile Activities Act 1969, 6; Center for Civilians in Conflict, 'Civilians' Perceptions of the Compensation Process in Iraq' 8–9, 11–12 <https://civiliansinconflict.org/wp-content/uploads/2018/11/2018.MENA_.We-Hope-But-Are-Hopeless.CompReport.Web_-1.pdf> accessed 7 March 2024; Edwin Kaseke, 'Social Security in Zimbabwe' (1988) 3 Journal of Social Development in Africa 5, 12.

[49] For a critique of tort law's high costs and delayed justice, see, for example: Geoffrey WR Palmer, *Compensation for Incapacity: A Study of Law and Social Change in New Zealand and Australia* (OUP 1979) 23–27; Richard H Gaskins, *Environmental Accidents: Personal Injury and Public Responsibility* (Temple UP 1989) 305–6.

[50] *Koohi v United States* 976 F2d 1328 (1992) 1330–31; Thomas Tugendhat and Laura Croft, 'The Fog of Law: An Introduction to the Legal Erosion of British Fighting Power' (Policy Exchange 2013) 54 <https://policyexchange.org.uk/wp-content/uploads/2016/09/the-fog-of-law.pdf> accessed 7 March 2024. See also the explanatory notes to Draft Bill 2645 Handling Lawsuits against the Operations of the Security Forces in Judea and Samaria and Gaza (Amendment 4) 1997; Draft Bill

difficulties by diverting claims from the civil courts system into designated bodies. As the examples above demonstrate, these bodies can have a lower evidentiary threshold and can grant payments without proof of the wrongdoing that resulted in the loss, which grants them the potential to be more cost- and time-efficient, though they are not necessarily so.

The second rationale for the existence of a state-operated insurance scheme is that it is aimed at achieving a political goal. For instance, when Israel first enacted its payment scheme for victims of hostile activities in 1957, it was meant to provide a positive incentive for individuals to dwell in border settlements, where they were exposed to higher risks from enemy states.[51] Another possible political goal that this payment scheme might have aimed at is promoting solidarity, with the state being collectively responsible for the losses sustained by a few members of the community.[52]

Despite the differences among the nature, scope, and motives of the various state-operated insurance schemes, it seems that in the context of an infliction of belligerent losses they generally share what I refer to as an internal/external dichotomy.[53] Insurance schemes are internal in the sense that they usually provide coverage for losses that are sustained by the state's own nationals.[54]

3173 Civil Wrongs (State Liability) (Amendment 7) 2005; Draft Bill 387 Civil Wrongs (State Liability) (Amendment 8) 2008.

[51] Draft Bill 274 Border Settlements Victims (Pensions) 1956, 170.

[52] Uri Yanay, 'Civil Casualties of Hostile Actions' (1993) 40 Social Security 35, 36. This goal is especially clear in the explanatory notes of two of the Bills that were introduced to amend the Compensation for Victims of Hostile Activities Act. In the first Bill, the status of family members of deceased victims of terrorist activities was equalized to that of family members of individuals who died during their military service by conferring a similar benefit, suggesting that the war effort has a military front and a civil front (Draft Bill 295 Compensation of Victims of Hostile Activities (Amendment No 27) (Family Member Missing Work) 2009). In the second Bill, it is stated that it is appropriate that Israel will aid its citizens who have been injured by terrorist activities, wherever they are in the world (Draft Bill 695 Compensation for Victims of Hostile Activities (Amendment No 34) (Compensation for Victims of Terrorist Activities Outside of Israel) 2017).

[53] There are other state-operated insurance schemes that do not share this dichotomy, such as the scheme operated by Germany in response to the war crimes Nazi Germany inflicted and the Canadian scheme aimed at providing payments for enforcing orders of the International Criminal Court in Canada. For a general overview of such payment schemes, see: International Committee of the Red Cross, 'Customary IHL: Practice Relating to Rule 150. Reparation' <https://ihl-databases.icrc.org/customary-ihl/eng/docs/v2_rul_rule150_sectionb#sectionb_ivnale> accessed 7 March 2024. However, the schemes that lack the internal/external dichotomy are generally aimed at providing payments for losses that did not arise from engaging in belligerent activities strictly speaking, but rather from a state or its agents conducting criminal activities.

[54] Israel extends the eligibility criteria for payments for bodily injuries to individuals who are citizens or residents of the state, even if the injuries were inflicted outside its jurisdiction (see: Section 1(5)(1) of the Compensation for Victims of Hostile Activities Act). Likewise, damage to property that is owned by nationals of Israel but that is located outside its territory can also qualify for payments (see: Sections 2–3 of the Property Tax and Compensation Fund Act (Payment for Damage) (Extra-Territorial Israeli Property) Regulations 1982).

Table 7.2 Internal/external dichotomy

	Citizenship of the payee	*Identity of the injurer*
Ex gratia	*Foreign (external)*	*The state (internal)*
Insurance scheme	*Domestic (internal)*	*Not the state (external)*
Tort liability	*Any (external/internal)*	*Any (external/internal)*

Yet, they are external in the sense that, generally, the insurance schemes cover losses that were not caused by the insuring state but rather by a foreign state or non-state actor.

The internal/external dichotomy is useful in analysing the other mechanisms of redress as well. The *ex gratia* payments dichotomy seems to be the mirror image of the dichotomy which exists in relation to the insurance schemes. *Ex gratia* payments are internal in the sense that they are awarded for losses that were inflicted by the state, and they are external in the sense that they are awarded to non-nationals. However, the internal/external dichotomy does not seem to exist in tort law, as it applies to both foreign and domestic individuals, whether they were injured by the state in which a claim is brought or by another individual or entity. Table 7.2 helps illustrating these points:

Considering this dichotomy, state-operated insurance schemes could be seen as a practical means of redressing belligerent losses that states' own nationals sustain in their own territories, and not as a means of redressing losses that are inflicted by states outside of their jurisdictions, on non-nationals. Yet, some scholars have suggested ways of extending the state-operated insurance to the realm of international armed conflicts.

For example, Yaël Ronen argues that an optimal reparations mechanism would be a domestic state-operated insurance scheme, accompanied by an inter-state claim for reimbursement.[55] According to Ronen, this scheme would have two stages. Initially, states would provide payments for their own nationals for losses they sustained during belligerent activities through a state-operated insurance scheme. Then, the insuring state could recover the costs it incurred from the payments it made to its population from the injuring state through an international claims mechanism.[56]

[55] Ronen (n 9) 219–22.

[56] Ronen does not elaborate on the nature of this international claims mechanism. But from her previous discussion about state claims, it is possible to infer that she is referring to one of three alternatives. The first alternative is that states will bring claims against each other in their ordinary courts. The second alternative is that claims will be brought to international tribunals. The third alternative is that claims will be negotiated on the political level and not adjudicated through any legal institution.

Ronen's suggestion both maintains and challenges the state-operated insurance schemes' internal/external dichotomy. The dichotomy is maintained in the sense that payments to injured individuals are made by states, to their nationals, for the losses they sustained by a foreign state or non-state actors. Still, the dichotomy is challenged in the sense that states are accountable for the injuries they inflict on non-nationals outside their jurisdictions through the international claims mechanism.

Another suggestion, which challenges the internal/external dichotomy to a greater extent, is made by Asaf Jacob. He argues that a third-party state-operated insurance scheme should be adopted in the particular context of the Israel–Palestine conflict. He maintains that Israel should enact a statutory entitlement scheme through which payments would be made to cover the costs of injuries Israel inflicts on civilians in the occupied territories while engaged in belligerent activities.[57] Abstracting from the particular context, we can see the twofold challenge to the internal/external dichotomy that Jacob's suggestion provides. First, payments are not made only for losses sustained by the insuring state's nationals. Second, eligibility for payments is extended to losses that the insuring state inflicts. Thus, Jacob's suggested insurance mechanism resembles the *ex gratia* payment schemes but makes payments a matter of the right that civilians hold, rather than a matter of the state's discretion.

IV. Advantages and Disadvantages

With a clearer understanding of the character of the *ex gratia* and state-operated insurance schemes, it is now possible to evaluate their respective advantages and disadvantages against those of tort liability. This evaluation is divided into two parts, based on the different categories of factors that will be used in this analysis. In the first part, I shall examine contingent empirical factors, such as the length, costs, location, language, consistency, transparency, payable amounts, and the identity of the administrating body of the three mechanisms for redress. Yet, as these factors are highly susceptible to variation, both between jurisdictions and in each jurisdiction over time, my exploration will be carried out in general terms, and I shall not attempt to provide an exhaustive account.[58] In the second part, I assess a structural formal factor, which

[57] Assaf Jacob, 'Immunity under Fire: State Immunity from Harm Caused due to "Combatant Activity"' (2003) 23 The Hebrew University Law Review 107, 175–77.

[58] Providing such an account, which captures the current value of these factors in all common law jurisdictions, will go beyond the scope of this chapter and book and is not required for the purpose of my argument.

is concerned with the ability of the three mechanisms to correct wrongs. This analysis shall outline the relative strengths and weakness of all three mechanisms of redress.

A. Contingent Empirical Factors

An analysis of these factors seems to produce inconclusive results. Some factors, such as the length, cost, and location of the redress mechanism, appear to indicate that the merits of tort liability are inferior to its alternatives. Other factors, for example the consistency and transparency of decisions, whether the payment amounts reflect the actual costs of the injuries, and the identity of the administrating body, seem to result in the contrary conclusion. Lastly, there are some factors that are shared by all three mechanisms, and so they have no bearing on their merits—for instance, possible language barriers.[59]

Let me further elaborate on this point. The long duration and high costs of tort litigation are well known and have been a source of criticism. Years can pass from submission of claim to a final binding ruling, especially if the parties appeal any procedural or substantive rulings.[60] Furthermore, the process is costly both to the parties, who often need to hire the services of lawyers, pay for the expenses of witnesses and court fees, and to the state that shoulders the operational costs of courts.

In comparison, both the *ex gratia* and state-operated insurance schemes have the potential to resolve claims more quickly and with lower costs. For example, the administration of the US *ex gratia* payments is made through ad hoc mechanisms, by submitting claims to judge advocates or project purchasing officers.[61] While approval and denial times of claims vary between brigades,

[59] For this reason, I will not assess this latter type of factors in further detail.

[60] For a critique of tort law's high costs and delayed justice, see, for instance: Palmer (n 49) 23–27; Gaskins (n 49) 305–6. In Israel, for example, obtaining a ruling in a civil claim takes, on average, about a year and half (Efrat Noyman, Yasmin Gueta, and Ido Baum, 'The Massive Backlog Exposed: How Many Cases Are Heard by Each Judge—And What Are They Trying to Hide' *The Marker* (14 February 2016) <https://www.themarker.com/law/1.2850257> accessed 7 March 2024; The Courts Administration Service, 'Yearly Report' 14, 19, 27 <https://www.gov.il/BlobFolder/reports/statistics_annual_2018/he/2018.pdf> accessed 7 March 2024). Similar issues with backlog could be found in many other jurisdictions (see: Ministry of the Attorney General, 'Ontario Civil Justice Review: First Report' (*Ontario Ministry of the Attorney General*, 1995) <https://www.attorneygeneral.jus.gov.on.ca/english/about/pubs/cjr/firstreport/backlog.php> accessed 16 December 2019; Joe Palazzolo, 'In Federal Courts, the Civil Cases Pile Up' *Wall Street Journal* (6 April 2015) <https://www.wsj.com/articles/in-federal-courts-civil-cases-pile-up-1428343746> accessed 7 March 2024; Lord Justice Briggs, 'Civil Courts Structure Review: Final Report' (2016) 29–30, 115–16 <https://www.judiciary.uk/wp-content/uploads/2016/07/civil-courts-structure-review-final-report-jul-16-final-1.pdf> accessed 7 March 2024.

[61] US Government Accountability Office (n 35) 32.

claims are generally resolved within days or weeks from the date of submission.[62] Moreover, individuals are not required to hire the services of lawyers or experts, and witnesses' statements are sufficient. Therefore, the costs that are associated with *ex gratia* payments can be lower than those that are associated with tort litigation.[63]

A similar result seems likely in relation to state-operated insurance schemes. The process of obtaining payment could be much shorter than tort litigation, spanning a few weeks to a few months, as claimants would only have to establish that they have been injured by the state from whom they seek redress. States already record information regarding the injuries they inflict in their operation logs. Given these records, as well as the fact that there is a need to establish only causation and not wrongdoing, it seems that many cases could be resolved more quickly than tort claims. Additionally, costs might also be lower in comparison, given that the bar for pursuing a claim successfully is establishing causation and not wrongdoing.[64]

The location in which the redress mechanism is administered also seems to be a potential source of criticism of tort litigation. As I argued in Chapter 1, the relevant forum to which tort claims for belligerent wrongs should be brought is the courts of the state affiliated with the wrongdoer. While bringing claims in these courts could be more effective in relation to the availability of information, enforceability of judgments, and avoiding issues relating to comity, there are accessibility concerns. Seeing my argument through would mean that injuries that arise from long-distance warfare, such as the operations conducted by UK forces in Afghanistan would have to be pursued via claims filed in UK courts. Requiring Afghan nationals to initiate international tort litigation to secure compensation would be expensive, time consuming, and administratively complicated. Consequently, it might either be out of reach for potential plaintiffs or sufficiently complicated to deter potential plaintiffs from pursuing claims.[65]

[62] Center for Civilians in Conflict, 'CIVIC, 2010' (n 34) 4–7; US Government Accountability Office (n 35) 45.

[63] Lindsey Cameron and Vincent Chetail, *Privatizing War: Private Military and Security Companies under Public International Law* (CUP 2013) 565.

[64] That said, the costs that are associated with state-operated insurance schemes might be higher than those of *ex gratia* payments. Ambiguity regarding causation may require expert evidence and demonstrating the scope and character of injuries is very likely to require expert testimony. Furthermore, it is not unreasonable to assume that individuals would hire the services of lawyers to ensure that their claims are successful. In this sense, the costs of a state-operated insurance scheme would not necessarily be too different from those of tort litigation.

[65] These accessibility concerns might not arise in close-range conflicts, when warfare is between neighbouring states. For example, Palestinian plaintiffs have been filing tort claims against Israel from the later 1960s. Moreover, these concerns are irrelevant for combat-related injuries that have been sustained by the awarding state's own residents.

In contrast to tort litigation, the administration of both *ex gratia* payments and state-operated insurance schemes could be located in the state in which the injury was inflicted. For example, the US *ex gratia* scheme is administered in the states in which the injuries were inflicted, and one of Israel's schemes is operated through its authorities in the occupied territories. Hence, in instances in which these schemes are available in the state where the injuries were inflicted, they are comparably more accessible than tort litigation.

That said, *ex gratia* payments, and to a certain degree state-operated insurance schemes as well, raise concerns in relation to consistency, transparency, redressing the actual costs of the injuries, enforceability, and the identity of the administrating body. The US' and Israel's *ex gratia* payment schemes illustrate these difficulties, and from the information that is publicly available, they appear to be representative of the issues that exist in other states' *ex gratia* schemes.

The United States operates three types of *ex gratia* payments: each has a different purpose and applies, in theory, to different circumstances. Yet, in practice, military units find them very hard to distinguish, and as such they are not applied in a coherent systematic fashion.[66] Interpretation of the scope of application of the various payment types (ie, which award is fitting according to the type of injury) and amounts paid for each type of injury vary between brigades, or even within the same brigade.[67] These factors, alongside the wide discretion for awarding payments and rejecting applications, contribute to the fact that the administration of the schemes can, and does, result in their inconsistent application.

Moreover, the amounts paid for the losses of civilians can be low and not reflective of the actual costs of the losses.[68] A death, for instance, will usually amount to 2,000 USD in solatia and 2,500 USD in condolence payments, while the average annual gross national income per capita in 2017 in Afghanistan was 560 USD, and in Iraq it was 4,630 USD.[69] These caps are deviated from only in exceptional cases, and even then the amount will not exceed 10,000 USD.[70]

[66] Center for Civilians in Conflict, 'CIVIC, 2010' (n 34) 4.

[67] For example, there is some inconsistency and confusion among the units regarding the definitions of condolence and battle damage payments, perhaps due to lack of proper guidance on the part of the Department of Defence, resulting in some units recording property damage as condolence payments and others as battle damage (Center for Civilians in Conflict, 'CIVIC, 2010' (n 34) 4–7; US Government Accountability Office (n 35) 3, 45).

[68] Yet, state-operated insurance schemes could be more reflective of the actual costs, if coverage is structured in this way. Whether or not that is the case depends on the particularities of each insurance scheme, and no information is available for review in this context.

[69] Center for Civilians in Conflict, 'CIVIC, 2010' (n 34) 6; World Bank, 'Afghanistan's GNI per Capita' <http://data.worldbank.org/indicator/NY.GNP.PCAP.CD/countries/AF-8S-XM?display = graph> accessed 10 June 2019.

[70] Center for Civilians in Conflict, 'CIVIC, 2010' (n 34) 6.

In addition, procedures for obtaining the *ex gratia* payments are not necessarily extensively transparent to the injured individuals and the general population. For example, none of the required forms and procedures or past decisions relating to Israel's *ex gratia* schemes are published and accessible.[71]

Lastly, in some instances, *ex gratia* and state-operated insurance schemes are operated by the injuring unit, as is the case with the US *ex gratia* scheme, or by the ministry in charge of combat operations, such as in Israel. Placing the same branch of government that inflicted the loss in charge of reviewing claims for payments and their administration, let alone the same ministry or unit, results in an inherently defective system.

In operating the *ex gratia* and state-operated insurance schemes, an executive branch is acting in a quasi-judicial capacity. While it might be arguable that in this capacity the executive should act in accordance with, and be held to, the standards of impartiality and fairness of the judicial process,[72] it is likely that the executive will nevertheless fail to fully abide by them. The purpose of the executive is to promote the public's interests through policy-making and its implementation. As such, there is a risk that public interests and the public's opinion will skew the operation or construction of the two schemes, moving away from the standards of impartiality and fairness. In those instances in which the injuring body also processes claims, there is an additional risk that the private interests of the injuring body will interfere with the proper administration of the payment scheme, mainly in order to reduce the degree of accountability for inflicting injuries. The fact that the schemes generally operate as the only available recourse, while tort litigation is barred, makes the inherent defectiveness of the schemes all the more problematic.[73]

Indeed, there are indications that the existing schemes are in fact skewed due to these considerations. For instance, the US *ex gratia* scheme is aimed at winning the hearts and minds of local populations so they will not be a

[71] And indeed, as stated above, many of the lawyers who represent Palestinian plaintiffs are often unaware of the various *ex gratia* payment schemes, as well as the military and district attorneys (Interview with Advocate Ben Ari (n 21)).

[72] TRS Allan, 'The Rule of Law' in David Dyzenhaus and Malcolm Thorburn (eds), *Philosophical Foundations of Constitutional Law* (OUP 2016) 214; TRS Allan, *Constitutional Justice* (OUP 2003) 145.

[73] That said, some might hold that there is nothing unfamiliar and objectionable in the executive acting in a quasi-judicial capacity and reviewing its own actions. The flaws that I have indicated thus far could also be found in, for example, immigration, human rights, and urban planning tribunals. As we accept the quasi-judicial operations of the executive in these familiar instances, the argument would go, we should likewise accept them in the context of the payment schemes. While this critique of the concerns I raise might be valid, it misinterprets my intent. I am not attempting to show that there is something generally wrong with the executive acting in a quasi-judicial fashion. Rather, I am illustrating that there are certain shortcomings to payment schemes in comparison to tort litigation in this particular respect.

hindrance to US war efforts.[74] The very purpose of the scheme seems to be oriented towards pursuing the US' public interests and not at safeguarding the private law rights of foreign individuals.

Another example could be found in the Israeli *ex gratia* payment scheme, which could be influenced by external political pressure. In the interview I conducted with Advocate Ben Ari, he mentioned that in one particular instance, in which a UK national was killed by the IDF, the United Kingdom applied tremendous amount of political pressure on Israel that only ended after Ben Ari met with the national's family and offered them a considerable payment through the *ex gratia* scheme.[75] Although Ben Ari did not specify the amount that was agreed upon, the estimate is in the millions of pounds. In comparison, the average payment for ordinary claims, which are not accompanied by the same level of international political pressure, is 33,000 ILS.[76]

There are also indications of bias in Israel's state-operated insurance scheme for victims of hostile activities. While according to the black letter of the law, all citizens and residents are eligible for payments under this scheme, only on rare occasions and following legal proceedings against the authorities have Israeli-Palestinians been able to obtain the 'victim status' required to be eligible for the payments.[77]

In comparison, tort litigation could be much more consistent, transparent, and reflective of the actual costs of injuries, and it does not raise similar rule of law concerns.[78] Laws, procedures for obtaining remedies, and courts' decisions

[74] Center for Civilians in Conflict, 'CIVIC, 2010' (n 34) 2–3.

[75] Interview with Advocate Ben Ari (n 21).

[76] Poliak (n 23) 1.

[77] It has been reported that the National Insurance enacted a policy in 2014, according to which it did not award this status and payments to Israeli-Palestinians who were injured in the context of violent protests: Nir Hasson, 'The State Recognized a Palestinian, Who Lost an Eye due to a Police Officer's Shooting of a Sponge Grenade, as a Victim of Hostile Activities' *Haaretz* (27 September 2017) <https://www.haaretz.co.il/news/politics/.premium-1.4473185> accessed 12 June 2019. In a recent case, a Palestinian's family had to sue the Ministry of Defense to obtain this status, after their relative died when a Hamas rocket hit the building in which he was situated: Tamir Steinman, 'A Palestinian Will Be Granted Victim of Hostile Activities Status' *Mako* (8 May 2019) <https://www.mako.co.il/news-military/security-q2_2019/Article-4ec7157d1779a61027.htm> accessed 12 June 2019. For Jewish Israelis under similar circumstances, the National Insurance seeks out victims of its own accord, in order to obtain for them the required status and dispense payments as quickly as possible: Baer (n 35) 3.

[78] Yet, a tort liability regime does not necessarily have to possess these qualities and could be discriminatory and biased. This appears to be a problem when comparing how, under Israel's tort law, tort claims brought to civilian courts by Palestinian plaintiffs against Israel for losses inflicted by its security forces are significantly less likely to succeed than those of Israeli plaintiffs. Meanwhile, claims by Israeli plaintiffs against the Palestinian Authority in the context of armed conflicts are much more likely to succeed—and awards are far higher due to punitive damages—in comparison to claims against Israel in this context. See, generally: Haim Abraham, 'Tort Liability, Combatant Activities, and the Question of Over-Deterrence' (2022) 47 Law & Social Inquiry 885, 903–13; Haim Abraham, 'Israel: Supreme Court's Double Standard on Liability Is Unfair to Palestinians' (*The Conversation*) <http://theconversation.com/israel-supreme-courts-double-standard-on-liability-is-unfair-to-palestinians-181969> accessed 11 August 2022; Haim Abraham, 'Discrimination in the Fight against Terror: Israeli

are publicly available. Binding precedent and the ability to appeal rulings can contribute to consistent treatment of similar cases, and, generally, tort liability is aimed at holding wrongdoers liable for the actual costs of the wrongful losses they have inflicted. Furthermore, as the courts are independent from the executive branch of governments, the risks of bias and impartiality could be—and to a certain extent are—mitigated.

That said, the partiality and unfairness that could be found in the *ex gratia* and state-operated insurance schemes could be eliminated or reduced in several ways. For example, judicial oversight, through a right to appeal to the ordinary independent courts over the executive's decisions in the operation of the payment schemes, could be made available.[79] Alternatively, the administration of the *ex gratia* payments or state-operated insurance schemes could be done through independent tribunals. Lastly, the schemes could operate as an optional alternative to tort litigation, and not as the only available route to obtaining redress. That is, individuals would have the ability to choose either the payment that is offered to them through the *ex gratia* or state-operated insurance schemes, or to bring a claim in tort to court. In adopting any of these suggestions, the inherent defectiveness of the payment schemes as expressions of self-judgment could be mitigated significantly.

As this discussion illustrates, there is no single mechanism of redress that is more meritorious than the other two. Still, there are two main benefits from considering these factors. First, they demonstrate that none of the three mechanisms can be discounted as a general rule. Second, they provide important insights to decision makers who are considering which mechanism should be implemented by shedding light on their respective advantages and disadvantages to potential claimants, defendants, and the administrating system.

Court Applies Jewish Nation-State Law' *Just Security* (21 September 2018) <https://www.justsecurity.org/60803/discrimination-fight-terror/> accessed 12 April 2020; Haim Abraham, Gilat Bachar, and Ceasefire Centre for Civilian Rights, 'Mapping Civilian Harm Claims against Israel and the Palestinian Authority' (2023) <https://civilian-harm-map.ceasefire.org/en/civilian-harm> accessed 4 October 2023.

[79] Making this point in a more general context, Trevor Allan has argued that: 'any doubts about the extent of [the executive's coercive] powers must be settled by an independent court, detached from the policymaking and public interest orientation of the other branches of government. The law can rule, in contradistinction to the shifting demands of public policy, only when the courts can enforce a boundary between law and the current governmental agenda' (Allan, 'The Rule of Law' (n 72) 211). In the US and Israeli *ex gratia* payment schemes, for example, there is no judicial oversight over the decision to grant payments or reject claims for payments.

B. Leaving Wrongs Uncorrected

In addition to the contingent empirical factors discussed above, there is a structural formal factor that requires consideration, which is the ability of each mechanism to correct wrongs. In order to correct wrongs, three requirements must be met. First, the wrongdoer is required to see to it that the wronged individual is compensated. Second, compensation should be for the wrong that the wrongdoer inflicted. Third, the compensation should reflect the full worth of the wrong. Meeting these requirements results in the restoration of the parties' relationship by expressing that one of them wronged the other, and vindicating the rights and social standing of the injured individual as a free and equal agent.[80]

Yet, the three mechanisms of redress correct wrongs and achieve the restorative and expressive functions that stem from wrongs being corrected to various degrees. I now turn to show that tort liability corrects wrongs fully, state-operated insurance schemes could be said to correct wrongs only under a limited set of circumstances, and *ex gratia* payments do not seem to correct wrongs at all. This assertion is, perhaps, unsurprising, given that tort liability is aimed at realizing and discharging with corrective justice duties, while *ex gratia* payments and state-operated insurance schemes seem to be oriented at obtaining some form of distributive justice.[81] Nevertheless, it is important to conduct this analysis, as we need to have an understanding of what is lost when tort liability is set aside in favour of its alternatives.[82] As the discussion below shall demonstrate, without tort liability we lose the ability of individuals to turn

[80] Steven D Smith, 'The Critics and the "Crisis": A Reassessment of Current Conceptions of Tort Law' (1987) 72 Cornell Law Review 765, 785; David Enoch, 'Tort Liability and Taking Responsibility' in John Oberdiek (ed), *Philosophical Foundations of the Law of Torts* (OUP 2014) 252; Scott Hershovitz, 'Treating Wrongs as Wrongs: An Expressive Argument for Tort Law' (2018) 10 Journal of Tort Law 405, 435; Ernest J Weinrib, *The Idea of Private Law* (OUP 2012) 107; Arthur Ripstein, *Private Wrongs* (Harvard UP 2016) 233–34. The idea of vindicating one's social standing should not be understood as a defence of individuals' honour. Tort law is not about the preservation of honour in an honour-based society (John CP Goldberg, 'History, Theory, and Tort: Four Theses' (2018) 11 Journal of Tort Law 17, 24). Rather, the vindication of one's social standing upholds the idea of each person's status as an independent agent, who is free to use her means to pursue her goals and shape her life (Allan, 'The Rule of Law' (n 72) 204).

[81] Note, both state-operated insurance schemes and *ex gratia* payments could be framed in a way that does not necessarily portray compliance with notions of distributive justice, such as with the US *ex gratia* payments that are aimed at 'winning hearts and minds', and some of Israel's state-operated insurance schemes that try to incentivize settlements in conflict-prone areas. Yet, despite the declared goals that might accompany these schemes, at their core they are payments to individuals for losses they sustain while a benefit is gained by the public. It is in this sense that they are an expression of distributive justice.

[82] Hershovitz (n 80) 446.

to the courts' authoritative power to enforce their rights, vindicate their social standing, and restore their normative relationships with their wrongdoers.

Let me begin by examining tort liability. Corrective justice duties are discharged through an imposition of tort liability when a defendant is found to have wronged the plaintiff, is held liable for the wrong she inflicted, and compensates the plaintiff. Through this procedure, the wrong is rectified, the relationship between the parties is restored, wrongdoing is acknowledged, and the social standing of the injured individual is vindicated. These elements require further unpacking.

For example, what does it mean to rectify a wrong? As a factual matter, certain wrongs cannot be undone.[83] Loss of life, limb, or property is not restored when compensation is paid. Still, compensation can restore the normative relationship between the injured and the wrongdoer. By inflicting a wrongful loss, the wrongdoer disturbs the injured individual's ability to enjoy her rights as a free and equal agent.[84] Compensation corrects the wrong in the sense that it is the means through which the violated rights and equal status are vindicated.[85] Thus, tort liability brings the relationship between the parties back into its rightful normative condition, even though the factual loss or social relationship might not have been restored.[86]

By understanding what it means to correct wrongs, restoring the parties' relationship, and vindicating rights, the meaning of an acknowledgement of wrongdoing and vindicating the injured individual's social standing comes into sharper focus. When a court holds that one individual wrongly injured another, it is acknowledging the wrongdoing that occurred. This acknowledgement exists independently of the injurer's own views and statements. A defendant could explicitly acknowledge her wrongdoing, for instance by saying 'I am taking responsibility for my wrongful actions'. Yet, her acknowledgement can also be implicit,[87] for example, if the wrongdoer complies with an order

[83] See John Goldberg's criticism of this aspect of corrective justice: John CP Goldberg, 'Twentieth-Century Tort Theory' (2003) 9 Georgetown Law Journal 513, 576.

[84] Weinrib, *The Idea of Private Law* (n 80) 84; Ripstein, *Private Wrongs* (n 80) 30; Martin Stone, 'The Significance of Doing and Suffering' in Gerald J Postema (ed), *Philosophy and the Law of Torts* (CUP 2001) 159; Jules Coleman, 'Tort Law and Tort Theory: Preliminary Reflections on Method' in Gerald J Postema (ed), *Philosophy and the Law of Torts* (CUP 2001) 203.

[85] Steven Smith argues that an imposition of tort liability vindicates the injured individual's rights in another sense, as it not only reinforces the violated norm but also restores the injured individual's confidence in the legal order more generally (Smith (n 80) 792).

[86] Ernest J Weinrib, 'Corrective Justice in a Nutshell' (2002) 52 University of Toronto Law Journal 349, 354; Seth Lazar, 'Corrective Justice and the Possibility of Rectification' (2008) 11 Ethical Theory and Moral Practice 355, 356; Richard Posner, 'The Concept of Corrective Justice in Recent Theories of Tort Law' (1981) 10 Journal of Legal Studies 187, 191–93; John Gardner, 'What Is Tort Law For? Part 1: The Place of Corrective Justice' (2011) 30 Law and Philosophy 1, 37.

[87] For a discussion on the difference between taking responsibility explicitly and implicitly, see: Enoch (n 80) 260.

of compensation, without admitting she has acted wrongfully—or even if she continues to argue that she did no wrong.

The court's explicit acknowledgement of wrongdoing through its ruling, coupled with the defendant's implicit acknowledgement through payment, supplies all of the relevant expressive value. A wrong has been inflicted, a wrongdoer has been identified, and the rights and duties of the parties have been clearly demarcated. This is the meaning of vindicating individuals' social standing through tort law. It is the ability to turn to the authoritative force of the courts to show that we have been wronged and that we are free and equal agents, and to enforce our rights.[88]

State-operated insurance schemes fall short of obtaining the same results in full, although they are able to meet some of the requirements of corrective justice and achieve some of its effects. These schemes could meet the first requirement, according to which the wrongdoer must see to it that the wronged individual is compensated. As the state is the insurer, it could be paying the individuals whom it injured, even foreign nationals.[89] Yet, these schemes are not paying individuals for wrongs they suffered. Rather, they are paying for losses while remaining agnostic in relation to their wrongful or non-wrongful nature. Moreover, the amounts paid do not necessarily reflect the full cost of the losses, and recoverability under the insurance coverage could be capped at a lower amount. Still, the normative relationship between the parties is restored either when the insurance provides full coverage for the losses or when the injured individual forgoes any claims they may have for the difference between the costs of the losses and the payment.[90] That said, in all other cases,

[88] Hershovitz (n 80) 435, 446. This is not to say that there is no expressive value to the fact that a defendant does not simply pay the amount of compensation a court orders her to but admits her wrongdoing as well—or, alternatively, if she continues to deny any wrongdoing on her part and has a third party pay the compensation instead, as an act of protest against the court's ruling. Acting in such ways has moral and social significance. Yet, these actions go beyond what is the relevant value to the particular discussion at hand, that is, to articulate that the wrongdoer inflicted a wrong on the injured individual, whose rights and social standing are vindicated through tort litigation.

[89] Asaf Jacob's suggestion for Israel to create a state-operated insurance scheme for non-nationals, Palestinians, whom it injures through its combatant activities follows this structure. Yet, this structure is not maintained in ordinary cases of insurance. In these cases, payment is made by someone other than the wrongdoer (the insurer), for a reason that is related to, but distinct from, the actual wrong (an acknowledgement of a contractual obligation). Furthermore, the wrongdoer is making a payment for someone other than the wronged individual, *ex ante*, for a potential wrong rather than the particular wrong for which the insurance will eventually pay. Hence, payments for wrongs capture only one side to the relationship between the injurer and the injured individual, and consequently do not correct the wrongs in the relevant way: Gary T Schwartz, 'Empiricism and Tort Law' (2002) 2002 University of Illinois Law Review 1067, 1070; Gary T Schwartz, 'The Ethics and the Economics of Tort Liability Insurance' (1990) 75 Cornell Law Review 313, 334–36; Weinrib, 'Corrective Justice in a Nutshell' (n 86) 350.

[90] The ability of state-operated insurance schemes to restore the parties' relationship by letting matters drop is not unique, and it could also occur in out-of-court settlements. By reaching a settlement, parties to the agreement can agree to pay and receive a sum that does not necessarily reflect the full cost

the state-operated insurance scheme does not seem to repair the relationship between the parties.

Furthermore, state-operated insurance schemes do not vindicate the injured individual's rights or social standing as forcefully as tort liability. As payment is made without a determination that the loss is wrongful, it only expresses that an insurance-eligible right the injured individual possesses has been violated. There is no designation of wrongdoing, nor is there a statement about whether rights were wrongfully violated.[91] Furthermore, out-of-court settlement could only be said to repair the relationship of the parties because it is a mutual process, in which all parties agree to let matters drop and so return their relationship to its correct state. However, no such effect can be achieved when the mechanism is one sided, in which the state has full discretion over the payment process in its entirety, and the individual has no alternative recourse. In this sense, state-operated insurance schemes seem to repair the parties' relationship when individuals have a choice to pursue redress through it or through alternative means, and when injured individuals let all matters beyond those covered by the insurance drop.

Ex gratia payments meet even fewer of the requirements of corrective justice and do not seem to achieve any of its effects. In fact, the only requirement that appears to be fulfilled is that the injurer will see to it that the individual they injured will be compensated. In this context, the state that inflicted the injury is offering payment for the injured individual. However, while payment is made in relation to a loss, it is not made for inflicting it, let alone for the infliction of a wrong. Rather, it is an expression of sympathy or grace, which is made despite a lack of any legal obligation to offer payment and without acknowledging any wrongdoing on the part of the injuring state. Furthermore, as I have indicated above, *ex gratia* payments are often made for low sums that do not reflect the full costs of the losses that were inflicted.[92] Consequently, these payments do not restore the relationship between the parties, nor do they vindicate the

of the losses suffered by the injured individual. Nor do the agreements have to explicitly recognize that a wrong has been inflicted. Nonetheless, these agreements appear to restore the relationship between the parties, as they agree to drop all claims against one another and accept the payment. In doing so, the parties are choosing to let bygones be bygones, thus repairing their relationship.

[91] In this sense, state-operated insurance schemes are different from an insurance policy that provides coverage for tort liability. In these cases, the injured individual's rights and social standing are vindicated by the court, and payment of compensation through insurance does not rule out these expressive functions (Hershovitz (n 80) 435).

[92] Luke Moffett notes that *ex gratia* payments are also often insufficient to dispatch with states' obligations under international human rights to provide effective remedy. See: Luke Moffett, *Reparations and War: Finding Balance in Repairing the Past* (1st edn, OUP 2023) 267.

injured individuals' rights or social standing, even when injured individuals agree to receive payment, unless the injured individuals decide to let matters drop.

It is helpful to analyse the extent of the similarity between *ex gratia* payments and out-of-court settlements. Indeed, in out-of-court settlements—in which the wrongdoer voluntarily offers to pay, for the wrong she inflicted, an amount that reflects its cost, and the injured individual accepts this payment—the requirements of corrective justice seem to have been met. For instance, if I accidently break my colleague's mug, I offer to pay for a new one, and she accepts my offer and payment. Under these circumstances, corrective justice duties have been discharged, the wrong is fully rectified, the normative relationship between my colleague and myself is restored, and her rights and social standing are vindicated. Nevertheless, this is not the structure of *ex gratia* payments. Out-of-court settlements are a mutual process of negotiations, which can occur before or after proceedings have been initiated, whereas *ex gratia* payments are a one-sided mechanism in which the state has full discretion over who will be paid, under what circumstances, and what the scope of payment will be. The only ways in which injured individuals can influence this process are by deciding whether to apply for payment, whether to accept the payment that has been offered to them, or to let matters drop.

While accepting or rejecting *ex gratia* payments does not restore the parties' relationship or vindicate the injured individuals' rights and social standing, there may still be some ramifications. Being a free and equal agent means that the injured individual cannot be forced to accept an offer of payment by the wrongdoer. However, refusing to accept a payment, as well as deciding to accept one, can result in the injured individual being barred from pursuing her legal claim, due to a statute of limitation or other procedural bars.[93] The resulting effect is one of closure. Corrective justice duties that would otherwise remain are exhausted in the sense that no legal recourse can be taken against them and the matter is considered settled.[94] It is not that corrective justice has been done, but rather that the matter is considered concluded. Under these conditions, the relationship between the parties is not restored, yet it is repositioned as the new correct relationship.

As this discussion illustrates, an imposition of tort liability is more capable of meeting the requirements of corrective justice than *ex gratia* payments and

[93] On an analysis of the legal closure that statutes of limitations provide, see: Arthur Ripstein, 'The Rule of Law and Time's Arrow' in Lisa M Austin and Dennis Klimchuk (eds), *Private Law and the Rule of Law* (OUP 2014) 308.
[94] ibid 325.

state-operated insurance schemes. Consequently, tort liability restores the parties' relationship and vindicates individuals' rights and social standing with a definitiveness and force that are lacking in its alternatives.[95] Put differently, tort liability is a mechanism that enables individuals to pursue accountability judgments, whereas the *ex gratia* and state-operated insurance schemes do not.

Tort liability is preferable, in this sense, to *ex gratia* payments and state-operated insurance schemes. If and when tort liability is done away with in favour of its alternatives, individuals lose the ability to turn to the courts' authoritative power to enforce their rights, vindicate their social standing, and restore their normative relationship with their wrongdoers. Whether or not this is a price that we are willing to pay, or if the benefits from such a choice surpasses its costs, is entirely contingent.

V. Conclusions

In this chapter, I set out to evaluate and compare the advantages and disadvantages of three mechanisms for redressing losses that are inflicted during war: tort liability, state-operated insurance schemes, and *ex gratia* payments. My analysis suggests that in some respects, the alternatives to tort liability schemes fall short of it, while in other respects they can be more effective or successful. Certain factors, such as the length, cost, and location of the redress mechanism, appear to indicate that tort liability is inferior to its alternatives, to a certain extent. Other factors, for example the consistency and transparency of decisions, whether the payment amounts reflect the actual costs of the injuries, the identity of the administrating body, and the ability to correct wrongs, seem to result in the contrary conclusion.

Some instances in which tort liability has been set aside for other mechanisms of redress are well known. New Zealand replaced its tort liability for negligent actions with a national fund.[96] Many jurisdictions use worker compensation schemes and motor vehicle compensation schemes that do away, to various degrees, with tort liability.[97] Therefore, the idea of having a mechanism other than tort law for redressing losses that are inflicted during war is not

[95] Smith (n 80) 785; Enoch (n 80) 252; Hershovitz (n 80) 435; Weinrib, *The Idea of Private Law* (n 80) 107; Ripstein, *Private Wrongs* (n 80) 233–34.

[96] Section 5 of the Accident Compensation Act.

[97] See, for example: Workers Compensation Act 1987 [New South Wales]; Workplace Safety and Insurance Act 1997, SO 1997, c 16 [Ontario]; Compensation for Victims of Traffic Accidents 1975 [Israel].

entirely novel. Furthermore, there may be reasons for operating an alternative to tort liability, which in some forms would be justified as they will be better, in one way or another, than bringing claims in tort.[98] However, from a substantive rule of law perspective, individuals' access to compensation through private law is key to rights enforcement and public officials' accountability, and as such is the basic starting point. Limitation of the right to redress under private law requires proper justification.

In the particular context of infliction of losses during war, and considering the way in which the alternatives to tort liability are administered, there does not seem to be a strong reason to prefer *ex gratia* and state-operated insurance schemes over tort liability. The inadequacies of *ex gratia* payments and state-operated insurance schemes are sufficiently weighty to question their desirability and effectiveness as the currently used mechanisms of redress. Moreover, although tort liability has its shortcomings, they do not reach the degree that they rule out tort liability completely as a relevant mechanism of redress, and the benefits that arise from tort liability are substantial.

Indeed, tort litigation is long and costly, and merely the distance between the parties in the context of long-range warfare could constitute a barrier to potential plaintiffs. Yet, these issues are not unique to the context of liability for belligerent wrongs, and they arise in peacetime as well. There are ways to resolve these difficulties without stripping individuals of the ability to bring tort claims against their wrongdoers.

These hurdles alone do not seem to justify the abolition of tort liability. Limiting or abolishing individuals' ability to bring tort claims must be properly justified, and as the discussion in Chapter 3 demonstrates, a sufficient justification does not exist in relation to losses that are inflicted during battle. The force of this conclusion is amplified in light of the analysis of advantages and disadvantages of the alternatives to tort liability that I have conducted in this chapter. This analysis shows that tort liability is not replaced by an ideal, or even marginally superior, alternative, and so barring individuals' access to tort remedies is all the less justified.

I believe that the deficiencies of the current forms of providing redress for losses that are inflicted during battle indicate that choosing them over a tort liability regime comes at too high a cost. Taking away civilians' ability to bring

[98] For an argument that alternatives might be better suited for achieving corrective justice, see: Arthur Ripstein, *Equality, Responsibility, and the Law* (CUP 1998) 20–21. For an argument that the adversarial structure of tort litigation is an impediment for reparative justice, and that consequently monetary compensation and apologies should be offered outside of litigation, see: Jennifer M Page, 'Reparations for Police Killings' (2019) 17 Perspectives on Politics 958, 963–66.

a claim in tort takes away their power to stand on their rights. The effects of this power are potentially significant even if only a few individuals use it.[99] The cost of removing this power, coupled with the deficiencies of the current mechanisms of redress, is sufficient to support the argument that revisions to the mechanisms of redress are needed. Furthermore, given tort law's ability to achieve corrective justice as well as its expressive value, it seems to be a preferable means of redressing belligerent wrongs to its current alternatives.

[99] The effects of tort liability in this context could be significant in a variety of ways. For example, individual plaintiffs can bring class actions, the amount of compensation could be large, and the legal and political ramifications could be widespread. All of these effects can be achieved even if not all potential plaintiffs bring their claims to court (see, for instance: *Jam v Int'l Fin Corp* 139 S Ct 759 (US, 27 February 2019); Owen Bowcott, 'Mau Mau Lawsuit due to Begin at High Court' *The Guardian* (22 May 2016) <https://www.theguardian.com/law/2016/may/22/mau-mau-kenya-compensation-lawsuit-high-court> accessed 29 December 2019; Keith Schneider, 'A Valley of Death for the Navajo Uranium Miners' *The New York Times* (3 May 1993) <https://www.nytimes.com/1993/05/03/us/a-valley-of-death-for-the-navajo-uranium-miners.html> accessed 29 December 2019).

8

Conclusions: A Case for Tort Liability for Belligerent Wrongs

In 1940, Dixon J held that 'to concede that any civil liability can rest upon a member of the armed forces for supposedly negligent acts or omissions in the course of an actual engagement with the enemy is opposed alike to reason and to policy'.[1] Since then, courts have repeatedly rejected the possibility that they could and should be able to impose tort liability on their own states and their combatants and agents for losses inflicted on civilians during combat.[2] The analyses I conducted in previous chapters challenge the courts' unwavering position. I demonstrate that theory, policy, and doctrine support the conclusion that tort liability both could and should be available to address states' belligerent wrongs. The framework that I advance is not one of blanket immunity, nor is it one of complete liability. Rather, it is an account of liability that results in the conclusion that some, though not all, losses that are inflicted during war are wrongful and hence give rise to a claim in tort.

In Chapter 2, I established that private law rights remain relevant during warfare, and consequently their violation triggers ordinary corrective justice duties, unless a justification exists by way of inflicting a loss while complying with international humanitarian law and states' rules of engagement. Were private law rights irrelevant during warfare, or if it were impossible to articulate wrongdoing, tort law would necessarily be unavailable. However, as ordinary

[1] *Shaw Savill & Albion Co v Commonwealth* (1940) 66 CLR 344, 361–62.

[2] See, for example: *Koohi v United States* 976 F2d 1328 (1992) 1334–35 (holding that immunity from tort liability is justified as exercising caution might hinder overcoming the enemy; that compensating civilians who suffered a loss due to the negligence of US military forces specifically, while denying a remedy to those injured otherwise in the violent context of warfare would be unjust; and that as tort liability has a punitive dimension, imposing it on soldiers who acted under threat to life and limb is unwarranted); CA 5964/92 *Jamal Kasam Bani Uda v Israel* 57(4) PD 1 (2002) 7–8 (holding that combatant activities create special risks, with which tort law is ill-equipped to deal, and hence that tort law should not be an available remedy. Instead, a dedicated regime, which could distribute the special risks of warfare appropriately while accounting for their uniqueness and any international treaties states might be party to, ought to be implemented); *Smith v Ministry of Defence* [2013] 4 All ER 794, 830–31 (holding that imposing tort liability for combatant activities would be unjust as during active hostilities combatants have no time to exercise judgment).

Tort Liability in Warfare. Haim Abraham, Oxford University Press. © Haim Abraham 2024.
DOI: 10.1093/9780191997051.003.0008

private law rights and duties remain relevant, and there is a way of conceptualizing wrongdoing through belligerent activities, the preconditions for the availability of tort law exist and it could be relied upon. Furthermore, as states could redress the wrongs they inflict on civilians through tort law, there is a justification for its availability.

In Chapters 4, 5, and 6, I implement my account of belligerent wrongs, establishing that tort law doctrines could be used in this context, and that the resulting liability regime would be narrow and ordinary. Under the framework I propose, liability would be narrow due to the character of belligerent wrongs as losses that are inflicted in breach of international humanitarian law or states' rules of engagement are not justified. Liability would also be ordinary, as it corresponds to infringements of ordinary private law rights that give rise to ordinary private law duties. For example, directly attacking civilians would not constitute a new tort of 'indiscriminate attack', but the ordinary tort of battery. The distinctive moral and legal features of warfare have implications for determining what would meet the requirement of acting with intent, that is necessary for an intentional tort to be established (Chapter 4), and for what could constitute the required standard of care in negligence (Chapter 5). These distinctive features could also be used to identify non-delegable duties in warfare (Chapter 6). Nevertheless, there is nothing about warfare that necessarily renders the doctrines of intentional torts, negligence, and direct and vicarious liability inherently inapplicable. Put differently, the analyses in Chapters 2, 4, 5, and 6 demonstrate that tort law could be used to redress belligerent wrongs.

In Chapters 3 and 7, I provide additional rationales for the conclusion that tort law should be available to address losses combatants and states inflict through warfare. In Chapter 3, I illustrate that a substantive rule of law approach requires private law remedies to be available to redress wrongs committed by public officials and bodies, as a means of protecting the rule of law. Furthermore, I show that limitations of private law remedies must be properly justified. Yet, none of the reasons offered by legislatures and courts for the blanket immunity from tort liability for losses inflicted by states during combatant activities are appropriate justifications, from a substantive rule of law perspective. On this view, tort liability ought to be available, at the very least, to address the wrongs committed by the state against civilians, as a bulwark against abuse and misuse of public power. In addition to the lack of appropriate justification for states' immunity from tort liability, Chapter 7 demonstrates that the shortcomings of tort liability do not outweigh its contribution to the rule of law and individuals' ability to turn to the authoritative power of the courts to vindicate their rights. Moreover, *ex gratia* payments and state-operated insurance schemes are neither ideal alternatives nor are they significantly superior to tort liability. Taken together, Chapters 3 and 7 indicate that there are good normative and policy reasons for tort law to be an available recourse with which to redress belligerent wrongs.

The upshot of my arguments is that the current legal regime in many common law jurisdictions, under which states enjoy blanket, or near-blanket, immunity from tort liability for belligerent wrongs, is not legally or morally justified. In reaching this conclusion, the framework I advance in this book aligns with two general trends that started in the mid-twentieth century. The first is a move to eliminate states' immunity from liability in private law, and in particular in tort law. In this sense, the framework I am proposing is yet another way in which sovereign immunity is constrained.[3] My conceptualizing of the relationship and interdependency of private law, the law of war, and the rule of law advances peace and legality by demonstrating that even during warfare a sovereign's discretion and authority are bound by law, not just by what is within its de facto power. As my analysis of substantive rule of law principles in Chapter 3 shows, a state is not simply the mechanism of exercising power over individuals but an institution of governing the public for the public's good. This notion imposes certain limitations on states' power and provides reasons for limiting or abolishing states' immunities from tort liability for losses inflicted through combat.

The second trend is the abandonment of the position that human rights do not apply during armed conflict.[4] My book continues and furthers this trend by demonstrating that even during war individuals enjoy certain protections of their private law rights, and a wrongful violation of these rights warrants an effective remedy. The obligation to redress belligerent wrongs is independent of whether a state won or lost in combat, as well as whether engaging in warfare is *ad bellum* just or unjust. Rather, a corrective justice duty of compensation would arise when a loss was inflicted while infringing international humanitarian law or the state's rules of engagement.

A few critiques could still be raised against the tort liability regime I advance in this book, which ought to be addressed. One such example follows the reasoning of the Supreme Court of Canada majority's opinion in *Nevsun*

[3] As Julius Ebbinghaus wrote: 'You cannot tame tyrants by theories; but neither can you do so, surely, without them' (Julius Ebbinghaus, 'The Law of Humanity and the Limits of State Power' (1953) 3 The Philosophical Quarterly 14, 14).

[4] David Luban, 'Human Rights Thinking and the Laws of War' in Jens David Ohlin (ed), *Theoretical Boundaries of Armed Conflict and Human Rights* (CUP 2016) 46, 48–49, 60–61; Jens David Ohlin, 'Acting as a Sovereign versus Acting as a Belligerent' in Jens David Ohlin (ed), *Theoretical Boundaries of Armed Conflict and Human Rights* (CUP 2016) 120, 151–54.

Resources Ltd v Araya. In this case, Eritrean workers claimed that they were forced to work in a mine partially owned by the Canadian company 'Nevsun', and while working in the mine they were subject to torture and cruel and inhuman treatment. The Supreme Court of Canada was asked to overturn lower courts' rulings that had dismissed Nevsun's motion to strike the workers' pleadings. The majority rejected the appeal, and in *obiter* held that ordinary tort law doctrines would be insufficient for responding to the character of the alleged wrongs, and a more appropriate remedy would recognize a new tort of violating customary international law, or provide a direct remedy for the breach of customary international law through the common law:

> While courts can, of course, address the extent and seriousness of harm arising from civil wrongs with tools like an award of punitive damages, these responses may be inadequate when it comes to the violation of the norms prohibiting forced labour; slavery; cruel, inhuman or degrading treatment; or crimes against humanity. The profound harm resulting from their violation is sufficiently distinct in nature from those of existing torts . . . [R]eliance on existing domestic torts may not 'do justice to the specific principles that already are, or should be, in place with respect to the human rights norm' . . . A good argument can be made that appropriately remedying these violations requires different and stronger responses than typical tort claims, given the public nature and importance of the violated rights involved, the gravity of their breach, the impact on the domestic and global rights objectives, and the need to deter subsequent breaches.[5]

The majority's suggestion is that tort law *might* be inappropriate—since the character of the violations does not correspond to the character of the harms redressed by existing tort doctrines—or even incapable of fully capturing and repairing the harms caused. Yet, the dissenting view rejected the need to acknowledge a new tort, holding that the alleged wrongs could be addressed by existing tort doctrines, even if increased damages were needed to reflect the gravity of the harm or deter against similar wrongs from being inflicted in the future. The dissenting view also suggested that acknowledging a new tort to fully signal the degree of harm in violating customary international law was not a proper justification, as the main value of tort law is not expressive.[6]

[5] *Nevsun Resources Ltd v Araya* [2020] 1 SCR 166, 236–38.
[6] ibid 275–76.

The doctrinal disagreement between the majority and the minority about whether a new tort should be recognized is jurisdiction-specific, and instead, I want to focus on the broader policy and normative questions that lie at the heart of the majority's obiter. From a policy perspective, determining whether recognizing a new tort of violating customary international law would be better than using existing torts depends ultimately on how one defines and measures the term 'better'. Throughout the book, I offer policy considerations to support the claim that existing tort law is a useful mechanism with which to address belligerent wrongs, and in some respects, it is superior to *ex gratia* payments and state-operated insurance schemes. However, I did not assess how a hypothetical new tort would measure against existing doctrines. Such a new tort would still have all of the drawbacks and advantages ordinary tort proceedings entail, with the main difference—according to the majority's opinion—being its expressive value and ability to capture and redress the wrong in full. This new tort would be able to signal clearly that torture is not simply an extremely harmful form of battery.

As a matter of positive law, a new tort of violating customary international law could be established, but it is not necessarily 'better' than ordinary existing tort doctrines. The majority's suggestion that a new tort could better deter breaches of customary international law is not based on theoretical or empirical examination of the claim, and similar arguments made in the context of tort liability during warfare have been refuted. Would the expressive value of a tort of violating customary international law deter potential wrongdoers more than ordinary aggravated damages or punitive damages? Perhaps, if the right market conditions existed to support such a conclusion, but we lack the information needed to reach a definitive answer.

Alternatively, would a new tort be better in the sense of its expressive value capturing the character and scope of the wrong more accurately than existing tort doctrines? The answer to this question seems to depend on whether one views torture as a type of battery that is extremely harmful or something more than that. Under the former view, through aggravated or punitive damages, the expressive value of battery would be the same as a new tort of violating customary international law. However, if torture is not merely an extreme version of battery, there would be a difference between the expressive value of the two torts. Nevertheless, I find it challenging to deem the latter view as coherent with the structure of private law, which, generally, does not consider factors such as 'the public nature and importance of the violated rights involved',[7] that

[7] ibid.

the majority opinion suggested ought to be considered. Rather, the focus is on the wrongful infringement of the plaintiff's rights by the defendant, leaving aside other external factors.

Accordingly, it seems that a new tort of violating customary international law is not necessarily preferable to ordinary tort doctrines. Nor is it the case that ordinary tort doctrines cannot properly respond to wrongs committed through acts that also violate customary international law. The account of tort liability for belligerent torts that I advance in the book remains a compelling and coherent avenue through which rights could be vindicated and wrongs addressed.

Another possible critique that could be levied against my account is that international law is better suited than domestic tort law to respond to wrongful losses that states inflict on civilians during warfare. The argument might be that when engaging in belligerent activities, states and combatants are engaging in public functions that have no private analogue, and therefore applying tort law to them would amount to incorporating public law rights and obligations into private law. In addition, it could be argued that the scope of loss and the character of armed conflict require resolutions and remedies that are attentive to, and stem from, the norms that govern international relations.

While I addressed these arguments in Chapters 1 and 2, it is helpful to reiterate why they do not undermine the account of tort liability for belligerent wrongs that I am proposing, and also why my account does not exclude the possibility for remedies to be extended to individuals under other bodies of law. Indeed, the authority to engage in combatant activities is one that is governed by international humanitarian law, which is of a public character. However, the fact that a public official uses her public powers does not mean that she cannot commit any torts in the process. Several torts, such as abuse of process, false imprisonment, malicious prosecution, and misfeasance in public office, address instances in which the use of public power has resulted in a private law wrong. It would be challenging to make sense of these torts were we to accept the stance that in fulfilling a public function it is impossible to commit private law wrongs. I have argued that warfare is no different in this sense. There are ways to engage in combat whereby if a loss materialized, it would be non-wrongful—namely when combatant activities comply with international humanitarian law and the rules of engagement; and there are ways of engaging in warfare that would result in an infliction of a wrongful loss, that is, if the loss came about by breaching one or both of these norms.

Moreover, as my account of tort liability for belligerent wrongs is informed by the norms that govern armed conflict, I offer an account of liability that is structured in accordance with the distinctive features of warfare. The scope of loss and the character of armed conflict are accounted for, and they are not viewed as extreme ways of engaging in ordinary peaceful activities, which would result in every combatant activity giving rise to liability in tort. Nor does my account view warfare as an instance in which states can act with absolute privilege that would mean no private law wrong could be inflicted or redressed, resulting in blanket immunity. Instead, I advance a liability regime that is ordinary and narrow, which could complement liability under international law,[8] and does not reject the possibility that international law could develop to address civilians' losses in warfare. The converse also seems true; the potential availability of recourse for civilians under international law does not necessarily exclude the possibility of offering redress under domestic tort law.

Nevertheless, it could be argued that the tort liability regime I present in this book would only be feasible in jurisdictions which have courts that are capable of independent judicial review of their states' actions. Moreover, even in these jurisdictions, the state would not have an incentive to eliminate or narrow its immunity from tort liability for combatant activities for foreign nationals, considering that such recourse is not available for their own nationals in the courts of other states.

These are challenging critiques that are grounded in the political motivations states may or may not have to relinquish their immunity from tort liability. The arguments I advance in this book are not political, but normative. I offer a framework that limits sovereign immunity and enhances the protection of individuals' rights by offering a means of holding states accountable for wrongdoing during warfare. While some political aspects are addressed for the purpose of context, engaging in a deep political theory analysis goes beyond the scope of this book.

Still, several possible political reasons for adopting my framework could be identified here, leaving further analysis to subsequent scholarship. First, states that value human rights and the rule of law should have an interest in offering a means of redress for wrongs that they inflict. As discussed in Chapter 3, providing a means with which individuals can vindicate their rights and hold public bodies and officials accountable for misuse and abuse of authority is

[8] Elsewhere I argued that having two liability regimes, one for individuals under domestic tort law and one for states under international law, could ensure that all wrongs have a remedy through one body of law or another, and might incentivize states to offer effective remedies to civilians. See: Haim Abraham, 'Frameworks for Accountability: How Domestic Tort Law Can Inform the Development of International Law of State Responsibility in Armed Conflicts' (2023) 64 Virginia Journal of International Law Online 1, 22.

fundamental to promoting the rule of law. To put it somewhat bluntly, allowing individuals to bring claims in tort to redress belligerent wrongs is the right thing to do. It responds to the moral corrective justice obligations states have to amend belligerent wrongs, which I articulated in Chapter 2, and as I show in Chapter 7, tort law is superior to its existing alternatives.

Second, reciprocity—in the sense of tort liability being an available remedy for a state's own civilians against a foreign state, in return for similar liability being available for the foreign state's civilians against the domestic state—is not a relevant normative question. It could be a political one. Moving away from a regime of blanket immunity from tort liability could be key in creating the conditions that would ultimately motivate other jurisdictions to amend their law as well. In fact, the trend to limit domestic and foreign states' immunity from tort liability developed in this fashion in the mid-twentieth century, when a few states unilaterally exposed themselves and foreign states to tort liability.

Third, although my focus in this book is on common law jurisdictions and assumes that courts are capable of independent review of state conduct, the core abstract conceptualization regarding tort liability for belligerent wrongs could be relevant to other legal systems. Even in the abstract, my framework could offer guidance through which it is possible to evaluate and concretize norms regarding state liability in accordance with local traditions. Indeed, my account of tort liability for belligerent wrongs could only be effective in practice to the degree that jurisdictions have an independent and functioning judiciary. Yet, it also offers resources for critiquing those jurisdictions that do not have these qualities.

My aspiration in this book is to establish that civilians could, and ought to, have the ability to seek a remedy for wrongs they sustain during warfare as a matter of right, and not merely as the consequence of states' goodwill, policy goals, or political pressures. In my pursuit of this aim, I add to existing scholarship that demonstrates how even during warfare, which is one of the most extreme and difficult of times, morality and law have something to say,[9] and rights and duties can be understood.[10] Although war appears to be the epitome of chaos and disorder, it, too, is regulated by legal norms.[11] Courts can and

[9] Arthur Ripstein, 'Just War, Regular War, and Perpetual Peace' (2016) 107 Kant-Studien 179, 195.

[10] Arthur Ripstein, 'Political Independence, Territorial Integrity and Private Law Analogies' (2019) 24 Kantian Review 573, 590.

[11] Oona A Hathaway and Scott Shapiro, *The Internationalists: How a Radical Plan to Outlaw War Remade the World* (Simon & Schuster 2017) 35.

should be able to review whether a state's claim that an emergency has arisen is justified, as well as the actions taken in response to these emergencies.[12] Making mistakes, even in combat, is part of being human; providing a right to a remedy for those who suffer from our mistakes is part of what keeps us humane.

[12] David Dyzenhaus, 'The Puzzle of Martial Law' (2009) 59 University of Toronto Law Journal 1, 38.

Index

For the benefit of digital users, indexed terms that span two pages (e.g., 52–53) may, on occasion, appear on only one of those pages.